JUNK DNA

Unlocking the Hidden Secrets of Your DNA

Joseph R. Scogna, Jr.

Kathy M. Scogna

Life Energy Publications

www.LifeEnergyResearch.com

Junk DNA
Unlocking the Hidden Secrets of Your DNA

Note: This book is based on the life energy research and work of Joseph R. Scogna, Jr. and includes material from *The Promethion*, *SAF Simplified* & Manuals, and especially *The Origins of Genetic Behavior*. The purpose of this book is to educate. It is suggested that the reader consider his or her own unique set of circumstances before embarking on any health or spiritual quest. If symptoms are present, the reader is encouraged to consult the proper health or spiritual advisor.

www.LifeEnergyResearch.com
SAF® is a registered trademark.

Book layout and design by Kathy M. Scogna
Cover Design by David Eaton

Junk DNA: Unlocking the Hidden Secrets of Your DNA

Includes illustrations, index
1. DNA-RNA 2. Junk DNA 3. 128 Sensory Channels (Senses)
4. Crystal Structures 5. Survival Mechanisms 6. Energetic Medicine
I. Joseph R. Scogna, Jr. author II Kathy M. Scogna, author, editor III .Title

ISBN-13: 978-1502336613 (CreateSpace-Assigned)
ISBN-10: 1502336618

Dedicated to
the Children of Earth

All creatures great and small
We share a lineage
We are family

Reach out, touch someone.....

Ancient Hand Painting in Cave, 11000-7000 BC
Cueva de los Manas, Argentina
Pigment was mixed with saliva (DNA!) then
blown thru a bone or hollow reed to make
the negative of the hand.

To Joe Scogna, my love and my light, who has enriched my life in so many ways

And to the dear ones in our gene pool —
Rev. Joshua E. Lickter, Rachel & Elliott Lickter; Jezra Lickter;
Nic & Stephanie Scogna; Kalli Scogna; Jason Scogna

Families are so important!

Rev. Helen Miller Moore & Tom Moore and family; Jon & Barrie Miller
Gollinger and family; Char & Judith Miller and family;
Niki Miller & Bill Oswald and family;
Pat Crivelli Crane and family; Robert Scogna and family; Jack & Lois Scogna and family;
Rob & Debbie Scogna Moir and family; and the late Peter Scogna

Table of Contents

To the Reader

Congratulations!

If you're starting to read this book, *Junk DNA: Unlocking the Hidden Secrets of Your DNA,* then it's very likely that Life Energy Research's awareness programs have captivated your attention and you're on a personal quest to learn more! I commend you on your decision. Now prepare yourself for the enlightenment you will embark upon reading Joseph Scogna's remarkable insights to the overall understanding of body, mind, spirit, emotions and the effects our environment has upon us at all times.

This book reads like a cosmology of understandings in our human condition and what affects us throughout our lives. When you look up at the heavens in the night sky, you realize we do indeed live in an ever-changing Universe; as small as we are, we are still a part of it, so we have this inner need to comprehend it. It is that inner voice that calls to us to know this reality and ourselves! Then, as our consciousness awakens further, we become increasingly curious to learn more and take positive action.

Music is a reminder that a well-orchestrated complexity can produce something beautiful. You're on a quest now to be the conductor of your own symphony, and this book, along with other SAF® reading material, are your guides!

It is your job to discern and make sure that everything works in harmony to serve you in your lifetime on Earth. When you walk forth with this understanding then you can truly help others in the healing arts. Each one of us is a healer. Remember?

With profound respect, I honor Kathy M. Scogna for the remarkable scholarship, editing and production to make Joe Scogna's brilliant research even more available and understandable.

In our changing world, this body of work stands as a lighthouse on a stormy coast, guiding us through these changing times to a new port—to our future practice of medicine and health for humanity. Those who read this book and embrace the understandings are truly the "Forerunners" the Hopi Bible speaks of that are coming!

Bruce L Erickson,
President of MotherEarth Media &
Director of the HEART Works Center
Santa Barbara, CA

Evolution and Creation

The chronological order of creation involves crystals, which are a manifestation of reality. All dreams initiated by Spirit effort to be reproduced in a crystalline structure, much like a painting is the crystallization of the artist's dream.

The auras of every living thing on the planet are replete with salt crystals that contain memory traces. Protein structures, part of the DNA-RNA molecule, stabilize a genetic blueprint, and the whole plan is laid in by a genetic planning mechanism (GPM) that facilitates billions of bits of information.

The GPM uses sensors that emanate from the mid-brain to scan the environment and pick up data for long term changes, so that bodies of the future will be better able to survive. It is almost a perfect system because the GPM automatically changes structure when the body is not surviving well and mirrors those energies in the environment that appear to be super-survivors.

Joe Scogna's explanation of how life

forms are altered by a natural process supports an evolutionist's position, but the concept of a genetic planning mechanism suggests an intelligent designer at work. Who designed the genetic planning mechanism?

As a visionary and researcher, Joe Scogna was himself an intelligent designer as he created innovative programs for health and generated many books de-lineating the processes that affect our well being.

I was privileged to work for Joe for 4 years. As I typed the original manuscript, the words: "In a grain of sand, we can see earth's history like a holographic image in its crystalline structure," were certainly a WOW moment for me. I was hooked!

Linda Schwank, Light Worker
Mt Penn, PA

I first met Joe Scogna in the early 1980s when I heard he was doing some unusual things in the healing industry. So was I! At our first meeting, he came into my office with an infrared sensing gun and a load of 5½ inch "floppy discs" for the old Apple computer system. As I found out, he was a "man with a mission" attempting to do several things at several places all at once, writing books and technical manuals, writing computer formats and script, seminars, teaching. It seemed he was always in a hurry; time was a premium for him.

It took a while to grasp the vast implications of his work. I realized then that he was doing things much beyond the time. As I began to unravel what it was and the depth, I knew it was important.

This book explains Joe's conception of DNA and how it relates to human healing. He understood DNA to be of a holistic nature; the unknown filler modern lab scientists call "junk DNA", if only because it doesn't fall in line with visible, physical and chemical guidelines.

DNA has been an area of special interest to me. I've been following the developments in the field ever since Watson and Crick first uncovered the structure of the DNA molecule in the early 1950s. At first it seemed clear that DNA had a gene for everything and it would be a simple matter to discover what these were. This was to usher in a whole new era of medicine: defective genes could be replaced; we could develop the ultimate medicine, the God-like rewriting of the basic molecule of life.

The race was on to see who would receive the accolade of decoding the genome. As the groundwork was laid for the new field of genetic medicine, the pharmaceutical interests were drooling at the monetary possibilities!

There have been many surprises in DNA lab work, surprises and shocks and changes of direction. At this time, it is certain there is not "a gene for this and a gene for that." Only a small fraction of DNA has been identified by present day lab researchers, with projections of 50 to 100 years before all is known.

The original "genetic medicine" idea has been left in a quandary. The field of epigenetics has re-surfaced and opened the door for information outside and beyond the structure of DNA presented by the lab scientist.

Joe Scogna's ideas are outside of mainstream studies and lab researchers and he very capably gets these across in this book. His concept of DNA is presented in a non-linear way, which allows us the ability to understand many human instincts and modes of action; with that understanding we are able to change our behaviors and patterns.

Enjoy the read!
Donald D. Mayfield, MA, NMD, DOM
Alternative Health & Prevention
Altamonte Springs, FL

Foreword

Joe printed his original DNA book *The Origins of Genetic Behavior* in 1985. It was in manuscript form then, and although not quite complete, it was filled with valuable information for humankind.

In the years since then, scientists worldwide have been exploring and making discoveries in DNA, which holds genetic information. Was Joe's work still valid?

Just as the discovery of fingerprints overturned criminal investigative work in the past centuries, so DNA discoveries have dramatically changed crime scene analysis. The wildly popular television crime shows provide dramatic renditions of true-life scenarios. This type of physical DNA has proven highly sellable. Big companies have jumped on the bandwagon and valuable patents are being issued; money acquired has funded yet more research. Physical DNA samples can help find criminals and release those falsely imprisoned, identify human remains, and track medical histories and family lineages.

The gene, to a biologist or chemist, is the functional and physical unit of heredity, which carries information from one generation to the next in a direct line: skin, hair and eye color, height, and some diseases are examples.

It has been said that human DNA is like a biological Internet, however, according to Russian scientists, only 2% of our DNA is physical or biological. Only 2% is

Kathy and Joe Scogna, June 1986

used for building proteins and for tracking crime scene information.

What of the remaining 98%? According to scientists in the lab, this is filler, some sort of genetic gibberish. Even Francis Crick (co-discoverer of the double helical structure) stated it was "little better than junk." And the name has stuck.

In 2003, scientists claimed all the DNA had been coded but they now admit most of the DNA material they have encountered is unknown, cannot be coded, and there is no money to be made with an unknown substance. What modern science does not understand or cannot see with current instruments is tossed into the category called "junk". However, on the other side of the world, the Russians are moving ahead with their own research on this unknown category, the hidden 98%.

In light of these developments, we have given Joe's early manuscript new life with a more compelling title: JUNK DNA: Unlocking the Hidden Secrets of Your DNA.

The information in this book is timely and timeless; a celebration of that hidden 98% because deep inside, we know the truth. There is no junk DNA. There is no genetic gibberish.

Human DNA is so much more than a biological Internet! Joe Scogna lectured and wrote about DNA-RNA in his teachings and books, of the connections between the elements, genetics, the holistic human being, and the Self Awareness Formula (SAF®) chain sequence.

In the early 1980s, Joe was creating his own computing system and was very familiar with computer science and its programming aspects, ROM (Read-Only Memory) and RAM. He nicknamed part of the DNA our RAM chip, the Random Access Memory chip we all have and can learn to access.

In 1984, he wrote:

"To a chemist, DNA is very rigid. The DNA addressed with SAF® is accessible through very intense mental and spiritual conditioning."

The rigidity that Joe pointed out is the purely physical structure that can be seen and mapped with instruments. The DNA that Joe embraced and wrote about was not just the physical DNA but rather the holistic DNA, the body, mind and spirit DNA of humankind and all life energy forms, all of this stored in our very own RAM chip.

When understood in this context, the entire composition and view of DNA changes. We see the inherited personality traits, our own emotional traumas and the emotional upsets and behavior patterns of our parents being acted out in our children and grandchildren, and the genetic plans and blueprints we have been bequeathed from ages past to understand and process. Yes, our DNA can be changed and altered in so many ways, by our own environment and our adventures and misadventures in life.

"The actions of the DNA and RNA are necessary to put the whole system into operation. The specific fluids that surround the DNA are in precise quantities, which can be translated by a crystalline mirror-like structure, like a laser beam, throughout the entire system. Thus the passages of processes, whether these are electrical, electrochemical or purely chemical, can follow a precise mirrored blueprint."

-Joseph R. Scogna, Jr.
Light, Dark: the Neuron and the Axon

What is the language of DNA in the crystalline structures that acts much like a laser beam? The vibration of sonic waves. Frequencies. This is a multi-way communication line, in and out, so that we have input as well: words read, spoken or sung; thoughts; emotions and other "emotional radiation"; as well as telepathic messages from a distance are involved in the process.

In the movie Superman, the infant Kal-El is sent in a crystal capsule to Earth, with ethereal sounds and images to teach him along the way. The crystals were then stored in a crystal cave for his future use. All knowledge was imbedded in the crystals.

How true this is! All the healing knowledge we humans need to access and know about has been imbedded and stored in the crystals of our own DNA. Crystals can transmit information to us, about survival, about our past and about healing. We just need to access, to listen, and be open to the possibilities.

The following quote was voiced by Jor-El of the red planet Krypton, as he bid his infant son farewell before sending him to Earth. It illustrates the dynamics of our DNA and the miraculous genetic planning mechanism you will read about in this book.

"You will travel far, my little Kal-El. But we will never leave you.

The richness of our lives shall be yours. All that I have, all that I've learned, everything I feel, all this, and more I bequeath to you, my son. You will carry me inside you all the days of your life.

You will make my strength your own, and see my life through your own eyes, as your life will be seen through mine. The son becomes the father, and the father, the son.

We will never leave you, even in the face of our deaths."

-Jor-El (Brando)
Superman, 1978 Film

What the reader will discover in *JUNK DNA: Unlocking the Hidden Secrets of Your DNA* is that we Earthlings have not just five major senses, but access to 128 different sensing channels to use to perceive and understand our world.

We are products of Planet Earth. In this book, we'll explore all the tracks of energy possible—hydrogen, water, light and heavy elements (gold, silver, lead), sugars, salts and crystals, proteins, fats— this is the hard-wiring of the universe, what a human being *is* and what makes up the earth as well. The earth's electromagnetic energy field is mirrored in our own electromagnetic energy field.

What has occurred on the earth from the beginning of time with its geological transformations and eras, with its progression of creatures and energies needing protection, all this has been left as tracings within our DNA.

The gravitational, radiational and magnetic flows in the solar system, the beginning life in the seas and on land with those biological tracings, and the sounds, utterances (languages) and the history of our species has been recorded as well.

We are products of our ancestors on a cellular level, going back even earlier than Stone Age man, with all the beliefs, traumas and behaviors intact; and products of our environment (learning, people, places and events), as well as being products of what we eat, breathe in and drink, all to be discovered and rectified, when necessary, by intense mental and spiritual conditioning.

This work embraces both creation and evolution as the reader will discover on these pages.

Darwin was not an atheist; to him, the evolution of energy was not by chance but by design.

The evolutionist, looking for visible

answers, gets down to the nitty-gritty, to the rocks and the layers of sediment that can be dated with different methods so there will be some official age to the earth and artifacts. To a scientist, a designation of age lends credibility to a time track and seems concrete, but the beginnings of humankind are a bit more hazy. When and how did it start?

The origin of this planetary system might seem to be by chance because we can't explain it fully and completely at the present time. If we don't relegate it to some force greater than us, then it is Electricity Unknown (Sensory Channel #70) and leaves us in the dark. (see page 189)

Certainly there has been life on earth as long as there has been a planet. If there was fire on earth, there was life. The planet is a life form just as we are.

The stretch of time of earth's history dwarfs a human's life history. Eighty or ninety years might seem old for a human but is nothing compared to billions of years.

At the conclusion of one seminar Joe gave, an attendee remarked; "This is genesis. We are studying genesis and the whole world will be affected."

The more educated we are in this self awareness process the better able we will be to help our self and others.

There is harmony in this universe; harmony and balance are built in. All we need is the key to unlock its secrets. This book is the key.

I'm so glad you're here! This is an awesome study for these challenging times: you're holding in your hands the key to the handbook for human healing!

Kathy M. Scogna
Stagecoach Ranch, California
Ides of March, 2014

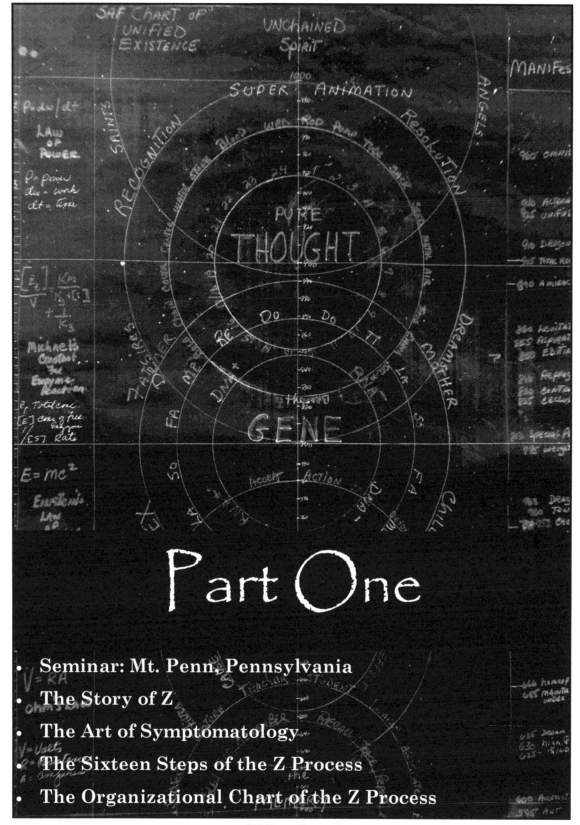

Part One

- **Seminar: Mt. Penn, Pennsylvania**
- **The Story of Z**
- **The Art of Symptomatology**
- **The Sixteen Steps of the Z Process**
- **The Organizational Chart of the Z Process**

Seminar: Mt Penn, Pennsylvania

Presenter:
Joseph R. Scogna, Jr.
President of Life Energy Foundation, Inc.

Attendees: Two dozen practitioners of various fields in the healing arts, from many parts of the country.

Seminars were held in classrooms of a township school, the headquarters of Life Energy. This section includes excerpts from several seminars and question and answer sessions.

JRS: This project on the Z Process was undertaken in order to understand what makes us humans operate smoothly and what breaks down that smooth operating ability into the fits and starts we have with life, the wrong directions we take, the emotional conundrums at home or work or school that permeate all we do.

We have a big problem in trying to solve the upsets of energy with human beings and trying to get them to be better. What is it we are attempting to do for them?

ATTENDEES voice their ideas:
To be symptom free
To balance the body
Better nutrition
Balance growth and development
To feel better; feel satisfied
To be healthy and happy
To reach their full potential
To be in-tune with the universe
Total awareness---

Joseph R. Scogna, Jr.

JRS: Total awareness! That's it! If we have that, we'd have all the rest.

He pointed to the blackboard behind him where he had drawn a chart: SAF Unified Chart of Existence, scaled from 0 to 1000.

JRS: At the top we see Unchained Spirit and Super Animation. Down at the bottom, at zero, we find spontaneous combustion, being vaporized. Here one minute; gone the next. Total magnetization, total gravity. Shackled spirits. (for partial chart, see page 15)

The angels and saints are up at the top. This is Superman, the uber-mensch of Carl Jung. What are some of Superman's abilities?

ATTENDEES talk all at once:
He stops bullets in mid-air by revers-

ing the magnetic flow...
Leaps tall buildings in a single bound-
He defies gravity– he can fly...
X-ray vision; he can see through walls... and people!
He can see through all matter...
Has great strength, can move the earth on its axis...
He can reverse time.....

JRS: Those are amazing abilities. I don't know about you but to be able to fly, to see through walls and people, to reverse time—that would be fantastic. With total awareness, we could bring about great healing.

If you read the Old Testament, you know that men and women lived to be hundreds of years old: Noah was 950 when he passed on. They had great understanding of time and incredible strength. The long dead Prophets appeared and disappeared at will, and reminded the people of what was written, what events were coming. Jesus appeared after his death and continued to teach.

Winged angels shared their visions with men and women; they often whispered warnings and important messages about the future.

The unchained spirit, super animation is shown at 1000. We are a long way off. Most people here and now are floating between 60 and 100, but we can and do move up and get better and acquire more abilities.

I am here to tell you that this is *not* a pipe dream. But, it isn't what you might think either, that we should want to be *like* Superman, an unchained spirit. It is that we *used to be* a race of super humans. We used to be up here, the masters of Life Energy!

We are people of Light.

But, if this is true, where did our abilities go? Look around. What the heck happened to us?

Well, what happened to Superman?

With so many great talents; flying, seeing through matter and reversing time; it seems he's all knowing and omniscient.

But his knowledge of chemistry is lacking. He certainly doesn't know much about kryptonite. That stuff scares the heck out of him. So you see, even a highly evolved man with super powers has some vulnerability and areas of knowledge to explore.

People on this planet, each one of us can be a super human, with mental telepathy, ESP, clairvoyance, many spiritual abilities, and yet still have areas to address. We're far from 1000, the top rung on that ladder.

Kryptonite caused Superman to lose his abilities. He became weak, he would fall asleep as if in a trance; we would say he was less unaware. What do we call that, when a substance makes us weak?

An allergy, right? Superman was allergic to kryptonite.

What is it we are allergic to? What makes us less aware, what makes us weak and not have the abilities we once possessed?

When we talk about allergies, we know that the frequency and wavelength is imbalanced; there is a jammed frequency, certain wavelengths of the body may be crushed. The classic reaction is the body saying, "I can't understand it; I've had enough."

When we're facing a substance that is indefinable, if we don't understand it, it sticks to us like glue. After a while, the glue, tar and mass bog down the channels of perception and acceptance. We are less aware, and weakened.

When I was playing basketball, I studied physics, specifically, gravity and energy in the body because I wanted to jump higher and run faster!

What we all experience when we try to increase our stamina, our abilities, and in some cases in attempts to just get through the day, we run headlong into resistance. This is a block; opposing energies that stand in our way. So I studied Ohm's Law and other axioms of physics from way back to understand it and how to get past that resistance. What followed was an intense and protracted study of the elements; collecting and combining the relationships of the elements and all the healing arts we as a human race have acquired through time.

It was a massive project, all the way back, from the earliest man forward: tribal medicine and rituals, acupuncture, Egyptian and Greek healing, and pressure applied to the magnetic electrical switching points, what we call the meridians. Those healing arts were juxtaposed to the science of energy, our modern day science. That's all in *The Promethion.*

I rewrote the Periodic Table to make sense with all the healing arts, ancient and modern, to understand all the personalities and the expressions of energy that have been donated by these different cultures throughout history.

You'll even find the gas krypton in *The Promethion*: its very name is Greek for "hidden". As the beginning of the sixth octave, Krypton is one of the eight electromagnetic and electroplasmic anchors of our energy field.

Krypton, changed slightly for the comics into "kryptonite", might have been deadly for Superman but we absolutely need it for balance.

Prometheus, the Titan, stole energy from Zeus, a flame, and gave it to mankind. So, with *The Promethion*, we can take this energetic information from lost sciences and filter it back so people can use it to help themselves.

How can humans use this information in daily life? The essential foundations for the SAF® method are this book (*JUNK DNA*) and *The Promethion*. At the upper location point are the SAF® manuals (*SAF Simplified* is the book of choice); all these enhance and complete the others.

The Promethionic Interface cross-connects the Periodic Table of Elements with the SAF® numbering system. We tabulate mathematical probability into the mix and utilize SAF® to access the present time storage and inheritance located in the DNA.

ROM and RAM are highlights of the language of computer science. ROM, Read Only Memory, sets the overall parameters of the computer operating system and is not changeable. But RAM, Random Access Memory, is accessible and changeable. I am constantly adding new RAM programs to the Life Energy System.

We humans have our own ROM and RAM locked in our gene structures, our DNA. The Read-Only Memory is the scaffold, the framework that is not changeable, such as the sun shines, the sky is blue, the grass is green. This is the operating system of the universe hard-wired in. However, we also have Random Access Memory (RAM); our own DNA chip. This is our individuality; the events in our lives and our ancestors are stored here, in the DNA of our protein structures, in our organs and glands.

right: The logo of the flame was designed by Joe Scogna; it perfectly symbolizes his work. It is also an image of the sun and its rays that represent radiation, by which life is created and sustained. As a geometric form, the triangle creates the third dimension in the physical universe; matter becomes visible. Logo used by Joe in his Life Energy Research work.

The RAM chip is what we are studying here; how to get in and change that RAM chip. But first you have to accept that it exists. If you do that, half the battle is already won.

If we can possess the key to the automatic mechanisms that steer physical reality, the measure of control we can obtain is phenomenal.

Even if we cannot appear and disap-

The Promethion, along with JUNK DNA, are the foundations upon which the SAF® method rests. Although each can be read and enjoyed in their own right, they share a symbiotic relationship; each enhances the others.

The Promethion *offers a comprehensive study of the elements as these relate to our energy science, plus history and personality of the elements. Methods used through the ages for healing of all Life Energy forms on the planet include elemental mates, color, pressure to trigger points, herbs, foods and other remedies.*

*In **Junk DNA,** we discover what has been stored in our DNA since the inception of this planetary system, from the hardwired fabric of the universe to our individual inheritances and lifetime events. With access to the 128 sensing channels, we can better understand our world, improve our perceptions and gain valuable abilities.*

*Drawing from both these sources, **SAF Simplified** allows us to utilize the SAF® method in daily life. The reader will find all the numbering information, the organ and gland systems and the emotions that will help track events through time.*

With the information in these three books, humankind has a chance to expand spiritually and gain in awareness while helping others along the way.

pear physically, pass through walls, fly in the air, or do all the fantastic and fabulous things that the men of the Old Testament could do or that the enlightened alchemists in Arabia and Persia could do; even if these things cannot be accomplished in a lifetime, if we could change our mind automatically, if we could adjust our attitude about past events then we could program our thoughts and our dreams to pull and propel us towards that fantastic goal of someday controlling those patterns. If we could do this, it would be impossible to make us sad.

People might not see this because of their limiting factors on belief. As you move up in ability and get better and better, the only limiting factor is your belief mechanism.

I don't believe there is a limit because I believe in RAM. Random Access Memory.

We all have a RAM chip but for each person the chip has different circuits imbedded because our experiences in life have differed.

Through the SAF® chain sequence, we can examine the programs and subprograms that have been laid-in over time and have left us codes to follow. We can understand the whys and wherefores and in this process of recognition and understanding, the RAM is rewritten.

This is important. When we figure out <u>what</u> the program was and <u>how</u> it went in, we can reverse the process and allow it an exit. This is what happens with deprogramming.

This is the bright spot; this is how we can extricate ourselves. When we say "genetic changeover" in this work, this is what we are doing; we are changing over genetically the RAM part of this equation.

How is our RAM written in the first place? A computer is programmed by shock and electricity; our RAM in the DNA is no different. When we are trau-

matized or shocked (which is electric), programming and reprogramming begins. Allergy substances shock us, numb us, squash our super abilities, hinder our life and put those mental and spiritual abilities out of reach.

There are the common allergies such as to plants or foods, but there are many other substances that make us weak and often re-direct our thought patterns and behaviors. All radiant energies can cause us to be weaker, less aware, and can make us act as if we are not quite ourselves. Radiant energies include the elements, chemical fumes, high tension lines, extremely low frequency waves (ELFs), friends and family members, emotional radiation from arguments and especially traumatic events. (see page 49 for a partial list.)

We can gain entrance to our RAM programs by shock, electricity and trauma, but that is not under our control. We can also get in by the right sequence of approach. That sequence is the SAF® equation, the SAF® chain of numbers. It presents areas for us to examine and understand. Finding these equations, these chains of energy, is the essence of life.

Equations that have made tremendous quantum leaps in our energy science are Einstein's $E=MC_2$, Planck's Equation for Black Body Radiation, Ohm's Law of Resistance, and Michaelis Constant for Enzyme Reaction (see page 127). These equations are presents to humanity.

SAF® practitioners have the ability to write 100 equations a day, with a person's genetic bank and their energy, and to release a tremendous amount of electric charge. This is what SAF® work is for, to write those equations, to release that electric charge. This allows recognition and healing to happen.

The reader will find in this book that the genetic planning mechanism, the GPM, created and stored plans and programs that have aided our survival for the past several millennia, but often in modern times that plan is off balance and we are out of harmony. What are our symptoms trying to tell us? What are the aggravations about? What are the allergic substances that take our power away?

We will explore the Z Process and reactions people have encountered and expressed, but first it is important to understand a few definitions of our energy science—electric, electromagnetic and how this fits with the SAF® sequence of numbers.

Electric and Magnetic

Everyone talks about electromagnetic as if they know what it is. And they don't even know what electric is. We can't see it, and if we can't define it then we are operating a little behind the eight ball.

To make electricity, a magnet surrounded by coiled wires is rotated; the wires then become electrified with current.

When electric moves on the wire (current) this causes a magnetic field to surround it. Because there is balance in this universe, the two fields, electric and magnetic, are actually interconnected. A changing moving electric field will induce a magnetic field to surround it and a changing moving magnetic field will produce an electric field.

We are electrical beings, human electricity, and that movement, that energy creates a magnetic field around us. So we are magnets, too; we can pull things into us, we can become magnetized. We possess an electromagnetic field, as does the Earth and all other creatures in this planetary system.

Electric Charge

All matter has electric charge, held in balance, which means there is an equal number of negatively-charged electrons around a positively-charged nucleus (neutron and proton). Humans are larger versions of an atom. We are the macro to the microcosm of an atom, but a microcosm to the macrocosm of the greater universe. Humans are smaller versions of the universe.

Electric is a Spark and a Break

Electric is a particle, a fragment, a spark, a break phenomenon. When we strike a rock, especially flint or quartz, a spark flies off. The connection has been broken. Electric sparks are whittled, chipped off the magnet.

When we say someone has "excess electric charge" we mean they have a lot of excess electric that isn't balanced with the magnetic flow; they have a lot of breaks.

What was broken to create that?

We were once a whole electromagnetic unit and now we aren't. How can a human being have a break?

Through loss—you had money in the stock market and now it is gone. Pieces of it were taken. You had a nice girlfriend or a wonderful boyfriend and then they broke it off and went away. In these cases, you are left with excess electric, or charge; you are *upset*!

In life, the only thing that creates charge, that creates symptoms, is electric. And the only way to create electric is to have breaks. Breaks are traumatic events of one degree or another. Each of us has our own circumstances and history so we view our breaks differently but we all feel it. It is expressed as symptoms, either pains (added pressure) or sensations (lack of or missing pressure).

The SAF® sequence, or the chain of numbers, is a part of the energy program of an individual connected to the chromosomes, the gene structures as discussed in this book.

Working with the SAF® chain of numbers is a re-app, a re-application; you have a chance to change and fix things.

Atomically change the DNA

It is vitally important that we realize we are capable of atomically changing the chromosomal patterns. Science has been working with these ideas for quite some time. In test labs, mice and other mammals are used, plants, fish and microbes are studied, genetically modified, and studied again. Even humans are examined and studied like this. No one knows what the ramifications will be for this type of genetic experimentation on physical levels.

The changes in DNA by physical means is one thing but the utter disconnection of control between the DNA-RNA and the consciousness of the person is probably the most difficult and most important concept to understand and grasp in our lifetime.

This is serious business. We're not just playing around; you're really going in to fix something in the program. Now this might sound crazy, but not only do you fix the program for yourself, but you fix the programs of your children and your children's children, and all of the people in your genetic past, as well. They all get

fixed. Even the people that died 50 or 500 or 100,000 years ago, you fixed them, too. Because they're still there, in your DNA.

You've got to understand something about this environment; we're living in a space-time continuum. We've got a cookie-cutter situation here, where an impregnation on space is being made of this moment in time. Well, then where does it go? It goes into another dimension, into Time. It slides. We virtually have a continuous creation of energy, moment to moment to moment.

The Body has its own Language

The body doesn't speak English or any human language; we have to get it to speak to us in its terms, which is an electrical language. The pains and sensations that we feel are in a binary pattern of positive (pressure is there) and negative (space is there, something is missing). When the body is in trouble, something is either there that shouldn't be there (pressure), or something isn't there that should be there (space).

On a physical level, let's say there is arthritis in a thumb joint; it sends a message of pain. There is an excess of calcium and fluid in the joint (pressure). If we eat something and hydrochloric acid should be available in the stomach for digestion and it isn't, then we will get a deficiency signal, gas or belching.

The Endocrine Sense Channels Chart, also called the SAF Operative Chart, is the language the body speaks (page 193). We can use it to decipher the messages the body is sending us via our symptoms.

In the SAF® language, numbers have been assigned to the organ and gland systems, along with emotions, conditions, functions and many other categories, making SAF® a body-mind-spirit-emotion language.

We can learn this language; it is essential for an understanding of the SAF® method and for reading an SAF® chain of numbers.

Our organs and glands, which are our protein structures, hold recordings in that protein (DNA) of what has happened to us in the recent and distant past. It is *all* recorded—the good, the bad, and the ugly, across 128 sensory channels. When we identify which organs and glands are stressed the most, this tells us what emotions are stimulated and need to be addressed.

Electric Motions

Emotions are energy, e(lectric) motions, or electric motions. These are mental experiences with biochemical (physical) actions and these tell us how to be, how to feel. By connecting physical and emotional symptoms, especially through time and finding our patterns, this helps us increase our self- knowledge.

Every Chain Sequence has a Story to Tell

With training, we can learn to read the numerical sequence much like a grammatical sentence. The sequence presents a holographic image, a slice of life of the personal issue or trauma or whatever it is we are working on. (read: *SAF Simplified*)

The Heaviest Charge in the SAF® Sequence

When we look at an SAF® sequence of numbers and apply the electromagnetic principles to it, the heaviest charge, the most breaks and pressure are visible in the lead, the left number. It carries a positive charge. The central number or core has no charge, and the last number on the right carries negative charge. Almost everything is happening on the two ends of the chain sequence.

Breaks and Resolution

A fast and simple way to cause a break in someone is to interrupt—loudly— when a person is talking. The speaker will be upset and have some sort of symptom. That is a mild example and wouldn't groove its way into the genetic makeup as mightily as other types of breaks in relationships, love interests or business. When we have a close connection with someone and our survival is threatened, the breaks are much more intense.

If we live by laws and a law is broken, we will have breaks, charge.

If we believe in someone or something and our hopes are dashed, we will have breaks, charge.

If we follow a set of ethics, moral codes, civic codes, family codes or religious codes and we violate any of those, we are going to have electrical charge. That is karma.

In an intense break the most prevalent emotion is anger. When we sense this emotion in a partner, we know he or she has a break. If they aren't speaking about it the electricity, the tension, will build.

When they *do* tell us what it is, they will feel the discharge of energy. That is the "A-HA!" we hear expressed.

The break, the upset is resolved by the telling. It is fixed and life goes back to null charge, no pressure, no symptoms. This is the re-app in action.

Illusion

This universe is filled with illusions. The breaks and disconnections, loss and suffering, all an illusion. Many people have been given the illusion that they have a disconnection or a loss.

Music can do this. Sad, sappy tunes and words can make young women cry for hours about a lost boyfriend, who "died in a tragic car crash", when this event was merely a popular song, a recording on a record or CD.

Soap opera stars on television are "family" to the avid watcher, and the births, deaths, twist of personalities, and marriage break-ups are as real as life to them.

People are easily convinced something was lost even if they didn't own it in the first place. It may be a reminder of a similar circumstance in their own life or it may be imaginary. Both are breaks; both have charge. Imaginary ills are just as painful as real ones.

In these situations, for resolution and discharge of energy, another viewpoint of existence will present itself for view and acceptance. There will be a naturally occurring change of attitude.

How many SAF® sequences to run?

It is best to complete one issue or complaint at a time, and work with what appears. The client will never have the exact same chain twice, with the same ordering of numbers. There may be similar numbers, but these will be in a mixed order and so are telling of a new scenario to decipher, or a different viewpoint to observe and accept.

It would be unusual to have just one sequence for each issue or complaint. If it is a major lifetime event, each time it is

worked a different set of perceptions will surface to be examined. Even a seemingly minor event may require several looks; it might not be minor to the client. With the 128 Sensory Channels detailed in this book, each different examination of the sequence will present varying perspectives.

Journaling

The SAF® method is revealing of physical issues, for which remedies can be found, and of emotional conundrums, for which talk therapy is useful. As physical issues, emotions and ages are revealed in the sequence of numbers, talking to a practitioner and making the necessary connections relieves the pressure. But it is also a great idea to journal for several reasons.

If in the middle of personal work you suddenly have an experience or a revelation, write it out. Talking is fine, but we don't think with words, we think with images. Keeping a journal can be very effective. The energy moving from the brain and mind, down the muscular system into the arms and hands and fingers is further released by putting the images into language, putting it into words or illustrations with pen and paper.

This is the point where the energy in the mind and body is converted into mass as it is put on paper.

It is cathartic; if someone is really mad at another, encourage journaling, or the letter writing technique. It isn't necessary to actually send the letter; the point is it is out of the body, out of the mind and now into the physical universe, written on a piece of paper, where it belongs. Why hang onto it? Let it go. Journaling is a way to clean off the pistons and allow the processing to really flow.

The Future

What is the future of mankind? If we were to go 1,000 years into the future, what kind of program would suit people then?

I'm in total agreement with however we get to the future; religiously by being blessed, or by physical cleansing. Wherever we end up we are going to need a program, some kind of sequence. So our intelligence and our energy at this time must rise to an even greater level.

Every program you run has its obstacles. Working with clients on improvements with their energy and abilities is no different. So take your work with your clients seriously and reach for new heights and awareness levels.

We will explore some of the interesting programs that are lodged in the DNA crystals, categorized as the 16 Steps of the Z Process. On Step 7 the reader will find the 128 Sensory Channels, the perceptions that are at our disposal for sensing our world, even if we have lost touch with many of these abilities.

Our reactions to these sensing channels have created Z programs, little "zombie programs" that run in the background directing us how to act and react. When we access those programs through the Self Awareness Formulas, the idea is to understand them, which releases their energy and their hold over us.

Through our own personal work, we can catch a glimpse at how we have arrived in today's predicament of being somewhere between shackled and unchained spirits.

There is a way out! The Z Reactions we cherish begin on a spiritual level. It is an Idea, a Concept, a Postulate. This is most important to remember.

The Formula for Resolving Z

We must consent to the idea that such a thing exists in the first place (spiritual); let it exist in the second place (mental); and forget that it is there in the third place (physical).

Because this happens in the proper sequence, it is mechanically possible to understand and eliminate Z reactions.

1. Make people aware of the Z Process through the various Steps listed in this book.
2. Teach how it got that way, what the program was, how it went in. Deprogramming occurs through personal self awareness work with the SAF® method. Once the personal connections have been made, the power that the (former) unknown had over us, that directed us, has been illuminated and there will be an electric release (A-ha!).

The Story of Z

Zeta, Zed.

Zeta, Z was the 6th letter in the ancient Greek alphabet, meaning, *"I am, I am alive."* The letter Z indicates there is some "aliveness" present. Anchoring today's English language alphabet, Z is the final sound, the final word.

In electronics, Z stands for impedance, resistance; the resistive energies that are up against us, energies that keep us from reaching our full potential.

In mathematics, Z can represent an unknown factor and is found as such in various formulas, including Mandelbrot's fractal geometry equation.

Z also stands for zombie, a primal urge, sometimes seen as a supernatural power or entity that can animate a dead body. For our purposes, a Zombie or Z reaction is an action performed without thought, when it seems a person is hypnotized or deadened, or acting out in some bizarre manner they might not have done in a fully awakened state. Movies have explained zombie conditions as resulting from excess radiation or a virus, both invisible entities. Humans, it would seem by all the literature and movies, are fascinated and obsessed with zombies.

We human beings are replete with electrical impedances and blocks, with unknown factors, and invisible, living entities that help us, stop us or send us in the wrong direction. Z factors, those zombie-like mechanisms inside us, when triggered, get us to react as we were pro-grammed to do.

We recognize this is true when we overreact to a simple communication, and then wonder, "Was that me answering?" Or we make resolutions to lose weight, to stop smoking or drugging, to get a better job, to be kinder and we promptly forget the goal and revert to our old ways at the first opportunity. If we think or do any-thing that causes us to pause and wonder "Where did that come from?" "Why am I doing this?" then you understand about little zombie programs inside that "made you do it."

Invisible Entities

A few years back anyone who spoke of unseen energies or invisible entities within the human system was not understood. That was the realm of the super smart, the genius, or worse, the person was dipping into the regions of the unholy. They might as well have been speaking a foreign language.

Frequency. Vibration. Energetic Healing. Invisibilities and how the universe operates have been a mystery since the beginning of time. So you are in good company!

In the end, we must try and understand these terms in light of our own experience, our own life.

By examining the microcosm of the human, the tiniest speck of energy in the crystals of the DNA, which contain all our life pictures and events, we will understand this tiny speck of energy in the context of the larger organized entity, the composite of energies that is the holistic human being. These life pictures and events hold the key to our talents, abilities, as well as our weaknesses and shortcomings. And we can then find our place in the greater environment of the earth and the macrocosm that is the universe.

It is awesome. It is baffling. But it is understandable.

Just by reading this book, even if you don't understand or believe all of it, just the fact that you have allowed the information IN, you are helping to uplift humanity. We all have a long way to go to reach the unchained spirit.

The Genetic Planning Mechanism

For eons, since the inception of this planetary system, the genetic planning and programming mechanism (the GPM) has had the duty of seeing to it that humankind and all life forms survive. That is our directive:

TO SURVIVE

To carry out this directive, the genetic planning mechanism uses our gene chip. Events are constantly being evaluated and, when necessary to ensure our survival, new programs are written and put into action.

Many of the gene chip programs of the genetic planning mechanism are revealed in this work; these programs are the basic scaffolding of the universe.

Doing self awareness work will help you tap into these previously unknown programs and sequences that were written by the GPM during times of stress and trauma and stored in the DNA.

Feedback System

We receive information about our environment and our condition from an elaborate feedback system, the senses.

Dorland's Medical Dictionary defines the senses as *"a faculty which the human being possesses that allows him to perceive the condition and properties of things around him. A person can sense many things; thirst, hunger, equilibrium, time (intervals), well-being (euphoria), light, color, etc."*

Dorland's Medical Dictionary lists about 30 senses; in this book 128 sensory channels are presented.

All sense channels rely on the measurement of the same basic substance: *pressure.* Pressure is created by two or more objects in opposition. Physical, mental, and emotional pressures all exist; we judge how well we are doing by the degree of pressure we feel on all sense channels.

The density of matter (objects) is the study of the ratios of pressure to space of all objects—solid, liquid, gas.

Space and pressure vary to suit individual conditions. The human body contains more pressure and less space than does air, for example.

A simple scale of how we relate to this would show an increase of space and decrease of pressure as sensation; whereas an increase in pressure and a decrease in space is felt as pain.

Sensation can be likened to a feeling of space rushing in all around, pulling in a spiral, like a whirlpool, in an effort to correct the spacial distance between objects.

Pain, at first very slight, then more severe, increases as objects move closer in proximity than the natural spacial balance permits. The pain signal warns: Get back! Get back to the comfortable spacing of pressures.

There are many gradations and varia-

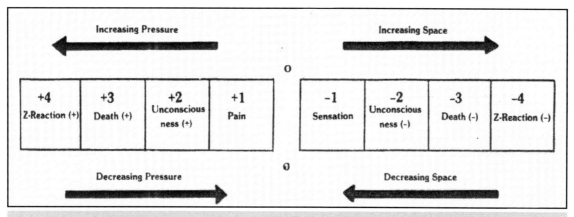

Expanded Scale for Sensing Pressure and the Z Reaction

tions of pressure. There are minor violations that produce slight pains and negligible sensations; the chronic offenders constantly suffer from illness and disease; and then there are the "major crimes", which sometimes result in an instant death sentence.

Z or Zombie Reaction

As we move through four different levels of pressurization, Z reactions are created, and can be discovered by any of us. (see the Expanded Scale for Sensing Pressure, above.)

+ or —1: At first we find the simple experience of either pain (pressure) or sensation (loss). We exercise and have sore muscles (pressure/pain), or we feel dizzy because we need water to drink (sensation/loss).

+ or —2: A second level includes two types of unconsciousness; one is induced by heavy pressure (pain) and the other by heavy loss or neglect.

+ or —3: A third level of pressure is found in the decay of cells and tissues, in which there can be death of certain cellular structures by over-pressurization or by being extremely depressurized.

+ or —4: The fourth level is the complete, total Z Reaction. It is considered only reachable by intolerable pressure or unbearable loss. Extremes of acidity or alkalinity are needed at this fourth level.

The reason why Z reacts the way it does is because of the preceding pressures and losses of pressures, levels 1-3 as seen on the chart above. These have made a groove, have been etched into one particular subject, idea or program of automatic blueprinting. When Z kicks in, it causes individual cells or groups of cells to react in a particular manner. If we were to take a spring device, press it down on a hard surface and then release it, the spring would return to its original position—balance— rapidly and automatically.

Our own system is much the same. When we create enough pressure or stress in our lives, we would say our system is spring-loaded. When there is too much of "something," there is always a flashback or recoil. It is an automatic, zombie response.

On these pressurization levels, there will be re-programming in our DNA to reformat our functioning level and adjust personality changes with the idea of better survival.

The first level is conscious and automatic, a discipline we can learn for focusing our mind to study and learn any subject, and for conditioning our body to perform amazing feats of athleticism, running in marathons, learning to paint, flying an airplane or swimming across the English Channel.

Examples of conscious Z reactions can be found in sports, such as a basketball player in training, who shoots a ball at the basket thousands and thousands of times in the same manner, at the same distance from the basket, utilizing the same muscles and intention. This will build up such a zombie-like pattern that he may be able to fire the ball into the basket without even looking.

The Guinness Book of World Records lists such feats, one player made 88 foul

---

Joe Scogna understood the Z principle and used it well. At age 14, he picked up a basketball for the first time. Not only did he teach himself to play, but within a year he was a stellar player, city-wide Philadelphia. By intense training of muscle and intention, in zombie-like fashion he could sink the ball, one right after the other, from anywhere on the court.

At one game, that had gone into double overtime, Joe had just intercepted the ball at the opposing team's end of the court. Attuned to everything around him—time, position of players, frenzy of the audience, geometric angles involved—he turned, rose up, aimed, and let the ball fly from his fingers just as the final buzzer sounded. The shouts were deafening, then complete silence as everyone watched that ball float thru the air to its desired spot – the home basket. Thunk!

The place exploded, both teams. They hadn't ever seen that ability in a high school kid.

---

shots in a row, blindfolded! Other players have made tremendous achievements that had been thought impossible, such as sinking 2,036 foul shots in a row. This kind of automaticity requires Z reactive force for its energy; in this way we can create our own RAM programs by training.

In all areas of life, we understand that "practice makes perfect". The repetitiveness of the physical action is required to create automatic patterns, whether it is done consciously or without thinking. This type of energy allows us to create any manifestation. A teenager who attempts to drive the family car for the first time is tentative, awkward and hasty, but in time, he can certainly maneuver it throughout his hometown, almost without thinking about it. In this case, the automaticity that has taken place within the teenage driver's mind and body is a form of Z reaction.

The Z reaction is desirable when we intend to improve our mind and gather knowledge of the universe. Throughout the entire cosmos, there are astronomical examples of Z reactive forces; the sun is a prime example. It can be construed as the only true automaticity that we must rely on, for if the sun were to be turned off, all other automaticities on this earth—all life— would cease.

Obviously, automatic reactive patterns are not necessarily a negative situation. Matter and energy can be taught to behave, to act voluntarily in predetermined patterns.

To better understand the Z reaction, we must dissect the components necessary to create one. In all phases of physical matter, there is a function to change. As all things are rapidly changing, shift-

The Z reactive force is a type of energy situation that allows matter and energy to behave by itself in predetermined patterns.

ing and rearranging, these are most certainly avoiding the Z reactive force, which can be painful. All energies in this planetary system are scheduled and patterned to be in equilibrium, or balance, so as to avoid the Z reaction. The chemical, elemental makeup of the environment is organized to prevent any violent pressurization or automatic dispersion (loss) of the patterns of energy laid into the environment.

In the 1940s, physicists Einstein, Bohr and others created servomechanisms for man's use by forcing certain elemental material to move more closely together than was natural. Nuclear devices demonstrate this theory. In creating the atomic bomb, these scientists violated the equilibrium and patterns set down for balance. An exploding atomic warhead is a manmade example of tremendous Z reactive force. During a nuclear explosion, the spring-loaded effect happens; there is an automatic retracing of all energies back to their rest positions.

A nuclear reactor, used to create electricity, accomplishes the same goal except its actions are ostensibly under more control than releasing a bomb.

The discovery of this phenomenon is not new; however, the application of its

(right) Atomic bomb blast. Atomic, hydrogen, neutron and dirty bombs are examples of tremendous Z reactive energy, manmade. The flashback (the blast), and then the fallout, are Z reactions. The victims are killed quickly and the deliverer more slowly.

force is now reaching into many innovative frontiers.

These demonstrate tremendous pressures. It takes pressure to create a Z reaction, even in a human.

Energies packed to a certain point that act as a servomechanism probably began with Stone Age man when he tamed "a piece of the sun" (fire) and learned it could be controlled, it was warming, provided light, it kept beasts at bay, and it would cook his food. The pent up energies locked into wood are released through flames and that energy is retraced back to a rest position, balance.

It is definitely up to the human mind, spirit and greater intelligence to program Z reactions, which are developed, propagated and controlled to a certain extent by our awareness level.

However, there are greater automaticities in the environment of which we should be aware.

Through the eons, the stories about vampires, zombies and unknown things that frighten people enough to make them leery of things that go bump in the night

are all based on the inability of man to conceive of and understand the Z reactive force.

The idea of a "vampire" existed for thousands of years across all cultures. When it first appeared in English literature in the early 1700s, it was perceived as reality. The idea is that a person who has been stricken by poisons would gradually be pressurized to a point of death; and yet beyond death, he would rise again in an automatic zombie-like fashion to prey upon the living. The energies in the system that are super pressurized will come back to haunt the living.

There can be many parallels drawn between a zombie or vampire of fiction and the complex degenerative diseases we see today, such as cancer, diabetes. And parallels can be found between our own stresses and past traumas that are still haunting us. The tragedy of a person not being able to locate the source of a recurring Z reaction that plagues him is visible in his chronic fear, depression, anxiety, superstition, disease and malaise; this is the state of humankind today.

Many misunderstood concepts that have never been solved are relegated to parapsychology, superstition, occultism, etc. An examination of these ideas reveals that many of the forces involved, depicted or dramatized are closely akin to the misunderstandings that we have about the Z Process and Z reactions today.

Conditions can only persist as long as they are automatically commanded to do so, inadvertently caused by the person himself. We add so much fuel to our own fires by ignorance and lack of awareness. Z reactions depend on unconsciousness, so all those things that dim our awareness have the potential for creating Z reactions of an unpredictable nature.

Because we live in a time continuum, the mysteries and unsolved concepts through the ages, up to and including our electronic age, have all been stored in our DNA. So it is prudent to learn as much as we can about our origins, how the universe operates so that we can be released of these unknowns that direct our actions.

The Alchemist and the Secret of Change

Ever since the earliest times, men have attempted to discover and to understand the invisible mechanics of the natural world. What makes the sun rise on one side of the earth and disappear on another? Why do stars twinkle? Why does the moon disappear? Why do rivers flow and water levels in the seas change?

Ever since recorded time, alchemy was a valued study, full of mysticism and unknowns. These researchers and natural philosophers, active in all parts of the ancient world – Egypt, the Middle East, China, India, South America, and Greece — laid the groundwork for religions and the scientist of many fields today.

Alchemists sought to understand the nature of life, immortality, and to better understand the connection of matter and energy and its intrinsic ability to change

---

Alchemy = Chemistry

The roots of the word "alchemy" demonstrate the spread of its principles.

- Egypt was Khem to the Arabs "the country of dark soil", known as "al-Khem."
- Our English word originates from the Arabic *al-kīmiyā'* or the chemistry
- Middle English: *alkamie*
- Old French: *alquemie*
- Medieval Latin: *alchymia*
- Late Greek: *khumeia*
- Greek (in Egypt): *Khēmia*

(left) The Egyptian Thoth (known as Hermes to the Greeks and Mercury to the Romans) is the founder of alchemy or Hermetic philosophy. He was a teacher of the occult, astrology, geometry and medicine.

The Egyptian alchemists made many advances with metals, ushering in the Bronze Age and the Iron Age.

We hear echoes of the tenets of Hermetic arts today in eastern philosophies: "As above, so below." (As in the macrocosm, so in the microcosm.)

Hermetic principle of vibration is found in nuclear physics: "Nothing rests, everything moves; everything vibrates." (Everything is energy.)

itself in quality, without destroying the quantity of energy.

We are still curious about this!

The transmutation process, the ability to change energies at will, was (and still is) a most sought after phenomenon on body, mind and spirit levels.

While early alchemic Greek philosophers determined the properties of the atom in 600 BC, on the other side of the world, the alchemic philosophy found its place as the Taoist religion.

The alchemist pursued the famed philosopher's stone, which, if discovered, would unlock the mysteries of life and the human body, as well as the ability to change base metals and lead into gold. While experimenting with the elements, they had seen these evolve and transmutate from one into another, and along the way made many discoveries in metallurgy. This set the stage for the various periodic tables of elements that men of

the occult and science have fashioned since the 1800s. (see pages 35, 64)

The elements are not static "things" as would seem by the printed charts and what we are taught in school but are instead pressure levels of Light that go

Alchemic symbols related the 7 known elements to the 7 known celestial bodies, and 7 days of the week.

Gold (Sun); Silver (Moon); Quicksilver (Mercury); Copper (Venus); Iron (Mars); Lead (Saturn); Tin (Jupiter).

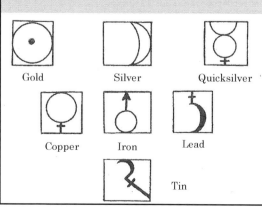

Gold	Silver	Quicksilver
Copper	Iron	Lead
Tin		

Objects, energies, and thoughts vibrate at different rates. There are many levels of vibrating energies that are hidden from the human being's five major sense perceptions of touching, tasting, smelling, hearing, and seeing.

through a life cycle of birth, growth, decay and death as do all processes on earth. All the elements above uranium are changed into other elements (transuranium elements).

In hot pursuit of the alchemist's dreams to create gold, as the first nuclear scientists studied the flow charts of nuclear decay they also learned to transmutate the elements. And they were able to create gold! Living in a materialistic society, this may have been their first order of business, and why not? However, the isotopes of gold produced (AU197 and AU195) are highly radioactive, and are of no monetary value.

The transmutation process in the human is under the guidance of the Willpower and Spirit of a person and can have many far-reaching benefits. Just let your imagination go and think of all the incredible feats that could be performed if we completely understood and could manipulate the transmutation process for ourselves. With this knowledge and ability, we could fly; teleport; live for hundreds of years as the early men of the Bible did, cause spontaneous healings, and do many miraculous things.

Stories such as these have been passed down through the ages and are now usually relegated to folklore tales of Arabia, Persia, and other mystical civilizations existing thousands of years before Christ.

This may still seem the stuff of science fiction but science has often followed art. The ideas and diagrams of the very creative often become facts, as demonstrated by Leonardo da Vinci and his flying machine, Ben Franklin and electricity (positive and negative energy, lightning rods for protection), and Jack Coggins, a science fiction writer whose illustration of a moon landing vehicle in 1952 became a reality a few short years later.

Although we cannot teletransport with our present technology, a "matter transmitter" was proposed by Edward Mitchell in 1877. So "Beam me up, Scotty" might not be far off!

And so, while it is true that the alchemist of old did not have instruments to see atomic level quantities, they made some fantastic primordial scientific discoveries with their ability to imagine, to postulate and to perceive through the mind's eye, a process called clairvoyance, what it would be like to visit microscopic, invisible areas.

Folklore annals do relate that there was a small group of alchemists who discovered the exact process for changing energy into matter and matter into energy, and they published their results in ancient texts and tablets, a trail for us to follow.

Transmutation in Humans

The DNA-RNA molecule and the genetic structures are part of a fantastic controlling mechanism that manipulates

(right top) Elemental Structure by William Crookes (1832-1919). An active dowser and spiritualist, Crookes was knighted by the Queen and President of The Royal Society.

Periodic Tables in Occult Chemistry

Occult Chemistry proposes that the structure of the elements can be assessed through clairvoyant observation, using the microscopic vision of the third eye, a method used by alchemists thru the ages, shamans, psychics and "Indian yogis, who are able to make themselves very small so that the atom can be observed," explained B. Jinarajadasa, of India, in 1933.

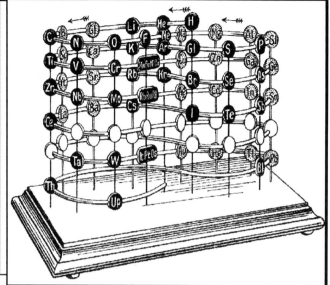

THE PERIODIC LAW
(after Crookes)

(left) The Periodic Law chart, based on Crookes' work, shows the flow and movement of the elements and their connections, and we can almost see the movement of a pendulum as it was dowsed by William Crookes.

The number affixed to an element is the number of "Anu" (not electrons) which compose the element. Anu is Sanskrit for the fundamental unit of physical matter. Along the top are the shapes of the Anu.

This Chart was published by The Theosophical Society, Adyar, Madras, India, 1933.

the transmutation process in the human being. When we consider the cycle of birth, growth, maturity, decay and death of the human body, we can easily see over a period of time that the structure, form, and energy, in visible and invisible quantities, radically changes. Transmutation occurs.

These changes occur at very slow speeds. We are living in and are a part of the changes, so when we try to view them, we can only perceive motionlessness. And thus, without very sophisticated equipment, we need to develop a highly tuned sense of imagination or clairvoyance to be able to visualize the rapidity of the changes taking place on atomic levels.

The Magic of Change

The rates of change in the environment are the vehicle for the wonder of the electromagnetic phenomenon. Essentially, objects, energies and even thoughts vibrate at different rates. There are many levels of vibrating energies that are hidden from the human being's five major sense perceptions of touching, tasting, smelling, hearing, and seeing. Step Seven in this book details 128 sense perceptions to which we humans have access.

The automatic functions that operate the human systems – nervous system, respiratory, cardiovascular, digestive, endocrine systems and many of the sub-miniature control centers — are on total automatic response. Although there are invisible quantities at work within the human body, these quantities or energies are not inconceivable. These were postulated thousands of years ago by the ancient alchemist and natural philosopher. The atom in particular was something not seeable to the naked eye and therefore not understood or accepted until our modern age.

Today, with betatrons and atom smashers, we have incredible technologies to photograph the energies that emit from the nucleus of an atom, seen as orbiting paths and streaking signatures of energies. An observer can pick up the remnants of quarks, mesons, and pi-mesons; not the actual substance because this is invisible, but as Heisenberg's Uncertainty Principle states: *"We must bounce photons off the subatomic particle. This alters their trajectory but is the only way we can observe the action, after it has happened."*

These sub-entities are evidence of a pre-scale of energy that contains actions far beneath the perception of human facilities and even beneath sophisticated detecting devices in use today.

The discoveries of the tiniest of the tiny frontiers and conversely, the magnitude of giant red hot stars across the universe as well, give scientists and researchers a truly broad spectrum of energy change to consider.

Repetitive Energy Cycle

The changing or transmutation process of energy, which is used to convert the tiniest messages such as quarks and mesons into the largest stars, is a process known as a repetitive cycle.

The repetitive energy cycle process allows energy to grow into something we can see. Repeating the application of energy to any object in the environment causes its growth and realization. The tiny brush strokes repetitively applied to the canvas by a trained painter mature into a work of art we admire. The energies repeatedly applied to a fetus cause it to grow and mature until birth, when the born baby can commence the life cycle. The same repetitive energies, like winding a thread around itself, cause matter to grow into a state of eventual maturity. The human being, once grown, is subject to suppression by the environment. Those same repetitive radiation strokes that caused birth now cause decay and ageing: eventually dying, and yet living into a new and different form of existence.

A pattern must be repeated and grooved in. This is a powerful yet simple way that energy is stored to create magnificent clusters of particles out of the small, energetic building blocks.

The answer to the mysteries about human diseases that have plagued medical scientists and their patients can be found in the reverse or unwinding of this repetitive energy cycle concept. It is unwound to understand how the disease got that way in the first place. The variable amounts of exposure that a person has to certain environmental stimuli, such as viruses, bacteria, poisons, toxins, high tension lines, electronic smog, chemicals, pollution, electromagnetic fields and the like, cause conditions to turn on and off like a light bulb.

The confusions of time and exposure to certain allergenic substances have put researchers into a veritable spin. The automatic plans and programs originally installed into the body for survival can create symptomatic patterns that are as scrambled as a pile of 100 million jigsaw puzzle pieces.

This being the case, the odds are against fully detecting the extent and the roots of the disease process. Doctors are dealing with the tips of icebergs. The reason is simply this: all energy cycles, as miniature as they are, have been laid in as a <u>program</u> for the DNA.

The subatomic particles, which carry out genetic commands, are undetectable with present day microscopic technology; it has not yet reached the stage where it

right: The DNA (Deoxyribonucleic Acid) and RNA (Ribonucleic Acid) are the main henchmen for the genetic blueprint of man, animals and plants. These two basic acids project the delicate spiral of electric pressure that emit from the core of the cell in helical patterns. DNA contains the coded formula for a cell to make protein—with adenine, cytosine, guanine and thymine, with a sugar-phosphate backbone.

- *64 triplets of nucleotides in the DNA*
- *64 hexagrams of the I Ching*
- *64 electric pressure levels of The Promethion*
- *64 Dichotomy Sciences of SAF*

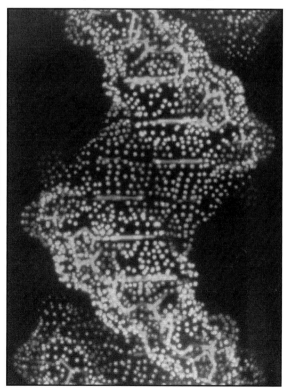

All energy cycles, as miniature as they are, have been laid in as a program for the DNA. The subatomic particles, which carry out genetic commands, are undetectable with present day microscopic technology. It has not yet reached the stage where it can decipher the automatic blueprints programmed into the DNA-RNA.

can find, much less decipher, the automatic blueprints programmed into the DNA-RNA.

Energy cycles are a DNA program. If we were to move into the DNA-RNA in some fashion, take the RAM program out, rewrite it and reinstall it, we could easily keep an individual from being sick and could eventually develop human systems with superhuman capabilities. None of us would program in arthritis; power and energy would be the goal.

Scientists, researchers and doctors attempt to acquire an inside view of the structure, movement and change of the physiochemical and electrical systems of the body. While each test (blood, hair, saliva, x-ray, CAT scans, MRIs, ultrasound, infrared and others) detects imprints and has a certain value, all are filled with inconsistencies and contradictions. They are hoping to find a peculiar pattern that will lead to the location, origin, or source of electromagnetic programming, the programming that will steer flesh into patterns of energy.

But just as the nuclear scientist attempted unsuccessfully to photograph the invisible, lab researchers are viewing the effect and not the cause. What they find visible is a fingerprint, an imprint on film of a moment in time after that structure already changed its pattern. At the moment in time of the actual change, the body is under the influence of some automatic impulse. Is it coming from the DNA-RNA or something smaller? At this point, researchers do not have the answer. However, the changed pattern is there.

Without "the answer", people today assign much of the explanation of the automatic invisible patterns of the body to deities, supreme beings or other sub-entities.

The energies locked within the core of life steer our patterns into the forms and shapes that allow us to witness beauty and ugliness. These patterns are programmed to repetitively change, and these changes add to or subtract from what we know and understand as reality.

The truth lies in the source of automatic programming. Automaticity, which is the realm of the Z reaction, is a discoverable phenomenon. We can mentally travel to exciting, brand new worlds that allow us to control our destiny. As we embark on this journey, know that it is a royal quest: to search for the awareness of knowing from where our energies come, how to use them, and how to program these for successful operations through life — then we can proclaim and reclaim our happiness.

The universe is filled with awe and mystery. The universe also holds the answers that operate its phenomena.

Once discovered, man is destined to reshape the universe with harmonic patterns that will glorify the cosmos.

The Art of Symptomatology

As far back as anyone can remember, to the beginning of recorded history many thousands of years ago and even before it was written down, man developed a segment of his communication abilities into the fine art of symptomatology, the study and knowledge of symptoms. Unlike electrochemical or electromagnetic testing processes, symptomatology depends directly on the analyzation and the evaluation of the individual by the individual. Being subjective, to be effective, the person must be cognizant of and be able to express his woes.

A symptom is defined as a change of characteristic in body and or mind: it can be a physical sensation or a pain, or could be a concept, an idea, attitude, emotion or a postulate.

In our Self Awareness work, we welcome symptoms, whether from physical issues or mentally triggered upsets. These are signals sent from within to alert us. The main goal in this process is to establish a base of testing that is personal in content. In this way, we can find patterns that are pertinent to each person.

It is mind boggling to consider the incredible complexity of the human system! But do not be discouraged. Whether a student, practitioner, or interested researcher, with modern technologies and the information made available by this research on Z reactions and the genetic programming, we can use guided information from infrared values or the special SAF® questionnaires, designed to illicit the information necessary to help trace down automatic responses that are indicative of patterns. These patterns will help to lead us to the source of confusion.

The special questionnaires, infrared values and the mathematical formula will create a sequence of numbers relating to the stressed organ and gland systems.

The questions are presented in categories, and cover the body systems, intertwined and complementary as these are.

For the seeker, it is as if he or she is being asked by a kindly, elderly homeopathic physician, who has studied the fine art of symptomatology. As a rule, this profession is well-versed in symptomatic patterns and has been since the system was organized in the 1700s. Much of this Life Energy and self awareness work is based on homeopathic principles.

Compare this type of symptomatology work with a visit to an allopathic (standard) physician. In that situation, when you gather your most pressing 5 or 10 symptoms and visit the neighborhood allopath to present these, the question you hear is, "which ONE of these symptoms would you like me to work on today?"

This scenario does not happen with SAF® work. ALL your symptoms mean something to you and therefore to this process.

But to be honest, doctors are extremely busy and do not have the time to sort through your particular complex symptoms and automatic responses.

This is personal work. We must each unravel this technical, complex situation for ourselves. We each have our own individual characteristic set of automatic responses, grooves etched and implanted in the circuitry of our own gene chip, our random access memory (RAM).

The Z reactions we experience are the result of confusions in our life. The source of the confusion is the Z Process and it has the answers; this is the programming we have been left to decipher. The point is not to eliminate the mechanism that is affecting us but to reduce its power. We, in this human body of ours, are in a balance of energies, an equilibrium of energies. To exist as a conglomeration of trillions of cells harmonically, we must be able to put our arms around the fact that there is some type of apparatus for maintaining homeostasis. This apparatus or procedure is found in the Z Process.

In the Process we find the genetic engineering that allows us to exist in a hostile environment. Wind, rain, the metals and elements, time and radiation constantly harass and provoke the human system and yet this system has been developed precisely to maintain its own status quo against all incoming pressure. Even though bodies are very fragile and timid in comparison with other structures in the environment, such as trees, megalithic mountains and vast areas of plains and oceans, the body still has the capability of being extremely resilient in the face of all this. Much of this depends on the Z Process. However, when the Z Process is out of balance or disturbed in some way, the body will decay, malform, dysfunction and send us symptoms.

The Z Process has remained hidden for so many thousands of years because of a lack of understanding of symptoms. When we become ill and are not operating at optimum function, the signals or symptoms are part of a Z reaction. It has been formulated and predetermined that a certain number of accidents will be repaired automatically; however, after a continual amount of stress or pressure to a particular area, the governing agents of the system take the cue from the engineer that guides them — energy must be transmutated to facilitate the new activity.

The interesting part about Z is that once it has been programmed in (whether consciously or unconsciously), it must later be programmed out, if no longer applicable. In the case of a basketball player, after training and playing hard for 15 years, the body is programmed for such activities. But if the player abruptly stops playing, the body then needs to go into a new transformation process. When there is a sudden end of training and conditioning, the former player may complain of bizarre symptoms and pains, which is actually the movement of energy as it changes the program within the system.

The Z Process, held in a dormant state by a perfectly balanced body, will manifest physio-electrical phenomena (symptoms) when disturbed. The particular type of symptomatology is an indicator of which particular Process is out of balance.

Knowledge of our symptoms is essential! All humans should be schooled in symptomatic patterns from the time they are children. Pain and sensation are invisible and so are not given the respect they deserve by the medical establishment. We therefore must do our own investigations and help ourselves as we can.

The knowledge of the cause and correction of symptomatology is the first step in the adventure of finding and controlling the Z Process. The environment has become such a suppressive situation to us, and the cell towers, chemicals, computers and electronics that affect us adversely, all add to our woes.

Ignorance (lack of knowledge) of our own symptom patterns has caused us to deny the possibilities that the automatic responses deep within the DNA-RNA molecule can be uncovered and controlled.

Programming

The idea of programming is taken directly from the same concept used in an analogue computer. The programmable computer chips are made of silicon dioxide, quartz crystals, which accept radiant energies and hold them in suspension until they are ready to be "read".

In the body, the amount of sand particles or silicon dioxide makes it a susceptible programming unit that can hold $10^{(24)}$ (one septillion) bits of information. This figure is substantiated by the electrical current coursing through the body, in combination with the cellular deposits of silicon dioxide and the sophistication of the human unit, in relation to present day technology. It does not postulate, however, the true capabilities of a complex apparatus like the human body.

The human body has a substantial amount of programmed material within; it has already been automatically programmed by Z Process. In other words, the musculoskeletal system, cardiovascular system, respiratory system, cardiopulmonary system, endocrine system, digestive system, and all of the other systems in the body on automatic response are being governed by master systems in the brain, mid-brain and the mind. Much of the mental control comes from the mind's guidance system, which is the person, the personality, the spirit.

Programming From the Earliest Moments in Time

The study of the human body and the Z Process, to be effective, must be examined from the earliest moment in time to the origin of creation and development of the earth, sun, solar system, planets, and man.

Long ago, Lucretius wrote: "To under-

"History is a cyclic poem written by Time upon the memories of man."

—Percy Bysshe Shelley

stand the world and the universe is to know the beginning, the causes."

Theoretically, the earth was formed several billion years ago and was subject to incredible geological changes through a succession of fiery periods of transmutation. The study of this phenomenon is not considered religious or irreligious, as it is totally an objective view of the changes and the metamorphoses that have taken place.

As mentioned previously, the genetic planning and programming mechanism, the GPM, has had the duty of seeing to it that humankind and all life forms survive. Carrying out this survival directive, the GPM has inscribed many programs into our DNA gene chip. These are the universal laws, the laws of nature that create a balanced and harmonious framework. All of us have these in our DNA, as do all life forms on the planet. Here too, are the unique and personal inherited and lifetime events, the good and the bad. These events are evaluated, recorded, and when under stress and trauma, new programs are written and put into action when necessary to ensure our survival.

When we wish to increase knowledge about this balance and harmony, through the Self Awareness Formulas (SAF®) we can tap into these previously unknown programs and sequences of ours.

The considerations as to the perpetrator of this creation must go in the direc-

"Everyone who is seriously involved in the pursuit of science becomes convinced that a Spirit is manifest in the laws of the universe— a Spirit vastly superior to that of man." — Albert Einstein

tion of one's own belief mechanism. If anyone doubts that a supreme being or master entity was involved in this process, then he is lost before he even starts. The greatest automaticity is the physical universe. It works by itself, under the guidance of Supreme thought. There is a hierarchy of intelligence in this planetary system, and this concept is something that one who seeks knowledge of the universe understands.

In 1859, Charles Darwin published his work, "The Origin of Species," in which he stated, *"There is grandeur in this view of life having been originally bereaved by the Creator into a few forms or into one; and that, whilst this planet has gone cycling on from so simple a beginning, endless forms most beautiful and most wonderful have been and are being evolved."*

The testimony of Darwin, that a Creator caused the initial development of energies on earth, in the solar system and beyond, points to an interesting understanding. Darwin, who closely studied the minute changes of energy that make each object characteristically its own, also recognized that the Creator instilled vast amounts of automaticity in everything on earth.

Therefore, it is up to each of us to study this automaticity and find out exactly how it relates to humankind and all life forms, and more especially, to our self.

The Sixteen Steps of the Z Process

Since the beginning of time to the present, an evolutionary structure has created certain well-developed, well-defined and extremely powerful levels of energies, which are the sixteen steps of the Z Process. The power and energy of these proc-

esses on a graded basis is what makes up the electrochemical system known as Homo *sapien.*

The Organizational Chart of the Z Process is a diagram of the step-by-step process that has occurred on Earth since the inception of the planet. This chart represents a hierarchy of energy and different graded levels of automaticity that act as servomechanisms for man's survival. The number of changes or transmutations that have taken place since the beginning of earth-recorded time delicately balances these sixteen steps.

Ever since the very beginning of earth, energies have extended great efforts to reproduce and it is this same duplicative process that causes the human being to behave the way he does. The patterns of energies on the chart that have been developed are specific graded levels of survival potential, from simple mechanisms to complex organisms.

The succession and pattern of LIFE ENERGY, as published here, is a complete memory imprint available in every speck of energy that exists on the earth. Not only do animals and man possess this information but also birds, insects, snakes, fish, shellfish, bacteria, sap, fat, proteins, salts, sugars and the elements as well. The fixed and stray movements of energy, which make up the full Electromagnetic Spectrum of energy, exist from the sun to the earth (see page 114).

This impressive record is no secret but is hidden from the average person. It contains the memory tracings of the story of creation to the present-day existence. The availability or access to this information is being realized with the help of modern technologies. However, man has always had an understanding of the progression or movement of energies in building block fashion to create more intelligent forms of life.

The discoveries of the DNA-RNA molecule brought Nobel Prizes to the researchers and awoke mankind to the concept that man was a collection of divisible parts even smaller than the cell. As seen by the Organizational Chart of the Z Process, the status of the cell or colony is not reached until about midway in the cycle. This means that energies must coordinate and construct certain pre-designed structures in order to be a whole organization, such as on the later Steps. The chart shows that half of the energy is spent ob-

---

The Organizational Chart of the Z Process

Step 1 – Radiation – Subatomic and Atomic Particles (electrons, neutrons, etc.)

Step 2 – The Light Elements

  (gases and the formation of water vapor)

Step 3 – Heavy Metals – (below cobalt to iridium)

Step 4 – Uranium and the Actinide Series (radioactive)

Step 5 – Sugars – (simple and complex)

Step 6 – Salts & Crystals – (compound, inert substances)

Step 7 – Protein Matrices — The 128 Sensory Channels. (consciousness begins)

Step 8 – Fats (nuts, seeds)

Step 9 – Milk, Sap, and Ooze

  (the beginning of life's organizations as humans relate to it)

Step 10 – Microbes, Plants, Bacterial Colonies

  (energies living in harmony and multiplying)

Step 11 – Crustaceans, Shellfish

  (those colonies on land and sea that develop protective armor)

Step 12 – Fish (the full spectrum of water-bound bodies that transform

  into reptilian or mammalian status)

Step 13 – Snakes and Reptiles

Step 14 – Insects

Step 15 – Birds

Step 16 – Animals and Mammals

The Organizational Chart of the Z Process is the key to understanding and finding the memory tracings from the story of creation to the present-day existence.

---

taining a building block-like organization.

In viewing the Organizational Chart, the sub-atomic particles, rays and other unseen, yet vital energies that spew forth from Supreme guided creativity in Step 1, form light elements, gases and water vapor in Step 2, which in turn precipitate heavy metals, Step 3. Metals condense and radiate their own fury to create forms of energy that can be used, stored and retrieved by intelligent life in Step 4. Sugars, salts, proteins and fats, found in Steps 5-8, are a progression of energy that is more or less structured like a finely tuned system of transistors, one begetting the other.

All these steps are necessary to develop the cell. Once the cell is constructed and there is capability of division, higher forms of life such as plants, crustaceans, fish, reptiles, insects, birds, animals and mammals can be developed.

No one can deny this organization for it is plain to see. The molecular structures, organizations and systems accompanying electrochemical processes are readily visible to the trained scientist and investigator. However, without a sophisticated electron microscope, it is imperative to learn the system of subtle, sublimated signals (symptoms) these energy levels have developed to communicate to intelligent forces (us), whether these signals are in a state of energy increase (pressure) or decrease (loss).

This information is essential so that we can continually keep the holistic human system in balance. Energy imbalance, sickness and disease are inevitable whenever any one of these Steps of energy overwhelm another. For instance, if there is too much radiation in the body, then the structures requiring the body to be organized and assembled will crumble. Excess radiation causes disruption of life's organized systems.

As we peruse the list of energy manifestations on the Organizational Chart, we begin to appreciate the magnitude of this study; each single step of energy produces its own particular set of symptomatology.

Once studied, and when used in conjunction with the SAF ® Questionnaires, Infrared, and the SAF Online Interpretations, we will discover which area of the body, mind or spirit, which step of energy is in active stimulation. The Z Processes of graded energy can communicate to intelligent life above it in the body to warn it of impending disaster on any level. It is a prime function of intelligent life to keep harmonic patterns moving between the developmental stages of energy within the system.

Just as the earth was formed in a systematic pattern of graded energy and intelligent life, so too, must an individual give respect to that pattern of graded energy and intelligent life if he or she wishes to keep it in harmony.

The symptomatology that emanates from an organized body of energy (when any of its steps of energy are missing or are in hypermotion) can be filed and listed under each particular step.

The explanations of the Steps will give the avid researcher and reader a better insight into the transition of energy that takes place from a Z Process through the Z reaction and finally, and ultimately, discharging or exhausting the energy on that level.

Part Two:
The Steps

- **Step One: Radiation**
- **Step Two: Light Elements**
- **Step Three: Heavy Metals**
- **Step Four: Actinide Series**
- **Step Five: Sugars**
- **Step Six: Salts & Crystals**
- **Step Seven: Protein Matrices**
  (128 Sensory Channels of Perception)
- **Step Eight: Fats**

Step One: Radiation

Radiation is the first grade of energy within the system. When we want to study the possibilities of symptomatic patterns, we must start at the very beginning of creation. As was expressed in the Book of Genesis:

"In the beginning, God created the heavens and the earth. ...and darkness was over the face of the deep.

And God said, "Let there be light", and there was light. And God saw that the light was good. And God separated the light from the darkness." Genesis 1:1, 1:3-4

Essentially, this same process is happening every microsecond at the speed of light (186,000 miles per second). The existence of the human body in its stabilized, balanced form, as well as all life forms on this planet, depends directly on the equilibrium of light radiation. This marvelous expression of energy comes from the will of its Creator, giving life variety.

Each time a human being postulates, thinks or poses new problems, he creates radiation and tantalizes the first step of electric pressure within his own system.

There have been many theories of the origin and creation of the earth and this text does not purport to replace any philosophy or idea of science or religion, but

"We know our God from His energies, but we do not claim that we can draw near to His essence."
--St. Basil the Great, Eastern Orthodox, (329-379 AD).

the knowledge of the Z Process does tend to overshadow primitive concepts.

For reasons of practicality, we must stabilize the activity and the energy that is imbued in the holistic human mechanism on physical, mental and spiritual levels. The cohesive force that connects these three separate concepts—body, mind and spirit—is dependent upon radiation.

Radiation is outreach.

It is creation.

It is the beginning of something that will manifest.

Without radiation, there could be no starting of any life form on this planet. It has been understood by historians through the ages that life grew out of the cosmos, out of whirling clouds of dust particles that formed into a darkened sphere. Essentially, man creates his own mental image pictures and his own view of himself, by way of these radiant particles. Each time that man uses these mechanisms, he must pay charges to the origin point of radiation. Consciously or unconsciously, each day of awakening, man must bless the day the sun was created. For without the sun's radiant rays, an action that began eons ago (historians believe it to be more than 4 billion years old) there would be no automatic activity on the planet, generated by others. If the sun were to turn off its light, all processes and life on earth would cease.

The glands and organs that are directly in control of these radiation ex-

The Winged Sun of Egypt. The sun was born of nothingness; it is fusion energy. In all cultures since the beginning, man has been fascinated by the mystery and power of the sun; as master of heaven and earth it creates and sustains life.

The worship of the Egyptian sun-god was first centered in the ancient city of Anu (On *of the Bible,* Heliopolis *of Greek and Roman writers).*

pressions are closely in tune with the wants and the desires of the mind and spirit of the individual. The glands and organs (stimulus-response mechanisms) translate this radiant information into cohesive energy and then ultimately nourish the entire body and the brain, especially from the cortex moving towards the mid-brain or hypothalamus area. The primitive brain, as the hypothalamus is sometimes called, is the seat of conversion for radiation into particles that will eventually become a living breathing structure.

The mental conditions, which precipitate physical phenomenon, are those generally termed psychosomatic; these psychosomatic ills, as a rule, make up a large percentage of the sicknesses in the present-day environment. These come about because of an inability to properly understand and control symptomatic patterns in the first place. Control of symptoms and illness must start with an organized intention on the part of the person to keep

the Z Process, the 16 Steps of graded energy, in balance.

The hypothalamus, itself being a nerve center, is a conglomeration of a mass. It is loosely clustered. The idea of radiation on this Step depends heavily on desire or the thought process itself. The hypothalamus seems to be that point of entry for many individuals to express energies of the mind into those that will be viewed on a physical level. (See the Endocrine Sense Channels Chart, also known as the SAF Operative Chart, page 193.)

Born of Nothingness:
Fusion Energy

Step One of the Z Process is born of nothingness, or fusion energy. This energy is that which creates light radiation from desire. ("Let there be light.")

Even though the hypothalamus is affected directly by this phenomenon, it is not the cause of it. To get at the cause, we must understand that the spirit, the personality or the willpower is the controlling

Holy books of mankind (the Bible, Tao Te Ching, Zend Avesta, and the Vedas), written by men of wisdom, always begin at creation, with similar creation stories.

The Lenape (eastern US woodland tribe) call the Great Spirit Grandfather: KESHELAMUKUM "He Who Creates Us By His Thoughts. (Cashman, The Circle of Lenapehoking.)

factor of the body. The Spirit is the one who generates radiation.

The hypothalamus is basically the receipt point in the physical sense of the area that aids in the transmission of symptom patterns to the rest of the body. In other words, the thought processes that are unleashed on the body will be relayed by way of the hypothalamus to the rest of the body to express these ideas and concepts in a physical way. This means that almost any thought that the individual has will be translated into some type of symptom. It is at this juncture where it may be the most difficult to track a symptomatic pattern, for we can have almost <u>any</u> thought we desire, depending on the environmental exposure and the hereditary transmission patterns.

When monitoring the genetic codes, people who have been educated or trained in particular ways will have very specific thought wave patterns. What we can gauge and evaluate on this Step One radiation level are the disturbances of transmission, not so much the direction of thought into flesh; but more, the disturbances that may occur <u>during</u> transmission.

If we can imagine this grade of radiation controlled by Thought as a transitory response, then we can take that one step further and visualize the holistic mechanism as an electrical conduction device that sends pictures and images to the body.

The device that man has developed that is the closest to duplicating this concept is the television. Images are collected

---

People are exposed to radiation and radiant energies every day and are unknowingly affected by it. These are not nearly as intense as a bomb but are much more insidious.

Examples:

*anger	*fluorescent lights
*arguments	*harsh light
*accidents	*radar
*injuries	*air travel
*sunlight	*car travel
*stress	*cigarette smoke
*poor diet	*crystals
*polluted water	*microwaves
*polluted air	*human contact
*sound pollution	*animal contact
*drugs	*vegetable contact
*worries	*electricity
*abuse	*anything that
*television	glows in the dark

ANY disease can be artificially created with the right amount of radiational energy exposure, as above.

---

on one end, sent, transmitted and received on the other end. The television is an apparatus that needs to be observed and understood if one wants to realize more fully the powers of the mind.

The connection from the spirit to the mental mechanism and then down to the physical levels (body) is the fruitful area of symptom patterns. Just as a telephone company or a computing device may have symptoms of electrical or program-

---

Both religion and science require a belief in God. For believers, God is in the beginning, and for physicists He is at the end of all considerations... To the former He is the foundation, to the latter, the crown of the edifice of every generalized world view.
                                                                 —Max Planck

The idea of radiation on this Step depends heavily on Desire or the Thought process itself. It is the Spirit that generates radiation. We can have almost any thought we desire, which will be translated into some type of symptom. Much depends on the environment around us and our hereditary transmission patterns.

ming disruption, so may the human being have symptoms when transmitting energy from a mental plane to a physical plane. We must consider the mental/spiritual apparatus in the Z Process. Without this connection, the rest of the manifestation of light radiation would be occluded and unknowable.

When analyzing the mechanisms that can be disrupted or imbalanced, we see a system that is devoid of heavy matter. The electrical system, which moves at light speeds, works primarily on energy patterns, and therefore, its symptomatology of dysfunction will basically be that of electrical phenomenon only, invisible to the naked eye. An example would be a headache (perhaps infrared could detect a headache, but to date no one has actually seen one.)

When studying the possibilities of radiant forces moving against other radiant forces, (human beings clashing with other human beings, their thoughts clashing with the thoughts of others, their actions clashing with the actions of others,) we can see that thought as radiation moves in particular patterns. These are rudimentary patterns. This means that the flow or force of the thought of a person can have some very basic malfunctions.

The Methodology of Thought

A determination must be made first of the direction of the flow of energy, either an outflow (a radiation thought pattern) or an inflow (a gravitation thought pattern). This would be either energy movement in a dispersing, explosive pattern away from us (radiational energy) or a collecting, implosive pattern in toward our center (gravitational energy).

When the environment strikes a person, such as when stung by a bee, hit by radio waves or a car, or attacked by emotions such as anger, antagonism and sympathy, energy is moving in toward the center.

When we are creating, or are in a creative mode, energy is radiating outward away from us. This developmental radiation experience is part of everyday life learned at a young age. The environment, however, has a much greater effect on us than we may realize.

Through the ages, humankind created a complete set of nomenclature to describe this energy travail. It has been written about and taught by scholars to show the entrapment of this society and its effects on us.

The Mass and Energy Scale

The main cause of concern on Step One radiation energy (that is, the energy that controls our thought process and our ability to create) is: PRESSURE.

Some pressures are perceivable and some are not. Physical, mental and spiritual pressures all exist; we judge how well we are doing and how we feel by the amount and type of pressure we feel. Whole sciences and studies have been developed to understand the rules of pressure and have been passed down to us.

But what exactly is pressure? Some people will call it stress, when in reality it is the product of two or more moving ener-

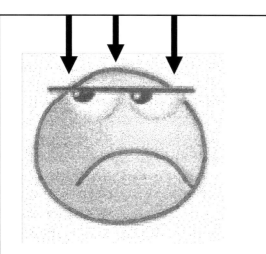

Emoticon for Depression
Pressure pushing down, as the pull of gravity.

gies in opposition.

All pressures will accumulate to form objects. A human being is a collection of trillions of pressures. A flower, an insect, rocks and minerals contain pressures. Even the air we breathe, although invisible to our eyes, contains pressure. The barometer measures atmospheric pressure and we do feel this.

The word Pressure comes to us from the Latin root word *pressare*, to press, to act upon by weight. The <u>type</u> of pressure is further defined by prefixes, useful descriptors of how the pressure affects a body:

In the English language, there are seven words (prefixes and definitions) from the same root word that describe our plight in the environment on earth and only one of them relates to our ability to fight back against the environmental pressure.

Depression

The Latin prefix De- means "down"; and when combined with *pressare*, "Depression" the pressure of gravity pushing down on a person.

Depression is a direction of radiational energy, unseen but certainly felt, which squashes our energy. It is an inhibitive type of energy, counter to the creative processes of an individual.

We continually fight against gravity on this planet; our lives are led in a battle against gravity. Were it not for gravity, man on this planet could easily become superman, with super human abilities. But because of this downward pressure, humanity lives in a constant state of depression, in which the pressure lowers the spirits, makes us gloomy, sad.

The level of Depression depends upon our ability to forestall or prevent gravity from squashing our thought processes too much. At this point in time when we attempt to rid ourselves of Depression, we still must acknowledge the aspects of gravity, on any plane. There will always be some resistance to our thought processes, but in actuality, resistance is always the primary concern to the radiant processes on a Step One basis. The ebb and flow of this radiant energy maneuver will always cause specific symptomatology. The sadness and the apathy, which are primary symptoms of this flow of energy, have been categorized under depression and graded with modifiers, such as mild, severe, and even suicidal.

Depression causes a blockage of mental thought, so that the picture-making process we use to realize our own potential and to propel us to action is darkened.

Another symptom that may be evident of this depression is unconsciousness, lessened awareness of our surroundings. At the same time, the body processes, those fluids and materials that are necessary for the enzymatic transfer of energy within the digestive system, are also hampered. The breathing is short and shallow; other evidence of this condition is a slowing down or clogging of the system. Those with chronic depression relate that their body generally feels heavy and pushed down. That may show as a sagging about the face, which can appear sunken and the countenance dark. Depressed people are squashed looking, as opposed to individuals who are happy and winning against the downward pressure (depression) of gravity.

The concept of gravity is evident in the word "grave," which comes to us from the Latin *gravis*, meaning heavy. It is a salient point that the graveness of any situation causes the weight of depression and what better description for a depression in the ground into which a deceased person is placed: a grave.

Repression

When the Latin prefix *Re-*, meaning "back, again and again", is added to *pressare*, we have "Repression", a condition of radiant energy that tends to restore a previous condition, to knock the individual backwards again and again.

The word Repression describes an energy situation in which a person takes one step forward and then three steps back. It is, in a sense, the action of energy being knocked unconscious. Repression is evident in the individual who gains a little and loses a lot. It is the type of failure process a person discovers when he invests in projects and plans that eventually cause his downfall. This type of energy situation generally depletes a person's overall being.

Repression is an energy condition that is demonstrated by chronic drug use. When a person uses a drug, he momentarily acquires a gain in confidence. The investiture in these types of substances and compounds are for temporary relief; however, unseen forces, repressive forces, which are possessed by and encapsulated in the chemical frequencies of the drug, operate against the person, the user, and knock him backwards into confusion and a less conscious state. Slowly and furtively, a drug acts in such a way as to reduce or diminish the amount of consciousness that an individual possesses. If we could draw a line from total consciousness to total unconsciousness, it would be seen that drug use and drug taking is about

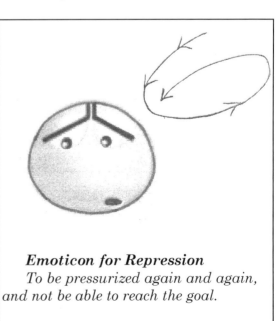

Emoticon for Repression
To be pressurized again and again, and not be able to reach the goal.

the most degraded process possible: the temporary gains that are made in well-being are quickly snuffed out by the residual chemical reactions that take place.

Individuals, who manifest Repression in a physical sense, may seem well and functioning one day and then very, very sick the next few days, until it is time to take the drug again.

This pattern is also observable in those who are addicted to foods, sugar, alcohol and many types of over-the-counter medicines. Their reactions are so closely aligned with the pattern of addiction that we can barely detect the real reason for their upset. And even when found out, the addictive item by that time has gained such a foothold in the organization of the body that it is difficult to uproot. The repressive process, which has captured so much of the consciousness of the person, has made the body a manifested control center that requires, even dictates, that the person take the addictive substance, whatever the drug of choice.

This addictive activity is part of our current social makeup but there are other factors that contribute to repression radiant energy. People with misguided and misdirected emotions often do the damage. The jungle scene of life puts one person's emotional conundrums up against another person's. The maze of misunderstanding itself is a chronic magnetized field of pressure that draws the curious to it: "Why is Daddy so upset?" "Who knows?"

Repression, and all pressures for that matter, fuel and feed themselves. There is no sense in adding to the melee with ignorance by adding chemical frequencies to the problem. Repression radiant energy is already here, alive and well, and living everywhere.

Impression

The Latin prefix, *Im-* means "on", so this type of pressure (Impression) has an effect produced on the mind, the senses or the feelings. This description of radiation is important to the human being because it is the pressure that implants ideas.

Impression leaves an imprint, a lasting mark that adheres to us like a tattoo. It is an energy that is frozen in position and causes the victim to remember, in chronic detail, traumatic scenes abhorrent to him.

A person who breaks up his marriage, splits up relationships, takes part in wartime events, loses loved ones and has trauma perpetrated against him has par-

Emoticon for Impression
Pressure has left its mark, a vague remembrance or belief. This is the pressure that implants ideas.

ticular images pressed into his mind that have left an indelible mark. The scars of these mental image pictures squash his energy against a screen too difficult for a person to erase in time. Time does not heal all wounds. Some will have these images implanted their whole lives and die with the visage of their torment etched across their thought patterns.

Without professional help, such an individual will demonstrate the anxiety, distress, torment and despair of having to think the same continual thoughts, over and over again. Rape victims, those who have been assaulted or who have witnessed terrible traumas acted out will replay the situation many times over in their minds, in which the faces, places and objects are extremely and powerfully excited, much like luminous neon tapestries.

This Impression radiation energy is replete with unconsciousness; however, the one signpost or symbolic tag that accompanies this confusion is always the memory of some significant portion of the upset. Once it has been implanted, the scenes are difficult and seem impossible to remove. And the despair or hopelessness that goes with the idea that one will never get rid of it, or "it will never get better" is the type of symptom pattern evident on those who are stricken with this energy condition.

In our present-day society, an impact or trauma is almost certain to befall every one of us. None of us are free from this, which guarantees that many of us will relay this type of radiant energy into the body.

Compression

The Latin prefix *Com-*, means "together", with *pressare*, to press together, to condense, to compact.

This type of Compression radiant energy condenses and compacts energy into a smaller, pressurized space. It is a see-saw type of distraction or disruption in that it ebbs and flows. It is present one moment and not the next. This type of energy has baffled scientists since the beginning of their study of human conditions. The trigger, which causes the Compression, is a moving or mobile entity outside of the individual.

Compression is a type of antagonism or distraction that teases or tantalizes the individual's energy systems. For example, a person can be highly allergic to some substance such as chocolate and when partaking of this material, the chemicals he is reactive to may drive energy inward toward the center of the body causing

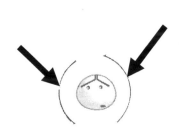

Emoticon for Compression
To be squeezed into a small pressurized space. The pressure comes from others, often unknown, who stop us from succeeding or even moving ahead.

pain, until it wears off. All the symptoms attached to this upset are evident when the individual is exposed to chocolate energies; however, later the effects gradually fade.

The types of symptomatology that may occur under the influence of a Compression form of radiation are almost infinite and therefore, impossible to detect by conscious thought alone. Without using sophisticated testing devices, people cannot discover what substances (persons, places or things) are acting as trigger mechanisms for the Z Process within their systems.

Items such as chocolate, milk, candy, cakes, sodas, people, etc. are not the actual culprit. These are triggers; these are triggering something that lies deep within the individual. It is so imbedded in the system that it is difficult for the person to put his finger on exactly what is causing his problems. He can blame the chocolate bar but realistically only an imbalance of the Z Process could cause his woes. These inequities of Z are connected to earlier traumas relating to particular grades of energy such as birds, milk, and radiation.

The testing procedures of SAF® (Self Awareness Formulas) follow symptom patterns and have come a long way in detecting the exact traumas; the times, dates, places, emotions and events for thousands of people. Collection methods include various subjective questionnaires of physical and emotional symptoms; and using Infrared for temperature values at organ and gland venting sites. With this sophisticated knowledge, researchers and participants can hunt down their own Z Process upsets.

The SAF® method is the only way to understand and control the mechanisms that haunt the human system and coerce the body into behaving irrationally.

Oppression

From the Latin prefix *Op-*, meaning "against, in opposition to". With Oppression there is an opposite pressure, to press against, to weigh heavily upon.

With Oppression, the energies of the person, when moving outward and forward, may be met head-on by the energies of another. For instance, if two people were vying for the same job, there may be an antagonism developed in the form of competition.

An example of Oppression in an obvious sense is demonstrated by the game of football. Team one is charging straight ahead (to the right) while Team two is charging straight at Team one; there is a clash. This collision of bodies (energies)

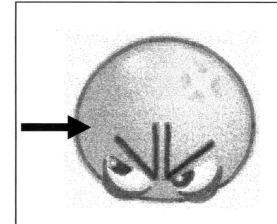

Emoticon of Oppression
Opposite pressure, from being opposed, by weight or constriction, mentally or physically.

causes a particular set of symptom patterns that we can directly observe.

Oppression is one type of organized radiational energy in which the person can see it coming right at him. This visual ability allows the person to stand his ground, push back, or confront that pressure. He may become angry and antagonized. If the individual were to become fearful, then the Oppression energy would meld into a more subtle form of radiation, suppression; Oppression is considered a milder form of suppression.

Oppression is the force that directly faces or attacks the individual and is responded to in one of two ways: the attacked person can either break and run, or face up to it and fight.

In either case, the radiant charges that fly toward the body are the type that stall or kick back pressure in the person's face.

Suppression

The Latin prefix *Sup-* means "under", to be pressed under. Suppression is an overwhelming type of condition.

Suppression radiation energy differs from depression in that suppression energy is not coming from above downward but from all sides. Imagine a pincushion and a hundred pins shoved in from every angle possible; this is an apt image of Suppression.

Suppression is "superior inward pressure", and is the worst type of pressure possible. The pressure squeezes, stops and blocks energy from all sides. It is an

insidious energy and is generally difficult to detect because its origins are unknown and unseen.

Suppression is such an overwhelming and yet subtle force and cogent pressure that most all humankind is blind to its activity.

By definition, Suppression must be invisible even to the person's mental viewpoint. It comes from "some unknown person or location," making it in the unconscious realm. Therefore, the suppressive pressure must be classified as something that occurs even on pre-radiation levels.

This unseen type of radiant energy is more easily felt through physical symptomatology. It may be something that a skilled person could view in another if he had the training to do so. In a sense, the view is not actually of the person's body

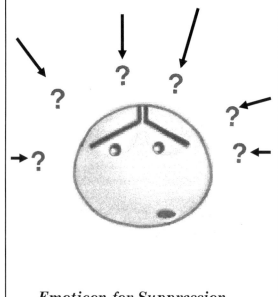

Emoticon for Suppression
This type of pressure has an unknown starting point but presses in from all sides. Don't know from whom or what???

but more of the body's statistics.

The suppressed person is failing. He is experiencing superior hidden pressure from many sides. Something or some person in the environment (source is unknown to him), is preventing his actions from becoming fruitful.

Expression

From the Latin prefix, E*x*- meaning "from, out". To press out, release, an outward manifestation of some feeling,

Expression is the only root word of "pressure" that we can use to radiate pressure outward from the body.

Expression is the only word to describe the type of pressure that we can create on our own.

Expression means to push energies out and away from the body and the mind by communication of thoughts, emotions, and ideas through various mediums.

Expression turns Depression upside down, pushing it upward.

Expression takes Repression and, again and again, knocks the energy back up the ladder towards total consciousness.

Expression takes an Impression, understands it, erases and dissolves its hold.

Expression takes Compression and loosens it, spreads it apart and dissipates it.

Expression takes Oppression and reverses its flow to allow it to release.

Expression takes Suppression from all directions and pushes it out and away from the body in 360 degrees from whence it came.

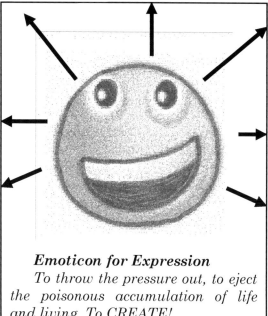

Emoticon for Expression
To throw the pressure out, to eject the poisonous accumulation of life and living. To CREATE!

Mankind, at this point in history, realizing the odds against him, has set up his own nomenclature and language to describe that the odds against him winning in this environment are six to one. This fact has been subtly implied by one of the most notable books we have for our language: the Dictionary.

In this way, we bet on our own mortality. We set goals and limitations for ourselves; we favor our self as the underdog. We have a unique sympathy for the underdog. We admire someone who "wins against all odds", however, this game has been set up so that the odds are against us.

Expression is the act of controlling harmonic, radiant patterns of energy moving out and away from the body into the environment, with little resistance. We can express ourselves verbally, through the arts, and more subtly by body expressions, feelings, facial features and communication.

In all the other instances and definitions of pressure, energy is moving in toward the center of the person, in which case, the environment wins and the individual loses.

The game started four billion years ago and is still being played. It is high time we learned the rules! With the constant application of intelligence and knowledge, the radiant energies of Depression, Repression, Impression, Compression, Oppression, and Suppression can all be controlled by our Expression.

The constant out-flow of radiant energy, of which the composite human being is capable, can be used much like a laser weapon against the forces of the environment.

Read on and discover more about the process of Z!

Step Two: Light Elements

The most powerful force beyond radiation is that of gaseous substances. The emission of hydrogen from the sun is the first building block of all the elements to follow, and all the Steps to follow.

Hydrogen is the basic substance of the universe; it is the lightest and the simplest element, often said to be in the etheric realm. It moves in such a furtive way, that its connection with the other gases, such as oxygen, nitrogen etc., create minor segments of life that eventually beget complex organizations such as animals and man. In essence, the composition of man is primarily water and gases. The heavier elements comprise such a minor part of the overall system as to be nearly insignificant by weight comparison.

The earth's classic memorial journey from the bowels of the sun, involves a complex process of creation that was comprised of many radiant expressions all at once. The blinding hot flash that caused the creation of the earth is recorded in the electromagnetic field as the memory banks of living, human entities on the planet today. The actual event took place billions of years ago and in sequence, developed a pattern of energy of which all living matter possessed a memory.

The hot fires, which molded the earth from whirling centrifugal (moving away from) and centripetal (moving toward a center) energies cast from the sun in its own shape, slowly began to congeal.

As the fires cooled down, molten energy masses of radiation in a radioactive symphony of disharmonic and harmonic light alike, degraded to heavier states of pressure. At that point in time, condensa-

Hydrogen from the Greek hydro, *meaning water and the suffix* —gen, *meaning to be born, creation.*

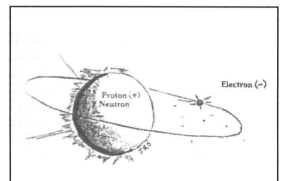

An atom of hydrogen, with a Proton (+), Neutron, and Electron (—).

Hydrogen makes up nearly 90% of the molecules in the universe. It is the product of fusion energy production of stars as well as the electroplasmic field of the human body (EPF). (see Sensory Channel #106) Illus. by Joseph R. Scogna, Jr.

*"I am the daughter of Earth and Water,
a nursling of the Skies;
I pass through the pores of the ocean
and shores,
I change, but I cannot die."*
The Cloud —Percy Bysshe Shelley

As the molten fires cooled, condensation of matter began and gave rise to gases, atmosphere and water.

tion of matter began, and as matter was first perpetrated, its energies were expressed in the form of gases. These gases gradually cooled, intermingled, and created atmosphere and water.

The corresponding human glands holding the most precise records of these events are the pituitary gland, which controls the water and fluid balance of the body, the lungs and the sinus cavities, which are merely gas chambers monitored by the pituitary gland to make sure that the individual is inhaling the correct mixture of gases. In a sense, the body is constantly monitoring the atmosphere to be sure that it is in accordance with the initial subscription laid down during the creation of the earth.

Breathing is one of the oldest, most recognizable activities in the human body. Even though it has been thought that creatures on earth did not begin to breath air until there was ample oxygen and photosynthesis, it is still a recording of earth history some 3 billion years ago when the planet *itself* began to breathe. The correct balance of the atmosphere is what the body is seeking in a specialized ratio form.

The kidneys and the urinary tract, as well as the sweat glands, participate in this harmonic achievement, for it is a condition that the body faithfully monitors every microsecond. When any of these factors are out of balance, that is, the water and gas mixtures, the body will become hopelessly imbalanced.

Sickness, illness and diseases such as mankind well knows today exist due to the fact that the primary gas and water imbalances in the body, created by unstable, environmental conditions, are allowed to persist. If environmental conditions were more stable as in the deep past, we would be more able to quickly and forthrightly correct the gas and water levels and stabilize the glands, organs and cellular responses responsible for the maintenance of these primordial levels; we could boast of never again being ill.

The symptomatic pattern that an individual displays during upsets of this era recorded in man's history is primarily heralded by upsets involving the lungs, bronchi and the sinuses. The most common manifestation of imbalances of this sort is the disease pneumonia, in which

Breathing is one of the oldest, most recognizable activities in the human body. Even though it has been thought that creatures on earth did not begin to breath air until there was ample oxygen and photosynthesis, we have within us a recording of earth history some 3 billion years ago when the planet <u>itself</u> began to breathe.

the body's gas and water balance becomes so topsy-turvy that water and oxygen begin to replace each other. The lung sacs fill up with the trapped water particles and mucus, and the individual begins to lose his ability to properly coordinate the water and gas balance.

The preliminary symptoms and signs of water imbalance are dizziness, vertigo and loss of coordination and equilibrium. This stems primarily from the middle ear syndrome, which develops because the brain and the primitive mid-brain mechanisms use this area of the body in order to aid in the body's electrical balance and coordination.

When the Step Two Z Process is askew, there will be difficulties in maintaining homeostatic water balance within the body. The sweat glands will be either overactive or under-active. The individual may have consistently dry, arid hands, feet or skin, or, conversely, may have tremendously sweaty palms, feet and skin.

Body odor may be atrocious. This is due to the fact that the water and gas mixtures are corroded with precipitates and poisons which add an extremely foul odor to the mixture. The facial expression of the individual is sunken, dull and

(below) Rock carving. Triple magnetic flow spiral, Newgrange, Ireland. According to Michael Poynder, Stone Age man understood earth energies, magnetic currents and water flows. They dowsed with pendulums to find underground sources and carved their findings on rock. Poynder, a dowser himself, found the spirals at many ancient sites in Ireland, and dowsed the sites for verification.

(above) OM Ireland, c.3500 BC. Ogham or Ogam (an ancient language) is pronounced OM in the Irish language.
(below) OM India, c.3500 BC. from Pi in the Sky *by Michael Poynder*

Photo: Tim O'Brien

cachectic (profound ill health). Disharmony of the system and gross imbalance is portrayed on a visage of crushing pressures.

The body will maintain the inability to correctly keep fluid in circulation and thus the individual may also be prone to swelling, edema, dropsy and other disorders.

The kidneys may also prove to be an area of great dysfunction, as the whole urinary tract may become engorged with precipitate minerals, deposits of stone and other calculi of debris.

The person who has violated the balance of the Step Two Z Process will definitely show signs of wasting. When the respiratory ability of the lungs is hampered greatly, the conversion of energy from the air into mineral combinations that balance the body will be lessened.

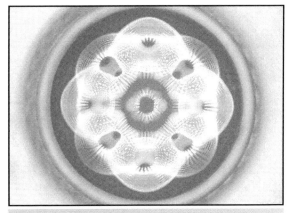

(above) Cymoglyph photo image of a drop of water responding to vibration, courtesy of Cuneyt Konuralp, MD from his light therapy and energetic explorations.

Well known present day work with water and vibration includes the photographs of Dr. Masaru Emoto. His "Messages from Water" books depict images of harmonics and disharmonics as frozen drops of water interpret these.

The practice of discovering and recording the vibrations of water has a history. (right) Ernst Chladni (1756-1827) used a violin bow to vibrate plates to determine the mode pattern and shape of sound for various items, including water.

Chladni also studied the velocity of different gases in special glass organ pipes, and examined such oddities as meteorites, stating these were of extraterrestrial origin, an idea for which he was castigated in his day.

Step Three: Heavy Metals

As the earth formed out of fire and molded itself into stages of gas and water, the homogeneous bands of collected light emitted by the gases charged with electrical particles began to take on a more characteristic and powerful pressure.

Storms, hurricanes, powerful winds, lightening and rains coalesced, disintegrated and dispersed into water vapor and freakish cloud formations. At length, this collection of energy, this folding and unfolding of electric pressures powered by the electromagnetic rays of the sun, began to change parts of the earth from their harmonic coordinated scenario into a more characteristic personified expression of pressure as the earth's vaporous status began to harden and compress.

At the same time, coincidentally, the formation of the <u>heavy metals</u> occurred. Heavy metal is that expression of the earth's personality in pressurized form, and refers to those metals that are below cobalt (Co) to iridium (Ir), which take in two full Octaves on the Periodic Table (see page 64).

Possessing Electric Charge is a Fundamental Aspect of all Matter

The characteristic crystalline formation of energy fashioned after the carbon prototypes formed in the second step of electric pressure, decidedly changed the face of the earth. The dimension of color, sound and vibration became much more localized and characteristic. In a sense, the earth took on a personality fraught with emotion and attitude. The earth began to live at this point.

The earth, itself a collection of harmonic energies, paved the way for the building blocks of matter and energy, which were to become the consistent, coordinated effort of cells called man.

The bubbly lightness of the gases formed in the second stage of energy (Step Two) coupled with the vaporous counterpart water helped to produce a situation that was ripe for the parade of heavy metals to follow. It is at this heavy metal level where the human being has memory traces of emotional status.

This level is the trigger point for the emotions, which are merely e (lectric) motions, or electric motions. By definition, emotional conditions presuppose that an individual has enough conducting material within to carry on electric motion. But in actual fact, the levels of emotional build-up are more so directly related to the heavier cobalt-to-iridium factors.

If we were to draw to scale the exact situation of pressure versus emotion, we would say that the bubbly, lighthearted excitement of gases and water vapor would have to be at the top of the scale. A

At this time period, the earth took on a personality fraught with emotion and attitude. The earth began to live at this point.

The Periodic Table of Elements

The elements and metals gold, silver, iron, tin, copper, lead and mercury were well known to the natural philosophers of antiquity; phosphorus made its official designation as an element in 1649. Experiments continued in all corners of the globe with many versions of the flows and structure of elements. In 1869, Russian Dmitri Mendeleev published a table with the then-known 63 elements. Based on this table, he predicted the existence of 10 new elements. He is considered the "Father of the Periodic Table." The table has been added to and used by scientists ever since. (see also the Occult Tables, page 35)

The horizontal rows represent periods, the vertical rows are the groups

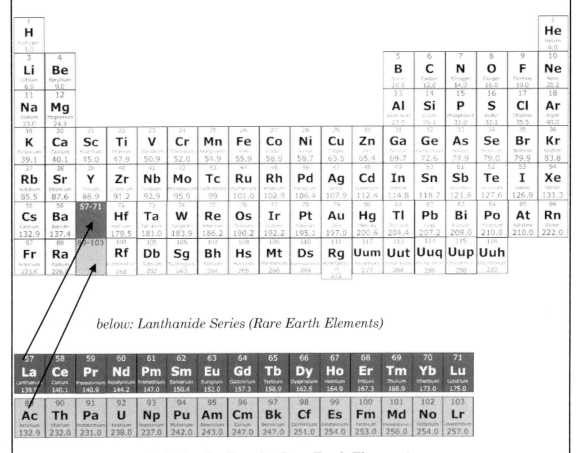

below: Lanthanide Series (Rare Earth Elements)

above: Actinide Series (Radioactive Rare Earth Elements)

In "The Promethion" the Table is divided into 64 electric pressure levels, with eight Octaves. This comprehensive study of the elements provides natural and sometimes ancient ways to achieve balance through its elemental mate and other minerals, nutrition, homeopathic remedies, herbs, color, light and pressure on specific switch terminals.

list of emotions would correspond directly to the build-up of electric pressure, for it is the power and the realm of the heavy metals to control the electrical motion present in the human body. Exhilaration, excitement and happiness must be considered at the top of the list. At this point, energies are totally free to move.

Enthusiasm (6.0)

With enthusiasm, to include exhilaration, excitement, euphoria and happiness, an individual still has much free, bubbly energy left untouched by the opposition of heavy metals. The energy that has developed is part of the second stage of electric pressure mentioned in previous paragraphs. The assignation of energy as an arbitrary number would be six points (out of six), with no formation of collected mass or pressure. In this case, elements from the gaseous state of nitrogen, oxygen, and hydrogen, to a point near phosphorus and silicon, would be considered the zone on the Periodic Table that closely aligns the emotional status of the individual. It is evident at this time that the body, being composed mostly of gaseous elements when happy and healthy, would express energies that are more closely aligned to these elements. In a sense, an individual goes through a subtle yet powerful transmutation process, which aligns his body to the gaseous state rather than to the heavy metal situation.

Conservatism (5.1)

At this position on the scale, the individual is beginning to lose part of his energy to pressure buildup. The gases in the body that were light, airy and bubbly are now beginning to condense into tighter, more acid-like particles, which remain in cluster form. The elements that this emotion readily mirrors are the line-up of metals from silicon to cobalt. This is the normal operating range for many human beings. It is the situation in which the perfect balance of zinc, manganese, chromium, copper, iron and nickel maintain an exacting coordinating effort of electric pressures within the body.

Antagonism (4.2)

An individual who is entering into an emotional band demonstrating that his energies are becoming bothered and disturbed, is antagonistic. One-third of his power is lost to stored condensed pressures that are more closely mirrored by the elements from cobalt to rhodium. The electric pressure within this emotional band is extremely gray.

People who are antagonized will dramatize more closely the disturbances that are part of the influence of the elements mentioned. Perhaps it is not important for a person to know that the elements in his body transmutate at fantastic rates, depending on his emotional status. However, to understand fully the Z Process, we must know and grasp that instantaneous transmutations of elemental energies within the body are the prime cause and effect relationship, which has a cause-effect mechanism between the mind and body. The situation that creates antagonism occurs due to the fact that heavy metals are out of balance, and these are also out of control. If we were able to easily control the transmutation process within the body, we would never again have the problem of a misplaced emotion, such as antagonism. We would never again have the problem of being unable to control ourselves under any circumstances. This, then, is the actual effect of the Z reaction, for it is that automatic response that is beneath us, causing all of our confusion and malaise.

Anger (3.3)

Anger is an emotional condition in which energies of the person have been directly pitted against energies of the body. The anger of the person seeks to confront and destroy the source of upset to him. It is a noble effort; however, the pressurization of the body is only equal to the free intelligence that is guiding the system. Therefore, the individual stands a 50/50 chance of winning an argument. However, that must be split down the middle again because half of his faculties

The Graph of Emotions

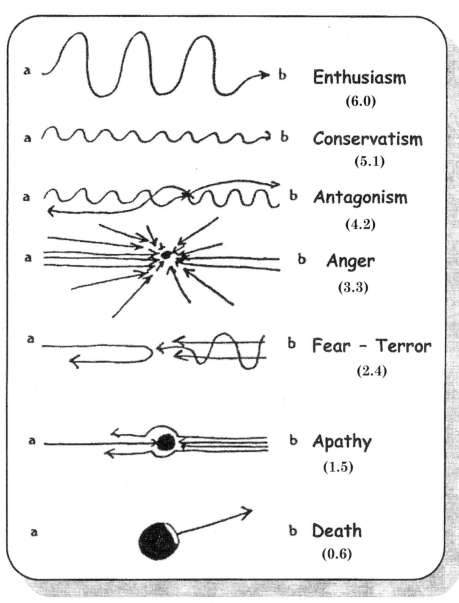

are lost to captured pressurization. This means that the individual stands a 4 to 1 chance of losing in this condition.

It is always at this point, when operating on this band of electric pressure (anger), that he definitely becomes ensnarled in captured energy masses, preventing him from operating at full capacity. The elements involved in this process are those in the band from cobalt to rhodium, which is the entranceway to pressures with which the individual feels he cannot cope. Anger is a 50/50 situation in which a person attempts to regain control so that he is not plagued by the upsets causing his problems. It is safe to say that the Step Three Z Process is very much a mental phenomenon. However, the expression of this phenomenon is definitely cast in physical terms; the anger shows itself clearly.

Fear-Terror (2.4)

In this band of energy, the individual finds himself almost totally overwhelmed by the collected masses and pressures surrounding him. The elements from rhodium to iridium are more powerfully compressed and more noticeably reactive and are those that help to create a situation where the person finds himself unable to do more; he can do nothing but cut and run in the other direction, almost as if he were shot out of a cannon. The two points of intelligence left to the individual (the two points of free energy) represent a 67% loss of power. It is at this point that an individual must make a decision to focus the remaining 33% of his energy on survival mechanisms and gutsy research so that he can get himself out of the mess in which he may find himself.

Apathy (1.5)

This is a zone of electric pressure in which the individual has almost completely ensnarled all of his energy. It is actually the point where the energies of the body readily transmutate to a latter band of heavy metals from rhodium to iridium. Many of the directives coming from the body are connected to this level of electric pressure. It heralds the death of this organism and the rebirth of a situation that has catapulted man into the fourth step of the Z Process.

Death (0.6)

On the elemental band just below the scale from cobalt to iridium is where we find death. It announces the rebirth of electric pressures into an awesome power which is, itself, a radioactive entity. In a sense, all the charts that depict the Z Process scale down in the same manner, in parallel courses, to reach the same goal. This level of electric pressure powers the Z reaction. It is a level of existence below death, and the level that is borne out of death. In a sense, it is the death of the old and the birth of a completely new form of energy. It is the point where energies snap back in the other direction.

If we were to imagine the Mass and Energy Scale (from Step One Radiation) closing in concentrically as we traverse down the scale from Depression to Suppression, and as an Expressive energy that gradually moves outward concentrically as we venture up the scale, we can view the next step of energy, the Actinide series, with a better understanding.

****

Step Three, the heavy metals, precipitates directly to Step Four, which is the primary area of the Z Process. Step Four is the first plateau of a solidly connected level of automaticity that will react immediately. Steps One, Two and Three are merely a prelude for Step Four. It is on Step Four that an individual will experience the tremendous awe and mystery of transmutation. It is Step 4 that is the set of automatic power that helps to create physical automaticity.

We must never forget that energies always start with Desire, work their way through a certain particular pattern, and there, at the end of that pattern, realize the automatic power of the disease process.

The Self Awareness Formulas (SAF®) is the study of life, the creation of life and its disease processes. Throughout all the processes of energy, there are pains and sensations. These pains and sensations cause dis-comfort, or dis-ease, and that is all it means.

Physicists teach that as energy moves out from the sun it causes a disease process on space.

And so it is on planet Earth; all disease processes begin with the sun.

Step Four: Actinide Series

The entire pattern of sixteen steps is more or less a depiction of the energies going through the cycle of creating and destroying the Z Process.

At Step Four, the Z Process has peaked. The energies from Step One (the radiant forces of thought), Step Two (the development of light elements and water), and Step Three (the emotional patterns that compress energy into matter) all pave the way for Step Four, the Actinide Series.

The Actinide Series are those radioactive elements that thrust or spring back energy onto the user.

This scenario is laid into the memory tracks of everything on planet Earth, for this happened billions of years ago in a scene that was played during the development of the Earth.

The energies of the sun, reaching out radiant forces into space to create the whirling, turning, fiery masses, which slowly vaporized into gaseous elements and water, and then slowly compressed into personalities fraught with emotions and captured pressures known today as the elements (especially the heavy met-

als), were due to pay back their perpetrator, the sun. Balance was necessary.

The energies from this act sprung backward, recoiled back toward the sun, and the expression of this springing-back action comes from the radioactive elements. The springing action is like a burst of sunshine when the pressure of the heavy metals became so severe and darkened that the physical laws could no longer permit its existence.

The creation of radiation was much like the dawning of a new sun. The energies, which sprung back, opened up the powers that man now uses for nuclear warheads and for the making of electricity. This atomic knowledge also opened the gates to much higher perceptive levels for humankind.

The energies of uranium and its sister elements pay back the sun by stretching radiation from their cores, electromagnetically, back to the sun. In a very real sense, this very situation is what the Z reaction plays off. When an individual has a sensitivity to or an acute perception of a certain material, what is being perceived is the action of that material snapping back against the user, just as uranium

The Actinide Series are radioactive elements. This means disintegration occurs until stability is reached. The elements pay back the sun by stretching radiant energies from their cores, electromagnetically, back to the sun.

89	90	91	92	93	94	95	96	97	98	99	100	101	102	103
Ac	Th	Pa	U	Np	Pu	Am	Cm	Bk	Cf	Es	Fm	Md	No	Lr
Actinium	Thorium	Protactinium	Uranium	Neptunium	Plutonium	Americium	Curium	Berkelium	Californium	Einsteinium	Fermium	Mendelevium	Nobelium	Lawrencium
132.9	232.0	231.0	238.0	237.0	242.0	243.0	247.0	247.0	251.0	254.0	253.0	256.0	254.0	257.0

The Z Process is the balance of power in the universe. It is insurance that equilibrium will be maintained. This concept confirms that whatever we do will eventually come back to us, someday, in some shape or form.

Spiritual precepts teach us of this concept: karma, "do unto others," and love one another.

snaps back against and toward the sun.

Examples of this "snap back" abound. We call this an allergy or an overload. We can eat only so much chocolate before that chocolate snaps a reaction back to us. We can consume only so many bananas before the bananas repay the eater. We can run only so far, so fast and so hard before the energies of the body snap back against the runner. We can inhale smoke and other chemicals, drink alcohol, have addictions and risky behaviors that are detrimental to the body for only so long before it will snap back and repay us in kind.

People who are devoid of the consciousness necessary to understand the Z Process will eventually drive their bodies down the energy-mass scale to the point where all their energies are gone and they are but a frozen mass. At that point, funeral directors make their income. At a wake, mourners stand around and look at the crushed, enervated mass that once was their friend or relative. That death, the deceased body, is a symbol of the person's inability to consciously transmutate energies, in balance, away from the pressures creating heavy metals that snap back.

Energy-free beings can exist in immortality when they are conscious of the fact that exposure to one particular substance, one particular environment, or one set of individuals, one circumstance, emotion or condition, without its rectification and release of energy, will cause death of particular zones and areas of the body which include the bones, muscles, cells, and tissues, but not necessarily death of the whole being.

Therefore, at this point, it is important to note the Z reaction is a warning — it hints at the understanding that an individual does not have to completely kill off the whole body. He only needs to destroy certain cells and tissues. Of the trillions of cells that compose the average human body, we can easily destroy 10-20,000 or even 100,000 cells and barely notice the loss. Those lost 100,000 cells may pass the dormancy of death, and may be released from the inertness, the stone-like quality of death into a new form of vampirism, a new form that may be called an allergy, a disease process, cancer, or some other term.

By whatever name, it is always the Z reaction. It is always payback time. When an individual pushes loads of energies, dead inert pressures past the death point, a new dawning of a sub-entity, which snaps against the body or the user, is evident. The system is spring-loaded and must be balanced.

This Z Process is the balance of power in the universe. It is insurance that equilibrium will be maintained. This concept confirms that whatever we do will eventually come back to us, someday, in some shape or form. The stuck particles will splash back against the body; just as the earth itself periodically experiences tremendous upheavals with earthquakes,

Heavy metals are chronologically imbedded in the memory tracks of all living things. The Periodic Table is not just the scale of descending electric pressures; it is a time track recording the creation of energy.

volcanoes, hurricanes and tornadoes.

Spiritual precepts teach us of this concept; karma, "do unto others" and love one another.

When we do not nurture an understanding of our life and livingness, then the usually calm, sedate living situations become breeding grounds for Z reactions. It is a constant struggle for us to continually maintain the awareness of all the possibilities that may exist of the Z Process. This is a very complex world. It is a training ground for those who wish to understand the many varieties of life on the planet.

The sixteen steps of electric pressure are but categories in which millions of separate subclasses of life exist. These subclasses and major classes of energy and living offer a test to each of us. It is a test of our ability to harmonize with these energies and create more power and energy.

We eventually understand that man in a more natural state, set free from deceit, deception and ignorance, easily existed in the environment and rarely created a Z problem that he could not handle and understand. However, in today's environment, with the air filled with bizarre chemicals, and the water loaded with filth and materials that even lab technicians find difficult to discern and label, with all the frequencies and assaults on our being, body, mind and spirit, we are hard pressed to maintain our energy levels. Take a look at the images of Earth on the next pages; so obscured with debris and space garbage. No wonder we fight against a tidal wave of depression, repression, impression, compression, oppression, and suppression, as detailed in Step One.

In a strict sense, the Z Process is the only tangible understanding man needs to possess to eliminate his ills; with this understanding and knowledge, he can live amongst the universe without developing any situation within himself that will eventually leach away or dissipate his power.

The ignorance that develops about the Z Process, and especially the Step Four reactivity in that process, is how man becomes pressurized via emotions and the heavy metal syndrome, which is further explained in *The Promethion*.

The US government conducted clinical studies after Hiroshima on the effects of heavy metals on people and animals, and how we can slip down the scale of heavy pressure until finally reaching the point of death.

We can consistently lose our grip on life by ignoring pressure buildup in the body. Ignorance of the Z Process begins first on a cellular level; on the most minute of the minute particles, the energetic level. Ignorance is the mistaken belief that not much attention needs to be paid to the smallest, the tiniest of energies. Eventually, that micro energetic pressure compounds into a gargantuan macro force.

Heavy metals are also chronologically imbedded in the memory tracks of all living things. The Periodic Table is not just the scale of descending electric pressures; it is a time track recording the creation of

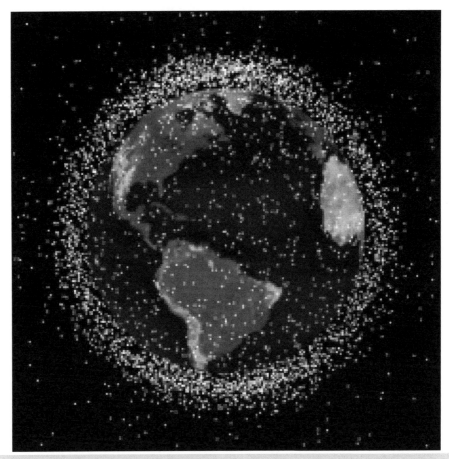

(above) Space debris obscures Earth

Earth from space, encircled with more than 800 satellites (alive and dead), plus space particles, parts and trash from different sources. More than 500,000 pieces are tracked by NASA as these orbit Earth.

energy. If the body is so closely attuned to the situation, if the body is so intimately connected with this pattern of energy that it is embedded deep within its genetic blueprint, then an individual stands the chance of earning the philosopher's stone that the alchemist so anxiously sought.

The information is so close at hand that we need only reach out and grab it. It is definitely connected to the present-day technologies that man is unleashing upon himself; he has created a situation where each individual must sink or swim.

For the next several decades, the pay-back, the debt is and will continue to be very high. Man has been pressurizing the planet to obtain automaticity and servo-mechanisms to do his bidding for him and now payback time has arrived. The environment is surfeited with radiation and rampant forces. Cancer and other degenerative diseases, which are all increasing in number and name and type, is evidence of that payback.

The incredible and increasing number of people, their pets and animals that are allergic to their own environments and each other, allergic to friends and family, allergic to plants, and especially allergic to the trappings of modern civilization, computers, phones, microwaves and electronics — all this is part of the payback.

The amount of criminal activity, decadence and hopelessness that exists today in the world, coupled with the outbreaks of war, famine, diseases, starvation and the other deprivations on physical, mental and spiritual levels, are all part and parcel of that payback system.

In the final analysis, it is up to each of us to discover the formulas; to rid our bodies, minds and spirits of energies that will entrap us in a pressurized situation that will one day soon spring back and attack the host (us).

(above) Satellites in orbit in the atmosphere are servomechanisms that humans use to operate the "civilized" world. Phones, computers, and cable, with transmissions of all kinds of government and personal information being relayed to and from the receivers and towers on the earth. Most countries have their own satellite systems.

Both these images on pages 72 and 73 are sobering. In today's environment, with the air and water and food filled with bizarre chemicals, and all the frequencies and invisible assaults on our being, body, mind and spirit, we are hard pressed to maintain our energy levels.

Looking at these images of our Mother planet (Earth), is it any wonder that we feel drained or zapped, that we fight against a tidal wave of depression, repression, impression, compression, oppression, and suppression?

We need to be mindful of the spring-loaded effect of what we do; the payback will be severe. *(artist David Dickinson, NASA)*

Step Five: Sugars: Simple & Complex

Up until this point, the action of energies has been mainly etheric. The boundaries set by the radiation levels, the elements and the spring-loaded, snap-back ability of Step Four, gives us a corridor or path to follow, which leads us to Step Five.

At Step Five, we observe a moment in history in which organic life begins. It is the part of chronological order that denotes the activity of the successive alignment of elements creating stored electric charge.

In a sense, Step Five is almost an enhancement of Step One, for at this stage, the rotation of the Z Process has moved into a second phase. Essentially, sugars are a mere reflection of radiation. In laboratory science, there is a parallel reaction between radiation and sugar. When radiation strikes the human body, sugar levels immediately rise then fall sharply. There is well-documented evidence that X-rays over a long period of time can create the condition of diabetes, in which there is excess sugar in the blood and urine, and the glucose monitoring system may become ineffective.

Sugar represents the first step of new life within the earth. It represents the organic life that begins a sequence of events involving inert chemicals (salts, proteins and fats). In this particular Step Five sequence, the alignment of energies from Steps One to Four helps to precipitate the energy factors usable by the human body.

Remember, in the first four steps raw radiation, gravitation and electric pressure was noted. As we enter the second quadrant, Steps Five to Eight, what is seen is the utilization of energies indigenous to living entities.

In the first quadrant (see below), Steps One to Four represent ethereal, electric energies, which are postulated. This group gives an individual more of the basic starting energies exuding from the spirit and the mind. Steps One to Four are ethereal ephemeral energies that are mostly invisible.

The second quadrant, Steps Five to Eight, shows the realization of life con-

1st quadrant: Steps 1-4	2nd quadrant, Steps 5-8
• Postulated energies: ethereal, ephemeral • Exudes from the Spirit and the Mind • Mostly invisible • Raw radiation, gravitation • Electric pressure	• Stationary substances • Associated with the body • Utilization of energies of living beings • Realization of life continuance • Visible to naked eye

Desires of humanity to create perfect forms, which is opposed by the environment in its effort to create its own shapes and forms, is mirrored in the DNA-RNA.

tinuance. These steps of energy are directly associated with the body, are more stationary substances that are visible to the naked eye.

The DNA-RNA, a collection of double helical energies comprising proteins, sugars, cellular salts and fats, is the expression of organic life, visible under a microscope, as opposed to ethereal thought, which is invisible. Today, scientists who make an inquest of the powers that control the genetic codes must look deeper, beyond the DNA-RNA, for Thought and desire in their most powerful and harmonic forms are what dictate the stimulus-response action which is replayed as sugar, salts, proteins, and fats. These four items—sugar, salts, proteins and fats—are the direct descendants of environmental stimuli and postulative thinking.

Desires of humanity to create perfect forms, which is opposed by the environment in its effort to create its own shapes and forms, is mirrored in the DNA-RNA. However, the genetic codes are merely a reaction to the stimulus-response mechanisms that caused their creation. The DNA-RNA molecules can be said to have chronologically originated, at this time in Earth's history, directly as a result of the interplay of powerful, imaginative forces. The energy forces of imagination, which spew forth from the desires, willpower and even the whim of intelligence and intelligent life, are what create the genetic codes that steer the body.

It is at this time that science must recognize that <u>function will denote structure</u>. If an individual desires to create a certain pattern of behavior, then the head, limbs, and trunk of the body will shape themselves into a particular form most advantageous to the completion of the individual's desires. In simple terms, those who work their bodies by exercise will reap the reflective benefit of muscular prowess to achieve their goals. The runner who exercises and practices vigorously shapes his body into a framework that may someday win a medal at the Olympics. A swimmer, who practices the strokes necessary to mold the arms and legs into a powerful cohesive force of energy, someday will be able to control the response necessary in living tissue to break a world's record. The artist, who trains his mind's eye, his brain and his hand to duplicate images in the environment, practices strokes thousands of times until one day his material, his creation becomes a masterpiece. The singer, born with the talent to harmonically arrange tones from the diaphragm and the voice, practices day in and day out to shape the body into an instrument that will someday bring her fame and fortune.

All these mechanisms are realizable through the Z Process. In effect, individuals who train themselves, knowingly and consciously, to shape and format the body into a certain automatic servo-response mechanism, will reap the benefits of con-

The energy forces of imagination, which spew forth from the desires, willpower and even the whim of intelligence and intelligent life, are what create the genetic codes that steer the body.

trolled Z reactions. The energies that are put down into cellular imprint, cyclically wind around, like copper wire around a pipe, over and over again until the potential for the unwinding of a fabulous performance of energy is created.

The energies a person possesses to transform thought into matter are part of the transmutation process that automatically induces the Step Five level of the Z Process.

It is a marvelous sight to behold when a person is able to control this process in which the degree of involvement is directly proportionate to the brain, hypothalamus, and the pituitary, more especially. The prevailing actions work exceedingly well to lay in commands for the genetic programming of the body.

The more startling and encouraging phenomenon is that these talents can be transmitted via the DNA-RNA to the offspring. Therefore, people with tremendous abilities who apply themselves towards learning to shape their bodies into instruments to perform tremendous feats of physical prowess, or complete fantastic, beautiful works of art, or to entertain with voice and songs from the heart, are realizing dreams and talents that are and will be passed down to generations and actually uplift the abilities of mankind.

There are so few world records and feats of energy that have not been surpassed by succeeding generations. Human beings, to maintain a certain exhilaration of life, defy the environment and the odds

Chemical diagrams of glucose and fructose, called simple sugars. A complex sugar is a complex carbohydrate. Both simple and complex add to our tally of needed energy; both are depleted by radiant energies in our environment.

against them constantly, and they produce even better grades of talent, beauty and intelligence. This is the quest of humanity.

However, on this step of the Z Process, a similar phenomenon can occur which is quite the opposite of the aforementioned pleasurable experience. Individuals who inadvertently lay commands into the body through disease conditions and wretched environments will not hand down talents and approbations, but instead disease, constant pain and suffering.

The woman who is a heavy drinker and smoker will pass this on to her young.

Individuals who maintain constant pressures on the body during activities such as working around oil refineries, heavy chemicals, hospitals with its radioactive wastes, widespread bacterial invasions and x-ray rooms and other dangerous environmental conditions will pass

As the field of water promotes its electric charge, the very next instantaneous creation of Life Energy is in the form of the simplest carbohydrate, glucose ($C_6H_{12}O_6$).

Sugar is the most unrestrained energy that exists. It is the pure energy needed by the body to produce power and energy. When in an unbalanced state, it causes rapid aging.

this, too, onto their young.

The ingestion of poisonous air, water, chemicals in the food chain and regrettable radioactive dust particles from nuclear bombs and testing, which pervade the environment, will also be passed along. The mutated genesis of cellular tissue that occurs in the present-day environment will be passed along and compounded tenfold in the generations to come.

And through all this, no one can fault Step Five of the Z Process, for it is merely a reflective energy force, which is there to aid and assist the intelligent and punish the ignorant. The punishment, however, is more or less the assignment of lessons to be learned on planet Earth. The survival potential of those who remain ignorant and unconscious to the Z Process is far less than those who effort to know its structure.

Even if one does not fully understand and comprehend the awe and power of this structure, this Process, he can at least say that he has taken his attention out of the darkness to peruse a world that promises health, happiness and beauty. The quality of life, of all life forms, is thus uplifted and improved.

The symptomatic patterns demonstrating upsets on the Step Five level are basically sugar imbalances: hypoglycemia, diabetes, gangrene and other upsets involving the dysfunction of balancing basic levels of energy in the body. The sugar or glucose levels are a precise, metabolic scale that presents a reading of exactly how much electric stress there is being brought to bear on the body itself.

The hypoglycemic is showing evidence of high states of radiation imbalance in the body, in which thoughts are becoming much more powerful than the realization of dreams. This is the daydreamer, the person with too many irons in the fire and none of them coming to fruition. We see this situation in someone who has taken on too many responsibilities without

---

Energy Patterns—Energy Usage Diabetes and Hypoglycemia

Diabetes and hypoglycemia are on the increase due to the quantum leaps made by electronics, which send out invisible frequencies and deplete our stores of glucose.

Graph One depicts the normal fluctuating curve of sugar usage.

Graph Two demonstrates the uptrend of fluctuations on the diabetic curve.

Graph Three depicts the fluctuations in the downward curve of a hypoglycemic person.

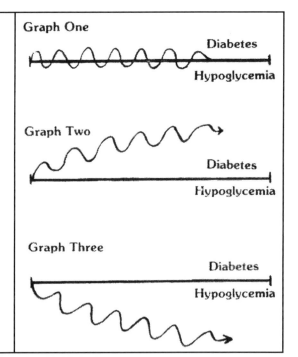

enough understanding and power to fulfill them. It is the reason why hypoglycemia has become a household word and a hobby; too many people have extended themselves far beyond their means. Their financial situations are influenced by extended credit, tantalization of the human mind by high-speed communication, television shows and ads and billboards that promise that if we just purchase a certain product – an expensive car or house or the latest facial creams – everything will be all right. Further down the line, these purchasers find that they are in over their heads and they are not able to culminate their financial commitments as easily as they had thought.

On the other hand, the diabetic is almost completely overwhelmed by responsibility. The sugar-glucose levels of his body are in a state where he has totally given up on the idea that he could win against the odds placed on him environmentally. The high sugar level readings basically trick researchers into believing that the "diabetic person" is surfeited with energy, when in actual fact he is inundated with unusable by-products of his inabilities to cope with the environment.

Humankind is experiencing sugar troubles on many levels, brought on by traumas, and these troubles reflect an area of disorder on the Step Five level of the Z Process.

Step Six: Salts & Crystals

The chronological order of creation, which developed a fine sensing mechanism for its own awareness, involves the study of crystals. (see The Axioms & Postulates of Crystals, page 87).

The crystal is part of the shape that is the manifestation of reality. It is a reflection of energy, the expression of its force and intent.

The crystallization of an artist's dreams is the fulfillment of his painting; a writer writes novels and stories to see them published, read and appreciated by the public.

An architect lays out plans so someday his building will be constructed and admired from a distance.

All dreams of mankind reflect an effort to be reproduced in a crystalline structure. The crystallization of desires is made manifest by Step 6 of the Z Process. At this point, energies coordinate to present solidity and finality; here a program is laid into the energy constructing the crystal: it shall last forever.

This lasting impression is what causes memory traces to transmit images and pictures that are retrievable on command. The energy masses hovering around the electromagnetic aura of every living thing on the planet are replete with salt crystals that contain memory traces. We need the crystal to prismatically separate light into certain patterns, which will be representative of the shapes, forms and events that have gone by, shapes, forms and

Energies coordinate to present solidity and finality. A program is laid into the energy constructing the crystal: "it shall last forever".

This lasting impression is what causes memory traces to transmit images and pictures that are retrievable on command.

events that have happened in the past.

In centuries past, people who used crystal balls as transmitters and receivers knew about the knowledge and power locked within the crystal artifact. Today, some may say this is superstitious, something from the occult, or a "new age" trend where the use of crystals is quite prevalent.

In a sense, each time a person perceives and makes recordings of the environment around him, the crystalline structure, comprised of the metallic entities listed on Steps 1, 2, 3, and 4, is fashioned in such a way so that as light shines through the crystals, a hologramic image will appear to remind the individual of a certain scenario. These crystalline structures cake up in layers, which are constantly recycled through the Earth's crust.

Archeologists, paleontologists and geology students who learn the past history of planet Earth are cognizant of the phenomenon of this layering. Within each particular layer, there is a different bank of memory crystals laid out in certain patterns. The fossils of living creatures im-

"In a crystal we have clear evidence of the existence of a formative life principle, and though we cannot understand the life of a crystal, it is nonetheless a living being."
from: "The Problem of Increasing Human Energy," by Nikola Tesla, June 1900

pressed into this crude representation of the memory tracing are not the actual fine-tuned crystalline structures that hold the information.

At an archeological dig, all we would need to do would be reach down and examine a grain of sand. Within that grain of sand is a crystalline structure, which, if we were able, we could transmit light energy through it and receive the information recorded some millions of years before. This information would not be so bland as a fossil! It would represent a full length, three-dimensional image that would reproduce the era from which the crystal came.

This idea may seem incredibly far-fetched, however, it is completely the opposite. It is the most scientific and advanced idea there is today on the planet, for these very same sand crystals can be fashioned into quartz crystals for watches, for radios and transmitters, or into the crystalline structures used as memory chips in computers. These memory chips are capable of handling thousands and thousands of bits of information in a very unsophisticated way.

The sum total of the existence of mankind can be found in every grain of sand and in every atom and subatomic particle. The recording is there, just as the recording is within each particular human entity.

Crystals in SAF® Sequences

With its distinction of being the most solid substance known in chemistry, the three dimensional crystal broadcasts and receives information to perpetuate some type of activity. If we want to listen to a local radio program, we are actually listening to a crystal as it converts vibrations into electric impulses.

A crystal is a terminal; it can receive or transmit to another location. We must have at least two terminals to have a conversation; information from one terminal moves across space and hopefully is received by the other terminal. If not, there is something wrong with one of the terminals; something has broken down.

The mind does not think in words or in numbers as we use in SAF® work; it thinks in pressures and geometric forms of crystals.

The crystals of SAF® work do have facets! But these do not resemble the near perfect "rock" we wear on our ring finger.

The SAF® program and method is based on crystalline structure; once we know its facets, then we can understand the whole crystal. What we see represented in the number sequence is a reflection of the entangled energies present in each of us.

The crystal is a tracing of what those energies look like, what the symptoms of the person are drawing in 3-D form, just as the numbers in the chain present an image of the organ and gland structures and the emotions that are active, entangled and stressed.

The dot and dash, though not technically crystals, were used in early radio telegraphy communication, which did transmit through crystals.

The dot is the unit of the code; in SAF® the DOT is a single organ or gland system, a location point, a terminal.

from: Greg Farmer

(left) A crystal radio receiver, also called a crystal set, is a very simple radio receiver. These can receive any type of radio frequency but usually it is in the AM band.

It needs no battery or power source— no electricity! It runs on the power received from radio waves by a long copper wire antenna. Its crystal detector was a piece of crystalline material, often galena.

The first crystal sets received wireless telegraphy signals broadcast by a transmitter that generated radio frequency electromagnetic waves.

The dash equates to the ROD in SAF® work, which depicts two location points (organs and glands). With two location points, we have two terminals, we have communication between the two, and this is broadcast out as the SAF® numbers.

In radio telegraphy, the dots and dashes were strung together into words for transmission (Morse Code); in SAF® we string together several organ and gland systems into numerical sentences. This transmission from the organs and glands is a message for us to interpret.

Color, Sound, Shape, Dimension, Time

The crystals of Step 6 control color, sound and other sense perceptions so the areas of the body most conveniently stricken when this level becomes imbalanced are the eyes, ears, nose – the senses in all their respects.

Colors may become distorted; the color-blind person is one who has an imbalance of Step Six. The automaticity of the body, set up to perceive the crystalline structures and the particular hue they emit will definitely be at a loss since the dis-

ruption of the crystalline formation is the primary cause of a malady. However, the pattern of the crystal's creation is the only other phenomenon or process to be considered. This pattern could be found on Steps One to Five.

If we are not able to perceive the crystal that controls our destiny, it would be a difficult task to eliminate it. Once the crystal is identified, then it can no longer operate behind the scenes as an unknown and automatic Z reaction.

By definition, as previously stated, the Z Process must be hidden and out of sight for it to maintain control over us; we must be unconscious to it.

The shape and dimension of things will also be distorted when Step 6 is not balanced. The ability to harmonize on this level allows our sight to operate proportionately with the environment. This is to say that when an individual is looking out from his body, energies, objects, motion, people, and places should be proportionately spaced. Individuals who have upsets or disturbances in Step 6 also have distortions of dimension and time. They are un-

(above) In a grain of sand we can see earth's history like a holographic image in its crystalline structure.

coordinated; they have difficulty seeing at any distance and generally require the use of glasses. Anyone who wears corrective glasses has an imbalance on this step.

Eyeglass lenses are made from silicon dioxide (silica, sand) and are shaped into certain curvatures that will enhance the environment to a particular view that is more desirable. This enhancement is made via a crystalline structure. Interestingly, the bends and distortions within the individual will also take shape in their view of the world. This can be a very clumsy and an inopportune failing for the individual in his quest to survive on an optimum level among his fellows. If he is severely myopic or astigmatic, if not corrected, he may become a mediocre achiever or underachiever because of his sight problems. In essence, because all the manifested surroundings in the environment are crystalline structures themselves, the imbalanced individual is having difficulties in communicating with other crystalline objects.

The set of glasses that a person must wear to correct vision is a light wave amplifier or deamplifier. If objects appear too large, then the lenses need to deamplify the intensity of energy coming from the environment. If the objects appear too small, then the glass needs to amplify the images, make them larger. Astigmatism is a combination of both situations. Cataracts, the dulling of the eye lens, are replaced with silicon lenses, and can often correct previous sight problems.

The blurriness and the out-of-focus condition mimics the person's sensing ability, which are set for a certain distance. Traumas have occurred in their life that have built up a residue of crystalline structures, which forces the person to see clearly only within certain ranges. The other ranges of sight are blocked out, so to speak; they are restricted zones of view.

A similar situation exists for someone who is deaf or hard of hearing. The hearing problem is due to restrictions placed upon him by the formation of disease processes, which are crystalline structures.

Crystals formed within a person (can be called salts) are devices that can take any shape. They are mainly the residues that exist in the body in lieu of water (H_2O). The athletic individual who has taken tremendous pride in fine-tuning his body will be composed of 75% to almost 90% water, the balance of the physical structure is comprised of certain inorganic mineral salts necessary for the transmis-

If we are not able to perceive the crystal that controls our destiny, it would be a difficult task to eliminate it. Once the crystal is identified, then it can no longer operate as an unknown and automatic Z reaction.

sion of electrical power: active ionides, elements, heavy metals, and gaseous substances. Ninety-nine percent of the body should be weightless.

The action of electric charge provides the illusory reality of weight when a person steps onto the bathroom scale. Electrical tension racing from the brain to the spine causes the downward, controlled depression, which will cause the person's weight to read on the scale. Without this downward pressure, a person can easily levitate from the ground and actually be weightless.

In a sense, it is herein stated that the depression, which we complain so dearly about, is 100% of the time self-induced. This is not to say we cannot get depressed about a certain condition or situation, but it must be a consideration on our part that we may be allowing something to cause our energies to continually move downward.

Crystalline structures transmit signals from the brain throughout the body. In a sick person, the body is composed of almost 50% crystalline structures and 50% water. The cancer patient is loaded with inert crystals. Someone who is ill or not in good physical shape almost always has an imbalance on the Step Six level. They are loaded with stuck memory. These crystals, which are held in the body, are those memory traces of which the individual refuses to let go.

Step Six is where we will find the psychopath who consistently and continually lives in the past. He cannot forget his past; he is upset with it because he lives with it. It lives inside him. This type person harbors his past as a crystal; he views his past like a gem. It is a mockery of a diamond existing within his body, for

> *Injuries and traumas to the body contain a large amount of crystalline structure (recordings).*

crystals do have facets and gleams to them. However, in this case the crystals are a very, very poor degraded form of diamond structure. The reason why an individual cannot get healthy is because he feels he cannot live without his past, he feels he cannot live without his crystals.

As William Faulkner so aptly put it in "Requiem for a Nun": *"The past is never dead. It is not even past."*

Individuals who do not want to clean themselves up, do not want to get rid of certain exudations lingering on their bodies, and who do not want to control their condition, will generally appear dirty, filthy and loaded with erratic, past memory traces. He or she may appear "dark". This person will have nightmares, flash thoughts and disjointed ideas. This may be a highly active person, because the body in certain aspects acts like a subentity. The crystalline structures that conglomerate in certain areas will cause so much noise and static interference in the operation of the body as to almost completely shut it down.

Since one tiny crystal can send thousands and thousands of messages per second, imagine what a trillion crystals could do lumped into one area! In most cases, injuries and traumas to the body contain a large amount of crystalline structure. The arthritis victim, someone with arteriosclerosis and any condition that involves the buildup of debris or dead masses, will have its own set of crystalline structures that will reflect energy in certain patterns and cause particular energy pictures to appear.

This is a frightening scenario. It is more terrifying than any horror movie that we can conceive! If we violate the laws of the Z Process, remain ignorant and allow the body to build up these particular pockets of crystals, then we leave ourselves open to having the wholesomeness of the body stained, regardless of any type of effort we may take to detoxify and cleanse. Simply washing with soap and water will not remove deeply imbedded crystalline structures within the body.

Crystals may form on the perimeter of the skin in some cases of pigmentation or deeper toward the core of the system. The more deadly crystalline structures are those that lodge in the core or mid-brain area, because when crystals move into the area of the mid-brain they can usurp the power of the brain itself. The energies that move to and fro, back and forth between the body, mind, brain and spirit can be short-circuited. New commands can be laid into the body that are undesirable.

The schizophrenic is a direct result of crystalline structures building up a wall within the mid-brain structure, which cuts off connections for proper functioning. The word schizophrenia comes to us from the Greek *scizo* (split) and *phrenic* (mind)—it manifests as a breakdown of the thought processes and emotional responses. The wall that builds up cuts the brain function in half and can actually separate the individual's identity. In extreme cases, many compartments can be created by the positioning of crystalline structures within the brain.

Note that this process is not limited to just the brain area. Sub-brain entities can be structured anywhere in the body. The easiest way to spot a person who has tendencies toward the upsets of Step Six is loss of mental control, heightened acuity of the sense perceptions and an increase in pain.

The Axioms & Postulates of Crystals

At least since the time of the Greek studies of Aristotle and Euclid (c. 300 BC), axioms and postulates have been recorded. An axiom is defined as an idea or concept that anyone would agree with upon hearing it. This accepted truth is found most often in studies of the sciences, mathematics and geometry.

A postulate is an idea proposed, usually based upon the basic premise of the axiom.

In the science of SAF®, axioms are considered the basic premises to be accepted first, before a comprehensive understanding can be achieved. In addition to the following axioms and postulates of Crystals, Life Energy axioms can be found in *The Promethion, Project Isis: The Fundamentals of Human Electricity,* and *SAF Simplified.*

Axiom C-1.1:

The Crystal is a manifestation of thought and desire.

Axiom C-1.2:

The Crystal is created by a collision of antagonistic forces generated by desire and thought. These antagonistic forces may be, but are not limited to genetic intention and environmental programs.

Axiom C-1.3:

Crystals are of infinite variety. They are and can be similar to one another but no two are ever exactly the same.

Axiom C-1.4:

The Crystal symbolizes the struggles of energy in an effort to liberate itself from the bonds of magnetic containment. It seeks to complete the actions of all antagonistic forces which are contained within the crystalline structure and return the electric energies to rest. Therefore, the Crystal is replete with magnetic-electric properties that have limiting abilities to control radiation and gravitation.

Axiom C-1.5:

Crystals send and receive energy transmissions.

Axiom C-1.6:

Crystals are programmable. Antagonistic energy in the form of magnetic or electric transmission can be added or subtracted from the structure.

Axiom C-1.7:

Crystals must have a core and a cortex. This means that the structure must be three dimensional although there can be a crystalline structure smaller than an atom or larger than a galaxy – A CRYSTAL IS A UNIVERSE.

Axiom C-1.8:

The Crystal is an enigma in itself. It is merely a representation of higher forces of energy. So, in this way, the Crystal is a symbol or code for some invisible or static force of energy. The Crystal may behave like a name of a person. It can function to represent the individual but is never the individual himself. However, the range of the power of a Crystal depends on the intention of the antagonistic forces which lie within its structure.

Axiom C-1.9:

A Crystal can be created or destroyed by unlocking the desires and intentions which intercept one another within its structure.

Axiom C-2.0:

Crystals are created in a pattern which involves the process of radiation and solidification common to all life. That pattern is:

Step 1: Radiation H+
Step 2: Light Elements
Step 3: Heavy Elements
Step 4: Uranium-radiation
Step 5: Sugars
Step 6: Salts
Step 7: Protein
Step 8: Fats

Axiom C-2.1:

The collision of radiant forces is necessary to create the core of a Crystal. Once created the Crystal has life-sustaining purposes. These purposes are embodied in the simple and complex languages which encode the postulates, intentions and desires of still forces* (guiding intelligence; hierarchies of intellect; and supreme intelligence).

Axiom C-2.2:

Crystals can degrade to heavier weight causing their once wholly electric or radiant cores to solidify even more and create light elements, such as magnesium, calcium, strontium, etc. All elements project and create, or effort to create, some kind of crystalline structure.

Axiom C-2.3:

Crystals, under extremes of pressure will degrade to heavier elements such as lead, gold, iridium, etc.

Axiom C-2.4:

Crystals can and will reach another state of radiant force which implodes toward gravitational forces. This level is designated by uranium. In the case of uranium, the element seethes with radiation and is unstable. The core and the cortex are both fragile in that they are going into decay.

Axiom C-2.5:

Complex Crystals create sugar which can be absorbed and used by higher, even more complex structures for energy. Sugar, much like uranium, is very heat labile and will degrade easily.

Axiom C-2.6:

Salts are the joining of Crystals to other Crystals – similar to linked box cars. This complex linking process is the

Special note: Stillness, still force or potential is the author's way of symbolizing the guiding intentions of spiritual energy. This is not mystic or etheric but empirical: there must be something of immense quiet power to conduct life.

The universe, composed of stillnesses and movement, creates a spectrum of motion wherein the Crystal mimics in symbological form the powers of the still. Since Crystals appear frozen or still, they cause individuals to attach great significance to them.

Diamonds, pearls, rubies, and sapphires, etc., mystify human beings because these gems signify the power of stillness.

In one commercial to sell diamonds the advertiser says, "Diamonds are forever."

basis of chemical bonds which unite similar elements and repel unlike elements.

Axiom C-2.7:

Proteins are crystalline structures which are extremely sensitive to electric stimulation allowing them to transmit messages in a grandiose style to accommodate larger structures of life.

Axiom C-2.8:

Fats are an insulator Crystal. They guide and direct electric-magnetic, channeling energies to higher states of proficiencies.

Axiom C-2.9:

The human being is a complex crystalline structure.

Axiom C-3.0

The human being has a core and a cortex of electric-magnetic structure.

Axiom C-3.1.

Vectors from the core of a human being produce phenomena which take the shape of the brain, bones, muscles, glands, organs, tissues and the cells themselves.

Axiom C-3.2:

Each manifestation of energy electric-magnetic: electric; magnetic, magnetic-electric is a process emanating a reliance on the core.

Axiom C-3.3:

There is a main core and there are sub-cores. Since crystalline structures are conical, helical, and pyramidal there can be cores, sub-cores, and the core of cores – a complex structure like a human being may have trillions of cores on hundreds of levels, but the structure is finite.

Axiom C-3.4:

A location is a moment. A moment is a collection of pressures and spaces which designate a certain coordinate in the body such as the tonsils, on a macro scale, and the sixth molecule on the tip of the lung on a micro scale. Coordinates can be <u>very</u> general on primitive scales and <u>extremely</u> precise on more advanced scales. The more precise, the closer to the <u>core</u>. The more general, the farther from the core and more exactly laden in the cortex.

Axiom C-3.5:

A core with moments will make a <u>chain</u> of energy electric and magnetic. The chain is composed of cores which are sub-cores and moments moving away from or going toward the core of all cores. (See *SAF Simplified* for more on creating and reading chains.)

Axiom C-3.6:

A particular flow of energy electric and magnetic must have a beginning or starting place. A <u>location core</u> is the start of a chain. When one moves the starting place then there can be a chain of energy. The chain always efforts to stop where it started, thus creating a completed circuit. If it does not stop where it started it is considered to be depended upon another core, sub-core, or core of cores.

Axiom C-3.7:

At the core of cores a great many chains are stored. If one were to dislodge or destroy this phenomena, all the chains depending upon that core would vanish. This vanishment is an effect of crystalline stillness and does not affect the controlling forces which placed the Crystal there. If one wishes to eliminate the manufacture of cores or chains he must eliminate the controlling postulates, which are energy masses of intangible value. Their significance is spiritual and bears the utmost potential.

Axiom C-3.8:

Vectors of energy which are unwanted can be eliminated by readjusting the program of data which directs the core, the sub-core and the chains of sub-cores connected to the idea of its existence – this holds for any manifestation of life energy no matter how complex.

Axiom C-3.9:

Complex organ functions and glandular activities depend heavily on the issue of programmed crystalline structures. All glands and organs rely on the output of the information within the core and thus are tuned to certain vectors or degrees from the center the way the hours are situated around a clock.

Axiom C-4.0:

Chains of one core represent rigidity and dislocation since they do not depend on another core (moment) for information.

- Chains of two cores are less chaotic; however, still without purpose.

- Chains of three cores are the manifestation of reality and mirror the traits of third dimensional objects: following all of the rules by which Crystals must abide.

- Chains of four cores represent stability.

- Chains of five cores are chaotic and disassociated and represent the character of humankind without intelligence.

- Chains of six cores are a balance of data which is the representation of the physical universe guided by intelligence.

All subsequent length chains have various meanings depending on the latter descriptions.

Axiom C-4.1:

The disease process in human beings is the result of conflicting impulses – these may be environmental or hereditary.

Axiom C-4.2:

Chains of one or two cores represent intangible and powerful sources for the creation of a disease state, whereas lengthy, more complex, visible chains are easier to dissolve.

Axiom C-4.3:

A chain must be located first by proper processing or it can hide from view.

Axiom C-4.4:

A chain must be run backwards toward its core to create its vanishment.

Postulate 1.0:

A graph can be drawn arbitrarily depicting the action of chains and cores around a central core (core of cores). (see following page)

This graph can appear like a clock and significantly aid the practitioner in discovering the true sequence of trauma and unintended programming so that it can be erased or eliminated.

Postulate 1.1:

The graph may serve as a grid for the interpretation of many phenomena of life. The inner circles are indicative of radiation forces and the outer lines are more representative of organic forces.

Inner Circles:
Circle One – Radiation (H+)
Circle Two – Light Elements
Circle Three – Heavy elements
Circle Four – Actinide series,
        Radiation (-)

Outer Circles:
Circle Five – Sugar
Circle Six – Salt
Circle Seven – Protein
Circle Eight – Fat

NOTE: At this time, the crystal coordinates have not been factored in to the SAF® sequence and chain creation process, therefore, crystals are not drawn for the SAF® chains.

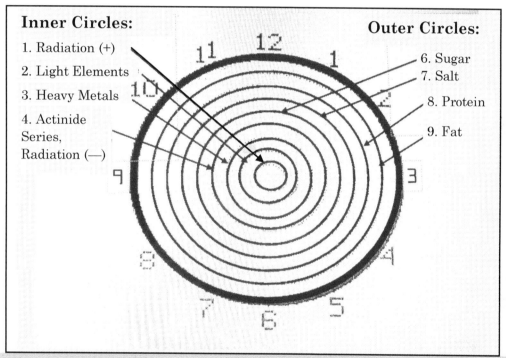

Inner Circles:

1. Radiation (+)
2. Light Elements
3. Heavy Metals
4. Actinide Series, Radiation (—)

Outer Circles:

6. Sugar
7. Salt
8. Protein
9. Fat

Crystals in their natural state are full of impurities. The colors change with different minerals, and the facets are usually scratched and dented as these are not highly polished in nature. Their shape is defined by the rock and earthly pressures and forces in which they grew.

There is energy locked into crystals. These have been used since ancient times for dowsing; drilled holes in crystal pendants indicate these were used as pendulums. Stone Age man used the pendulum to find many hidden water sources, magnetic force fields and energies of the earth, as well as measuring distances. Stone Age man left images carved into or painted on rock to note the location for those who would come later.

Step Seven: Protein Matrices
The 128 Sensory Channels

After the crystalline structures of energy establish themselves, they act as seeds to spawn new forms of energy.

The crystals themselves promote radio waves in double helical form. This is to say that twin beams of electricity exude or project from the crystals in transition. As we have read, Steps One to Five help program the crystals with data to be used in developing particular characteristics, identities and personalities of life forms, which will grow from them.

In Step Seven, the protein substances, which are part of the DNA-RNA molecule, stabilize a genetic blueprint. This plan of operation is delicately laid in after considering billions upon billions of bits of information, which the genetic planning mechanism of the body (generally called the electroplasmic entity) has constituted. (For a greater understanding of the Electroplasmic Field (EPF), see *The Threat of the Poison Reign*, and *The Promethion*, and *Perception Channels #105 and #106*.)

On the Step Seven level, life forms manifest and seek to survive by preventing changes of characteristic and broadcasting particular personality. The proboscis monkey, which sports a rather large swollen nose, developed that way by genetic engineering. For some reason, the genetic planning mechanism, the GPM of the monkey body, felt it was necessary for the animal to have that specific appearance. Somewhere back on the genetic line, a monkey who had slightly larger nasal features was a highly successful fighter, suitor and procreator. Perhaps the monkey had a close call in a fight with a panther and sustained a swollen nose; the brush with death increased the activity of his pineal gland and sexual prowess, and he was a sought after sexual partner. This alerted the monkey GPM that this model of monkey would be a better survivor than monkeys in that region with smaller noses. So, the monkey GPM went to work to construct subsequent models, which mimicked the appearance of the original larger-nosed monkey. The proliferation of the proboscis monkey is in much greater proportion than could normally have occurred via the offspring, in a direct genetic line, from the original monkey.

Likewise, the giraffe, originally living in forests that changed to plains and grasslands, has altered genetic programs. The GPM of the giraffe rewrote programs

Genetic planning mechanisms (GPMs) can easily copy information from the environment without the plant, animal or human having to be a direct descendant via the bloodline of a particular plant, animal or human.

so that all giraffes evolved and developed much longer necks in order to reach the best leaves on the few tall trees.

This is significant in that genetic planning mechanisms (GPMs) can easily copy information from the environment without the plant, animal or human having to be a direct descendant via the bloodline of a particular plant, animal or human.

The expressions of energy, which become crystalline structures, borrow much of their designs from impressions made upon them in the environment. This is the exact process that programs individuals to have cancer, heart disease, diabetes, arteriosclerosis and other nonessential conditions. For some logical reason, the genetic planning mechanisms of the body, expressed by the DNA-RNA molecule, takes information from the environment, which leads it to believe that if it fashions a human being, or any other living entity, after certain information received, that this being will definitely survive better than the last model.

This is the exact and precise impetus for the genetic planning mechanism (GPM). The GPM spends a good deal of time worrying about the future. It uses sensors, which emanate from the midbrain, to constantly scan the environment and pick up data for long-term changes in the design of the human. This is done so that bodies of the future will be able to survive in the environment as it is presented to the genetic planning mechanism. However, the same mechanism can be fooled by the environment into believing that what it is viewing is a message of survival, when in actuality it is a systematic plan of a disease process.

A system that employs graded Steps 1

-6, namely, absorbing radiation; absorbing light elements and water; absorbing heavy metals; radiating itself; developing power; and then developing crystalline structures that will radiate new and better life forms, will have certain mechanical difficulties.

First, we must realize the input system used by the GPM. It is one that was developed in chronological sequence with the origins of the earth.

There was a time on the planet when energies reached the point of super saturation.

Crystalline structures, or so called inorganic substances, began to take the information it had received from the environment and play it back, so to speak, just as we would play back a tape recording or listen to a record or CD.

The GPMs began to fashion organized systems, such as plants, animals and human beings, taking much of its energy and power from this era on the planet which approximately occurred some three billion years ago.

At a certain time on the planet after the great fires and the floods that cooled them, the heavy metals and radiant forces, which later produced tiny molecules of energies in the form of sugars, eventually developed compact, organized crystalline structures which exuded a spiral of radiant energy from which the DNA-RNA molecule draws its power. The memory of these incidents is what the DNA-RNA draws from automatically. If we were to disconnect the memory bank of the GPMs and prevent it from reliving that time on earth when a particular faculty was developed, then the body's automatic ability to not only develop plans for the future, but also reproduce itself, would be seriously hampered.

The gravitational input system that the GPM uses is subject to defect when energies are not properly stated. In other words, the GPM always carefully scans the relative pressurization of living entities to decide whether or not they are potent survivors. The GPM will consistently copy the effects of those entities in the environment that appear to be super-survivors. As in the case of the Proboscis monkey and the giraffe, the GPM was most certainly influenced by some prodigious act or actions that the original monkey or giraffe performed. If we understand the view that the genetic mechanism exists solely to structure organisms for improved surviving, then we can see that almost anything put into this mechanism, which resembles a better way or plan of surviving, will be carried out vehemently.

It is as if the genetic mechanism were the CEO of a large corporation and needed input from his surrounding officers so that he could direct the advertising campaign, the product line, the development and the entire structure of the workforce in order that the company could survive in present-day market circumstances.

Scales for Measuring

The input of forces from the environment is mainly of a radiant nature and will communicate certain concepts and principles, which the genetic mechanism constantly monitors with scales of acid/basic balance, comfort/discomfort, and pressure/spacial alignment.

Acid-Basic Scale

The acid/basic scale (acid-alkaline) is used primarily to monitor the degree of pressurization that matches or violates the original blueprint (see scale below). If the body has been scheduled to have a pH of 6.5 overall and the actual pH is 6.2, then the value judgment must be made on the part of the genetic planning mechanisms. The only question that arises is whether the individual is surviving or not. If the individual is surviving better at pH 6.2, then the genetic planning mechanisms will make changes to ensure that all the subsequent transmissions of en-

(below) The Acid-Basic Scale is the measure of pH, (potential of Hydrogen). It determines the acid or alkaline aspects by measuring electric pressure and space alignment, with water as the null point for analysis. While scientists follow a number scale and color, we humans can tell when we are 'off center' by our feelings: acidity causes pain, alkalinity causes sensation.

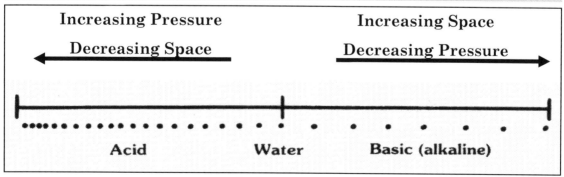

ergy, which the DNA commands the RNA to perform, will be at pH 6.2.

For every area that is acid (electric pressure), there must be another area of alkalinity (space) to balance it.

Pleasure & Discomfort Scale

The method employed by the genetic planning mechanism to govern whether or not the body is surviving, is by the pleasure and discomfort scale. This electrical scale is intrinsic to the brain. It measures the degree of pressure on the overall system. As was previously described in the Graph of Emotions, as a body becomes more and more pressurized, it is brought down, subsequently, to lower states of emotion and existence. The genetic planning mechanism (GPM) is consistently aware whether or not the individual is experiencing changes of energy that make him happy, or changes of energies that cause him sadness. The body uses this basic view electrically by measuring the amounts of pressure and space available to the body. Seeing as how the body, when depressurized and existent in its original, intended state, is a gaseous substance; and the body when totally pressurized turns into a crystalline structure like granite, the genetic planning mechanism uses this scale to fashion changes that will prevent it from inadvertently becoming a pile of frozen sadness.

This is almost a perfect system because it automatically changes structure when the body is not surviving.

Genetic Planning Mechanism Records All

The genetic planning mechanism changes the structure and mirrors those energies in the environment that appear to be surviving. If we went to a local swimming hole to relax and sunbathe for the day, the GPMs most certainly will record all that occurs while there. If it is a pleasurable experience, then the GPM will record that in great detail, in fact, so much incredible detail that the awareness of present-day scientists has not been able to comprehend it. The magnetic direction in which the body faces; the time of day; the color of the sky; all the minute characteristics of all the people who are present at the swimming hole, including such minor things as hair color, height, weight, size, color and type of attire, etc., all meticulously recorded and laid into the memory banks of the GPMs. If the person appears to be surviving, then this is noted automatically by registering on the scale of electric pressurization.

Positive vs. Negative Response

The body needs only to tense up and experience a frightful incident to trigger a negative response in the genetic planning mechanism (GPM). If the body receives a positive response, then the genetic plan will be enhanced; if there is a negative response then it will be altered to try to develop a new blueprint that is more survival oriented. The relative amount of change occurring during scenes that do not contain much force is relatively minor.

However, if some dramatic or traumatic incident occurred while we were trying to enjoy our day at the swimming hole, then this would make a more proportionate alteration in the system. For example, if a mother went to the swimming hole to relax and enjoy the water and all of a sudden her daughter began to struggle while she was swimming, threatening to drown, then the sensors and monitors for the GPM would be kicked on automatically for full sensitivity.

Depending upon the outcome of the incident, new information fed into the system may change existing programs. If the mother were able to reach her daughter and save her from drowning, then the GPM of the girl's body would be altered as well as the mother's. The GPM of the mother's body would be enhanced. Libations and praise does more to groove in an existing genetic program. However, when someone needs to be saved from drowning, such as the child in this incident, then the genetic mechanism busily attempts to change patterns of energies within the child's body so that she will survive the experience on her own the next time.

GPM is Organized

This is obviously a marvelous, automatic mechanism. In other examples of courage, fright, honor and dishonor, genetic mechanisms will monitor just the changes in pressure occurring during these instances, and all of the information necessary to either enhance or abandon existing blueprints will be available. Because the genetic planning mechanism has the capability of monitoring trillions of bits of information on and in the environment, it must be quite organized. The organization of this plan has been split into approximately 128 separate scanning sensors.

Our Sensing System

What is the particular sensing apparatus that the genetic planning mechanism uses to elicit data? The receipt of impact on the sensing measuring ability of the genetic planning mechanism is the same type of system used by all entities. The sense of pressure titillates the channels of energy that have been developed for just such an occasion. It is important to note that the sophistication of such a sensing system depends on the development of the prior steps that have been listed in Steps One to Six. This hierarchy of energy development helps to create crystalline structures that will receive information and translate it.

Over the eons in the development of the human body are minor crystalline structures that take information from the environment in the form of sight, sound, taste, smell and touch, for example, and have developed sophisticated sensing devices to reach as far as an organism can reach to pull information from the environment. The eyes, ears, mouth, nose, hands, feet, skin and many other sensing structures have taken millions of years of evolution and development beyond the first six steps to create. For example, a gaseous entity from Step One or Two would not need these types of structures. It would not need ears to hear, eyes to see; a nose to smell; a mouth with which to taste; skin to sense touches. These perceptions, external and internal perceptions, are automatic and can be experienced by any crystal.

Any crystal contains enough prismatic ability to separate radiation into the 128 channels that follow.

The development of this sensing system is as orderly and coordinated as the hierarchy of energies embodied in the Z Process itself. In a sense, these channels

"Our five senses enable us to perceive only a minute portion of the outside world."

—Nikola Tesla

were developed out of necessity to herald the development of the human being. But the construction of a fantastically organized collection of cells like a human being needed many guiding and molding phases of energy subsequent to the development of these sensing apparatuses.

At first glance, an individual may believe that these sense channels were developed after the body; however, as was previously explained, even a cloud of gas could contain all 128 perceptive channels without needing the crystalline representation or artifice to accompany it.

The creation of these sensing structures was merely a tribute or monument to trillions of cycles of use on a particular sense channel. In other words, it is the belief of the author that the ears and the eyes and all the other structures that involve the senses, such as the organs and the endocrine system, were developed primarily because those sense channels were used an astronomical number of times. The residue of crystals, which built up during the use of these sense channels, later became the structures that we easily recognize as present-day, normal body parts.

Each of these 128 Sensory Channels act by pressure; the Law of Comfortable Pressure and Space has been inscribed into the universal code. People, animals, plants, and objects should not become too crowded together, or too spread apart. The amount of opposition needed for all beings, animals, minerals and plant life to be happy and content adhere to this universal code:

All Pressure (objects) will be spaced a comfortable distance apart

This is a logical law and does not cause a lot of trouble to human beings unless it is violated. The body is first alerted by feelings, much like a warning shot overhead, then if the warning is not heeded, the punishment (pain) begins.

The following review of the 128 sensing channels will give the reader some idea as to the workability and feasibility of such sensing mechanisms. This preliminary synopsis is not to be taken as a total treatise on this system, for it would take hundreds of volumes of research data to amass a quality paper that would do it justice. At the same time, the reader should remember that these structures and sense mechanisms were born out of crystalline structures, which were shaped primarily by radiation.

It is unfortunate that many humans lack the ability to reach but a few perceptions. If we were to connect with all 128 sensory channels, we would have talents and abilities far beyond those of any mortal man. We can see as we study this material that if we were to have these talents and perceptions at our fingertips, we would be able to easily survive, and survive well in this environment.

Sensory Channel 1
TOUCH

More than any other sensory channel, the sense of touch acts as an advanced scout for the sensing of the organism. Touch is the point where the energies of the environment and the individual organism meet.

Largely as a result of observing the sensing mechanisms of bats, by which a sound frequency is emitted and bounces off an insect or object, the phenomenon of RADAR (Radio Detection and Ranging) was discovered and in use by 1940.

This type of communication system is the primary mechanism of which the sense of touch is composed. Essentially, a sensing beam is channeled in a 360-degree radius around the body to pick up any encroachment by the environment on the location that the organism has chosen to be its own.

This beam can sense all pressure levels. Touch transcends all the senses listed in this book as the Expanded Tactile Sense; in this capacity, it blossoms into sub-channels. Touch provides the entire range of "feelings" a human being possesses.

This Expanded Tactile Sense is sometimes called the sixth sense or extra-sensory perception (ESP). As the reader understands more about this process of self awareness and enlightenment, and works on personal issues for release of stuck and misdirected energies, he or she will discover an increase in many abilities, including mental telepathy and a greater appreciation for life and living.

Touch spans all wave pressure levels and gives a person the ability to perceive all pressures and forces.

Sensory Channel 2
TASTE

At a point in the development of the organism it became essential to harmonize with the outside energies. The taste sense acts as a toll keeper and regulator for the system.

The earliest crystalline structures realized that energies from the outside must be brought within itself to catalyze reactions that would sustain growth. This is seen today and mirrored in the action of eating. It was essential for the early

---

Eclipse, by Pink Floyd
All that you touch
All that you see
All that you taste
All you feel
All that you love
All that is now
All that is gone
All that is to come
And everything under the sun is in tune.

The Dark Side of the Moon, 1973

---

mechanisms of crystalline structures, which would branch out as proteinaceous substances, to develop a sense mechanism that would screen out particles that might be detrimental to its existence.

The sense of taste ultimately became the sense needed by the organism to prevent accidental ingestion of substances that would ultimately destroy it. Today, human beings possess a very dim appreciation of this sense as they shovel in food and drink past the objections of this delicate mechanism. Food and drink items, which are not nutritive and nourishing for the body, are ingested on a daily basis.

In a perfect world, with all senses functioning well, we should be able to detect all chemical substances via the sense of taste. We should be able to discern the exact chemical structure and electronic makeup of all substances by using this sense.

In many police and chemistry labs throughout the country, some of the primary tests used are those that involve the sense of taste, and the sense of smell (Channel #3) for the discerning research scientist still holds a vague appreciation for the ability of these mechanisms.

THE 128 SENSORY CHANNELS

1. Touch
2. Taste
3. Smell
4. Sound
5. Sight
6. Controlled Personal Motion
7. Angle (the shape of things)
8. Tone of Sound (quality, harmony)
9. Tone of Sight (quality)
10. Tempo
11. Amplitude (increase & decrease)
12. Acids (pressure)
13. Space (alkaline or base)
14. External Motion
15. Radiational Forces (planetary)
16. Gravitational Forces (planetary)
17. Birth (starting new cycle)
18. Growth (continuing of cycle)
19. Maturity (stagnation of cycle)
20. Decay (loss of cycle)
21. Death (end of cycle)
22. Skin Sensitivity
23. Perception of Hunger
24. Enzyme Activity
25. Vitamin Action
26. Digestive Activity
27. Mineral Action
28. Glandular Transaction (hormonal)
29. Magnetic Position (eight gyros)
30. Magnetic Reference 1 (people)
31. Magnetic Reference 2 (place)
32. Magnetic Reference 3 (planetary)
33. Protein (internal)
34. Protein (external proteins)
35. Fat Insulation (Stage 1)
36. Fat Insulation (Stage 2)
37. Fat Insulation (Stage 3)
38. Fat Insulation (Stage 4)
39. Fat External (Stage 1)
40. Fat External (Stage 2)
41. Fat External (Stage 3)
42. Fat External (Stage 4)
43. Sugars (spark)
44. Carbohydrates (stored spark)
45. Pain
46. Sensation
47. Unconscious Pain
48. Unconscious Sensation
49. Death from Pain
50. Death from Sensation
51. Z Reactions from Pain
52. Z Reactions from Sensation
53. Radiational Forces (especially male)
54. Gravitational Forces (especially female)
55. The Color Red-Violet
56. The Color Red
57. The Color Orange
58. The Color Yellow
59. The Color Green
60. The Color Blue
61. The Color Blue-Violet
62. The Sound DO
63. The Sound RE
64. The Sound MI

These 128 sensory mechanisms were born out of crystalline

God of Touch	God of Taste	God of Intelligence	*Egyptian Gods of the Senses*	God of Sight	God of Sound

65. The Sound FA
66. The Sound SO
67. The Sound LA
68. The Sound TI
69. Electricity Known
70. Electricity Unknown
71. Magnetic Situations Known
72. Magnetic Situations Unknown
73. Sense of Sequence—Time
74. Endocrine Sense Channels (emotions)
75. Thymus Activity
76. Tonsils Activity
77. Appendix Activity
78. Peyer's Patches
79. Protective Systems (Stage 1)
80. Protective Systems (Stage 2)
81. Protective Systems (Stage 3)
82. Heart (love)
83. Colon (hate)
84. Stomach (assimilation)
85. Sinuses & Anterior Pituitary
86. Liver Activity (transmutation)
87. Lung Activity (breathing)
88. Bronchi (capturing breath and holding)
89. Sex Organs
90. Bones & Muscles
91. Thyroid (carbon/nitrogen cycle)
92. Blood Vessels (Fear Phase 1)
93. Brain & Nervous System (Fear Phase 2)
94. Adrenal (Fear Phase 3)
95. Mind
96. Senses & Hypothalamus

97. Kidneys (perception of poisons)
98. Male — Female (hormone balance)
99. Skin (defense protection)
100. Solar Plexus & Pancreas
101. H_2O & Posterior Pituitary
102. Calcium & Parathyroid
103. Spleen (invasion reflex)
104. Lymphatic System
105. Electromagnetic Perception
106. Electroplasmic Perception
107. Hot or Heat
108. Cold or Coldness
109. Dryness (lack of water)
110. Beauty
111. Ugliness
112. Symbols & Language
113. Symbols & Mathematics
114. Intention
115. Postulate Composition
116. Counterpostulate
117. Lies
118. Truth
119. Perception of the Sun
120. Perception of the Solar System
121. Survival
122. Succumbing
123. Winning
124. Losing
125. Body Temperatures
126. Spirit (greater & lesser)
127. Universe
128. God

structures, which were shaped primarily by radiation.

Sensory Channel 3
SMELL

One of the more important sensing channels is the sense of smell. The energies that pervade the atmosphere in the form of gases are more deadly than anything else because the gases can invisibly pervade spaces and vie for areas that the organism may occupy. This is one of the primary considerations when developing a survival energy system.

In the beginning, energy was formed totally of radiation and then it molded into crystalline structures that had survival for their purpose. Therefore, it was essential to safeguard the structure by preventing the erosion of these structures by gases. The primary gas, which tends to rapidly degenerate crystalline structures, is oxygen. The oxidizing forces of the atmosphere cause the preliminary mechanism and protein substances to construct devices that would warn the organism that attrition by erosion was imminent.

The sense of smell was a primeval sensing structure and second only to the sense of touch, in that touch basically used radiant forces or radiation itself as a detecting mechanism, whereas the sense of smell detected the levels of gases.

Sensory Channel 4
SOUND

For sound to travel there must be mass, and it must be dense enough for molecules and atoms to clash, collide and bounce as these violate the Law of Comfortable Pressure and Space. Objects moving swiftly together and then apart create distinctive pitches and tones. These sounds carry through the environment as shock waves, frequencies. The sensing of energies crashing in the environment is

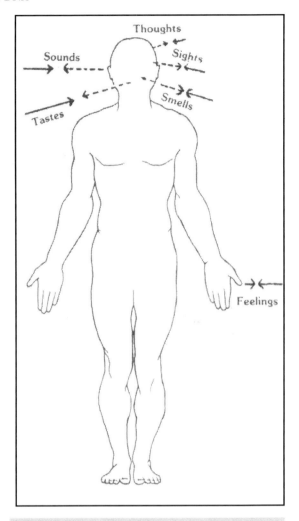

(above) Thoughts, plus the five major senses of the human: sight, sound, taste, smell, and touch. The Expanded Tactile Sense transcends and enhances all the other 128 senses noted in this book, as thoughts, in and out, add to the mix.

an art.

The quality of sound is not appreciated on this channel #4 for this level was developed early by crystalline structures to prevent the accidental connection with other crystalline structures that were too dense or too wispy.

This grade of sound is a mechanism that a person uses to harmonize with other structures. A sense of sound aids the individual in selecting environments suitable to his or her temperament. Sound is one ability that helps the person to locate similar structures so that procreation can begin. It is one of the few sensing tracks that adds asceticism to its energy.

Sensory Channel 5
SIGHT

The ability to discern light by viewing with electronic beams ultimately caused the development of the apparatus that we call the eyes. The energies used by a crystalline structure to locate objects in the environment were of a sophisticated, radiational quality. However, just as the experiment proved when testing bats in the early days of radar research, radiation sent outward to perceive must be bounced off objects and be re–received. The sight sense gives an individual the ability to grade shape, size and color. It is a more mature and developed sense of touch.

Clairvoyance, the ability to visualize accurately what cannot be seen with the eyes, is a heightened ability. Some are born with this ability; some are taught through awareness, meditation, and by being free of conflicting, disharmonic energies. It was more commonplace in less hectic society structures.

Sensory Channel 6
Controlled Personal Motion

The original crystalline structures highly regarded the ability to change position. All efforts were made to become mobile. In the sea, this characteristic was hampered by the tidal influences of the ocean. Just as the salmon today still efforts to swim upstream to spawn, birds move cross-current against the wind and other animals and species fight the elements, so did the early crystalline structures, which set out into the oceans as the primary salts that precipitated life.

In this sensing track, the ability to control one's own motion was a sense developed by crystalline structures to judge survival potential. The more one was able to control its own motions, the more survival prone it became. And so, structures caused changes in genetic planning mechanisms (GPMs) to program in a greater ability to be mobile. Mobility was equated with survival, while immobility was equated with death.

Even today, it is not hard to envision and juxtapose a powerful athlete with an ailing, arthritic man and view the difference. It is a day and night comparison. The athlete has hardly any restricted motion and is in almost perfect control of his organism. Conversely, the diseased and ailing person is almost completely restricted and has very little control of his movements.

GPMs, which perceive this scenario, effort to reconstruct the program in the diseased person's body so that future bodies in his genetic line may develop athletic prowess. Moreover, the GPM evaluates a lifetime of controlled personal motion and sets about to write a new program in the hopes that future generations will be more successful in environmental endeavors. However, it has been observed that a monkey wrench thrown into the GPM may actually cause the genetic blueprints to be interfered with so as to create a false picture. This falsehood comes in the form of faulty input data and somehow the GPM mistakenly aligns the individual with the wrong data. In this situation, the programming of future generations and the present host becomes more and more decrepit.

The accidents of genetic planning come about by variations and stupefactions in the genetic mechanisms themselves. This is to say that through an inability on the part of the GPMs to foresee errors in its own systems, the mechanism itself may become filled with erroneous data, which will cause it to temporarily or inadvertently program the body to be sick. This is the reason for congenital illnesses and other such hereditary, detrimental factors, for if the genetic program could rectify itself, it certainly would. It is consistently and always programmed to aid the survival of the mechanism and not to hamper it.

Sensory Channel 7
ANGLE
(the shape of things)

One of the more important sense perceptions used by the genetic planning mechanisms to maintain a foothold on the environment is its ability to perceive shapes and sizes of objects in the surroundings. This is the channel of energy that aids the person's sight mechanism to perceive the relative nearness and farness of objects, such as the collective energies of cars and trucks. Is the angle or shape very large (close, perhaps too close), or relatively small (far away)?

It is an extremely important consideration, for it aids the coordination of the individual with the environment and prevents him or her from having serious accidents.

Sensory Channel 8
TONE OF SOUND
(quality, harmony)

The tone of an object in vibration is an aesthetic sense. However, this type of harmony is directly parallel to the genetic sensing mechanisms which have an understanding of surviving and succumbing. If someone is out of harmony, sounds in the environment may become too dissonant and therefore emergency signals will be sent to the body to warn it to remove itself from the immediate surroundings lest it be traumatized.

This has a direct bearing on the shape and angle of energies in the environment, for it is the angle percent which gives the individual his ability to discern just how dangerously close he may be to objects, large and small. It is a warning mechanism to cause a person to remove his body from the area. For instance, if any person were to get too close to a Caterpillar tractor moving earth, the sight sense would kick in the sense of shape or angle. At that point, the angle of the tractor would be broadly communicating to the brain in the genetic mechanism that the person is extremely close to a large object. That, coupled with the sound bouncing off the body in a disharmonic way, will cause the person to be repulsed from the situation, automatically. In other words, the person's reflexes would kick in without volition or conscious control; he or she wouldn't have to think about it.

In another sense, the ability of the sensing mechanism to track energies in the environment via sound and sight give a person the advantage of keeping away from things that are small, yet deadly. A small bee with a potent stinger changes shape dramatically when moving too close

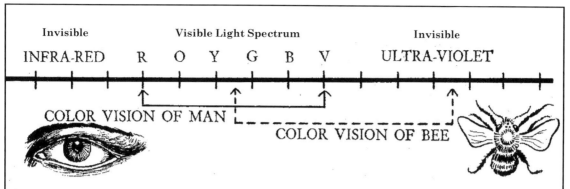

Color vision of a human (visible colors, red to violet) and of a bee (from yellow-green, then into the ultra-violet band of energy).

to the individual's body. At a distance, the size of the creature and its angle shape is relatively small. When perceived as being too close to the body, the ability of the sensing mechanisms to discern the insect's body as larger than it should be causes a reflex reaction. This, of course, is coupled with the disharmonic sound—the buzzing—which parallels and enhances the changing size of the bee's shape.

Sensory Channel 9
TONE OF SIGHT
(quality)

The harshness of light, its clarity and its softness, are trigger mechanisms that alert the individual he may be losing the ability to fine tune shapes and angles in the environment. The shape angle of collective energies, such as cars, trucks, buildings, people, etc. is the realm of Channel 7; however, on Channel 9, the tone of sight is relative to the ability to discern and capture the actual wavelength and curvature of magnetic structures within these larger objects. So, if a person is having difficulty with the tone of sight, then he is having an inability to "sharpen the picture".

Older television sets had a tone con-

trol. If we were to use it to demonstrate this principle, we would more clearly understand exactly what this sensing mechanism is capable of providing. The tone control on a television actually establishes a homeostasis of electrons on the screen. When the electrons are out of focus, bouncing around in a random pattern, our sense perception likewise becomes erratic and disharmonic. Thus, the picture that is displayed on the TV is fuzzy and out of focus.

Individuals may lose the same ability to a greater or lesser degree, and alert the genetic sensing mechanisms that he or she is beginning to succumb. The genetic sensing mechanisms rely on this sense trait to factor the individual's ability to visually confront environmental hazards. When the person begins to lose the sense of total control of the environment, then the genetic sense mechanisms jointly agree that the person is beginning to lose his ability to confront the trials and tribulations of life and living. This is usually the time when modern day man reaches for prescription eyeglasses. The glasses serve to sharpen the tone levels; however, the use of eyeglasses for correction, as a general rule, is an admission of the wearer's inability to confront subjects in daily life. Even though corrected with glasses, the overall quality of sight has still diminished.

Early crystalline substances that rode the seas used this fine-tuning sense to selectively pick out energies in the environment that would inhibit or enhance their purposes. The overall purpose of the crystal was to propagate itself. Therefore, anything that added to that endeavor was something that could be focused on with great clarity, and anything that inhibited the crystal's ability to promote itself would cause a blur in the imaging.

Today, individuals must thank the early crystalline substances for providing their eyeball with an almost perfect lens with which to view the environment.

Sensory Channel 10
TEMPO

The speed and random motion in the environment is of prime concern to the genetic planning mechanisms because this, too, is a level of survivability. An individual, who is in an area where the random motion is slightly more or greatly more than he or she can handle, will be either chronically or acutely overwhelmed by that environment. This situation of overwhelm is a signal that the energies of the organism are being destroyed. In a sense, this is the Z Process.

Early crystalline substances needed an ability to discern the speed of particles moving around them. It was impossible for crystalline substances floating in the seas to attach themselves to objects that were moving too rapidly, and it was equally difficult for these crystals to adhere to objects that were moving too slowly. In the latter case, objects moving too slowly would actually retard or prevent growth of the crystal. In a sense, the actual reason for the crystal's search for optimum random motion of particles in its vicinity was one of communication.

The interference and disturbance of energies around crystals when there is non-optimum random motion is illustrated by the human being today. For example, if we were to suddenly leave our home in the country and move to New York City, we may suffer a shock of "excess tempo". Objects, tall buildings, people, cars and other materials in the environs of the city may be moving so rapidly about us, they may throw us into a nervous convulsion. On the other hand, a person moving from a busy city to a country setting may find a disturbing quality or stillness of random motion that would set him or her into a detrimental pattern of boredom. In both cases, tempo is extremely important for survival; for the sickness of boredom is just as detrimental as the illness of anxiety. In both cases, the person has not been able to reach an optimum vibratory state.

It is, therefore, necessary for all living beings to align themselves with the proper tempo in their surroundings, lest they be doomed with an inability to properly communicate with themselves and others.

Sensory Channel 11
AMPLITUDE
(increasing & decreasing of power, pressure)

The measurement of environmental stresses and pressures is an essential task.

The early crystalline structures were able to assess the surrounding environment and its own internal structure for increases and decreases of radiation (pressure, stress), the increase or decrease of a vibration. This is a most necessary task in that it allows the crystal to predict changes that may be pleasant or unpleasant in its surroundings.

The scale of increasing and decreasing electric pressures around crystalline structures follows the precise pattern of surviving and succumbing or winning and losing, which the genetic planning mechanisms need to cipher.

Today, human beings are equipped with a multifaceted perception, allowing them to perceive whether there are increases or decreases of intensity on any of the sensing channels. This is a broad-range, overall sensing ability that allows us to measure energy changes on the major sense bands, such as touch, taste, smell, sound, and sight.

If an individual begins to lose his ability to sense the amplitude of electric pressure around him, it is the primary malfunction of the hypothalamus and the brain itself. However, it may even be a more intrinsic malfunction of the thalamus, that part of the body actually acting as an energy conductor, semi-conductor and capacitor. In other words, the tube-like structure in the base of the mid-brain takes energy from the environment, or from the internal workings of the body itself, and relays it from the brain to the body and from the body to the brain. This same structure has the capability of changing the intensity of electric pressure reception or transmission. The thalamus also maintains the ability to hold and capture stresses and pressures received as sensed impressions from the environment and within the body. Finally, the cells themselves maintain a miniature replica

of a thalamus structure, for it was from the cell that the body maintained its original blueprint to construct the thalamus in the first place.

When conditions destroy the sense capability of the cells and tissues to perceive amplitude in the environment or in the immediate area around the cell, the cell will then misjudge its relationship to environmental stresses. In this way, it is in jeopardy; it may not be able to correctly assess damage or inactivity to a structure of itself. This is seen most certainly in human beings when they lose perceptive sense and fall headlong into situations that ultimately lead to their downfall. The inability of the mind to learn its lesson from earlier crystalline structures to construct marvelous apparatus of the body causes human beings to lose their ability to judge when environmental pressures are becoming too severe for them to withstand with adequate comfort and longevity.

It is true that an individual digs his own grave by allowing bad habits and inconsistent patterns of living to wear away the protective mechanisms of the body. The person who drinks alcohol, smokes cigarettes, and keeps odd hours must certainly put a damper on his own perception of the body's dismay.

This, however, is a minor infraction when considering the lengths people go to to provide cures and excitement for themselves. Operations, medicines, and even over-the-counter poisons are ingested daily to provide some type of homeostatic mirage that the individual believes will keep him or her comfortable. The constant desire on the part of the person to entertain himself by sitting for long hours in front of a television or computer, and playing outlandish video games is reaching beyond his body's ability to tolerate them.

This is not to serve as condemnation of a person's right to exist in the mode to which he or she is accustomed. However, it is more a warning that dimming the warning mechanisms of the body, which are finely-tuned to perceive changes of possible harmful pressures to the body, is suicidal.

Sensory Channel 12
ACID (pressure)

The early crystals, which pervaded pristine seas of the earth, developed an ability to perceive acid conditions very early in their existence. The necessity to be aware of acids, which were the high pressure buildup of elements such as hydrogen and uranium, was a necessity to preserve the crystal's state of being. Essentially, the desire for the crystal to survive in its own comfortable state was greatly threatened by the presence of acid, for acid disintegrates crystals just as fire devours wood. One step too close to a strong acid and the crystal would evaporate. This ability to perceive acid conditions came directly from the hot fires that still burned millions of years after the creation of Earth.

The human being is a complex structure of acidity and alkalinity. The organism intermixes those particular periods in Earth's history when hot fires burned on the planet. For example, the whole act of digestion requires a high intensity of acidity, which is akin to a smoldering volcano. The energies that lie within the body are flexible enough to change their pH, thus causing sudden conditions of acidity, which can destroy cells. The actions of exercise and stress upon the muscular tissues create lactic acid, which is highly detrimental to the crystalline cellular structures within the body. And so, this drama of crystals trying to escape destruction by being able to perceive acid conditions continues. However, the sense channels of the human body are far inferior compared to the sense perceptions of the mind, which also are able to perceive high acid conditions.

Pains and sensations, which develop when acid states are more intense than they should be, are warning signals to genetic mechanisms of the body to change and restructure energies more tolerant to the stresses and pressures the individual may be receiving. In an electronic environment filled with radiation spewing forth from ubiquitous sources, such as occurs in the society of today, genetic planning mechanisms (GPMs) may be overrun with input, directing the genetic code to make gross changes to allow for conditions of high acidity.

The input from errant electric charges, microwaves, invisible chemical frequencies in food and air and water, virtually unheard of in past generations, make it essential for the GPMs to direct changes.

The organ imbalances that may persist in high acid states are those that may affect the stomach, the cells, the tissues, the bones, the muscles and the brain. An individual may be dizzy and lightheaded while suffering from pains in the stomach, the joints, the muscles, and perhaps deep in the bones. There may be signs of liver, pancreatic and adrenal troubles as well.

It is safe to assume that no organ can be safe from the buildup of acidity, which may go unchecked.

Sensory Channel 13
SPACE (alkaline or base)

Just as the early crystals detected a sense of building pressure around them as a survival reflex, so did they alternately develop an ability to perceive the emptiness of space, indicating to them that the potent electrical forces they needed to continue their survival were nowhere to be found. Alkalinity is a sense perception developed by crystalline structures to alert their control centers that energy, which may support their activities, is dwindling.

The human body perceives this very same condition and has become accustomed to the term hypoglycemia, whenever the surprising perception of alkalinity is registered.

Alkalinity is the direct opposite of acidity and because the body exists in a more efficient state when slightly acid, it is obviously essential for the genetic planning mechanism (GPM) to perceive when the body is receiving sense impressions that indicate the energies around the individual are non-supportive. The old saying "feeling alone in a room full of people" is an indicator of symbolization that is mentally used to describe conditions in which we may find ourselves. These conditions can be harmful because we may not have enough reactive material close at hand to sustain life's functions. This condition occurs when a man, who wants to build a house in the middle of the desert, can find no wood, or a woman who desires to play a game of tennis and finds an empty court with no ball, racket or other players. A similar alkaline condition results when a worker reports for work on a Monday and finds the building empty, or another who intends to drive a car and finds it out of gas. All these conditions are indicative of certain relative states of alkalinity.

The symptomatic patterns that may present themselves during states of alkalinity will be warning signals that the GPM is receiving signals of alkalinity. These signals may be confusing; however, they are conclusive when the individual senses the opening up of space or a lost, "gone" feeling. Possibly there may be fits of hysteria, anxiety, apprehension and extreme nervousness. A person who loses his perception for alkalinity may crave being left alone, but those who suffer temporary breakdowns of this perception may actually develop the fear of being left alone. Whatever the condition, the individual most certainly judges his response by the input of his surroundings and more especially from the people in his life.

Someone who suffers from inabilities to perceive space may have primary dysfunctions of the eyes, brain, middle ear and the solar plexus.

Sensory Channel 14
EXTERNAL MOTION
(movement of objects in the environment)

One of the primary concerns of crystalline structures was the relationship of external objects to itself. There was always a constant monitoring of the activities of other entities around them, which pervaded both the land and the seas. At this time in the evolution of the planet, crystalline structures developed the very mature sense on their own for perceiving the movements of objects relative to themselves. With sophisticated sensing abilities, crystals were able to track other energies at great distances at a 360-degree circumference.

The human body, painstakingly developed by the coordinated effort of crystalline structures over millions of years, eventually settled on a sensing device capable of tracking movement of other things in the environment with great perception. This external motion is a combination sense perception involving the senses of sight, sound and touch. It is a perception that can be finely tuned to allow athletes to perform great feats of prowess such as racquetball, tennis and other sports requiring keen hand and eye coordination.

Individuals who lose the ability to perceive environmental motion almost immediately suffer breakdowns of hypothalamic control. However, the input of radiation from the surroundings, plus the body's ability to analyze these things, directly depends upon the eyesight and the motor controls of the brain. Persons who develop deficiencies in this perception will have deteriorations of the spine and the bones, and the muscles will atrophy.

The ability to perceive environmental motion and movement external to the body is a finely tuned sense perception, which is coordinated by the pineal gland, as well. And because the pineal gland is involved with the pituitary gland, that master gland of all the endocrine system, it immediately relays sense information to the genetic planning mechanism (GPM) to try to adjust protein matrices in the hopes of constructing, on a makeshift basis, a more suitable muscular build and skeletal frame in the present time. If a person is playing a sport or doing an activity requiring great coordination, the GPM can be tapped and programmed to automatically control certain reflex actions to make the person more adept at his or her endeavor.

Sensory Channel 15
RADIATIONAL FORCES
(planetary)

The ability of crystals to perceive the actions of other energies in the environments surrounding them was developed into a sophisticated sensing mechanism that could observe the direction in which other energies traveled.

Radiational forces are particular energies that explode or move outward from a common center. This motion has been borrowed by every living entity seeking to survive. Trees, flowers, plants, animals, and all energies that move out from a common center, even the cell itself, are processes of radiational forces.

The characteristic radiational forces are those energies that shape themselves in particular specific objects that can be recognized by the genetic planning mechanism. A tree is really an explosion, almost frozen in motion. If the actions of a tree were sped up a trillion times from seedling to mature oak, we would witness a powerful, explosive force. Time-lapse photography can do this, but on a shorter time frame than the life of a mighty oak. It is the radiational sensing ability of crystalline structures, coupled with the sense of time, which organisms used to perceive the sequence of explosions created by life energy around it.

The ability of the body to recognize radiational forces is a relative talent from person to person; each of us has differing abilities in this regard. Even though the body itself has the capabilities of automatically determining radiational forces in the environment, it is the mind that

(top right) Radiational force explodes or moves outward from a center. every living entity uses this for survival.

(bottom right) Gravitational force moves inward, toward the center. It is a matter of viewpoint. Gravitational force can also feel like a pulling away.

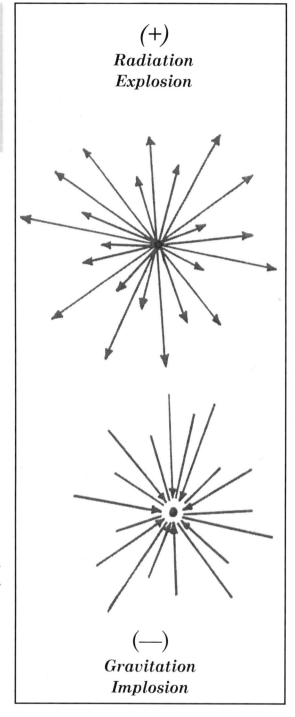

(+)
Radiation Explosion

(—)
Gravitation Implosion

must be trained to finely tune this ability. Energies that move from a common center towards the individual are radiational forces; of course, the largest and most well understood example of this is the sun itself. It explodes nuclear energies towards the earth in the form of many varied types of rays and particles, which strike the person and all life on the planet.

The perception of the person to note just how much and what type of radiational forces are attacking, in proportion to his ability to withstand it, is all-important. Those who lack this talent will find that sun bathing on the beach can be a horrifying experience. The rays of the sun are extremely sudden and formidable and it is those automatic mechanisms within the body that warn the individual that he may be getting too much of them.

Other radiational forces in the environment, such as other people, places and things, can also add to the potpourri of energies that move towards the center of the person. Simple conversation must be viewed as radiation being received by the mind and body. However, when conversation turns to anger and antagonism, then the intensity and frequency of this emotional radiation emitted from other people becomes deadly to a certain extent.

The environment is booby-trapped with many objects that can suddenly or powerfully direct energies towards us. A moving truck, barreling along down a side street at 40 or 50 miles per hour can present a tremendous problem to the sensing mechanisms that perceive radiant forces. If the truck is heading directly for the body, then this will be construed as a radiational force and the sense mechanisms that contain those forces and evaluate them will be stimulated. It is up to the person and the reflex actions of the body to move itself out of the way of danger.

When the human body is deficient in its ability to perceive this type of electric pressure, the body's reflexes will be much slower. If this is the case, the brain, the hypothalamus, the eye and the adrenal glands will be directly affected. However, the sense perception of radiational forces is built into every organ, tissue and cell of the body. It is an important part of endocrine function since glands work on their ability to perceive and control the stimulating effects of hormones that are transmitted from gland to gland. The body's endocrine system, and its entire glandular system for that matter, is built on an electric pressurized system that provides control of the input and output of hormones, enzymes, vitamins and minerals. Each gland is equipped with a finely tuned sense mechanism allowing it to perceive energies radiating to it from other glands, cells and tissues.

It is this channel, the ability to perceive radiational forces, that permits every functioning part of the body to meter the amounts of stimulation received from other vital energies within the body. For example, the anterior pituitary gland emits the thyroid-stimulating hormone (TSH) received directly by the thyroid. The thyroid, using the ability to sense radiational forces, accepts a certain amount of TSH until it is satisfied. At that point, a radiational signal is sent backward to the anterior pituitary to signal it to stop sending thyroid-stimulating hormones. The thyroid then radiates its hormonal product to the other glands and vital stimulating sites in the body which, in effect, perform the same action. They all accept a certain amount of radiation and then they radiate back to alert the origin or source that they have had enough.

Human beings, as a composite energy, act on the same type of information from the environment and relay this information to the mind, which then records it all for posterity.

A person losing his ability to sense radiational forces may show primary dysfunctions of the eyes, the brain and the adrenal glands. A person may experience fear, worry and feelings of inadequacy and weakness. The ability to coordinate body motion may become upset as well.

Sensory Channel 16
GRAVITATIONAL FORCES
(planetary)

The early crystals simultaneously developed the ability to perceive gravitational forces at the same time they developed the talent to accurately detect radiational forces.

Gravitational force is one that moves inward to a common center (see chart on previous page). Its energies are directed outward, and must be distinguished from a radiational force in that to the crystal, radiation moves inward towards its center, and to the outside forces, gravitation is being experienced when an individual feels a pull away from him.

All gravitational and radiational forces are a matter of viewpoint

Depending on where one is standing, it is the action of whether forces are moving away from or toward the individual. This is the essence of the ability to detect whether or not energies are perceived away from or toward the common center of the crystal. This is a very precise and important sense perception; it helps to locate the individual so that he or she can constantly stay out of harm's way in the vicinity of energies that may be too overwhelming.

The human body is very capably constructed to observe forces moving out and away or pulling inward. In essence, there can be just four types of motion that the body is most concerned with:

* Controlled radiational force, which is one that is pushed out away from the body on command from the body (for example, creating an artistic piece)

* Controlled gravitational force, one that is pulled in toward the body under control and command of the body (for example, eating)

* An uncontrolled radiational force thrust toward the body (for example, someone yelling in anger)

* An uncontrolled pulling away from the body (such as when someone dear to the person leaves or dies).

The sense perception for this type of energy, moving to and from the common center of the individual, is directly parallel with its ability to survive. Without a very finely tuned talent for perceiving these energies, body parts that are sensitive could be either overloaded with radiation or when expending out too much radiation be so deficient that they could be completely exhausted.

When radiation is thrust outward under control, the individual is more than likely expressing himself. He is creating creations, which are aimed at making him happy, fulfilled. One of the highest forms of perception is the ability to push energies out and away from the individual. To expand under control is the highest purpose.

When pulling energies inward under control, the person is admittedly deficient in materials needed to create his creations. He acknowledges he needs the assistance of outside forces. The human body is set up on a give-and-take basis, in which the body requires the ingestion of and the exhalation of gases in the atmosphere, as well as the consumption of energy-laden food particles, and gives back the expulsion of fecal matter. On all creation bands, the human body needs to take in as well as to put out, and this concept is aligned with the action of all energies in the universe: all energies in the universe operate on a give-and-take basis. Even the sun requires energies being drawn back inward to it in order to continue its own rhythmic cycle of creation.

When energies radiate toward the body uncontrolled, this could present a spectrum of destruction to the body, which can be as simple as the upset of being verbally assaulted, or as destructive as being hit by a fast moving object such as a bullet or a speeding car. It is very important for us to develop a sense of when there are increases and decreases of electric pressure in the form of radiation moving toward the body; our survival depends greatly on the ability to perceive these things.

When we experience uncontrolled gravitation or withdrawal, we are usually the victim of varying amounts of loss. What we are losing may not be very dear to us or it may be extremely important for our survival. The relative perception of how important another object is for one's survival is part of this sense perception. If we lose an article of clothing, there may

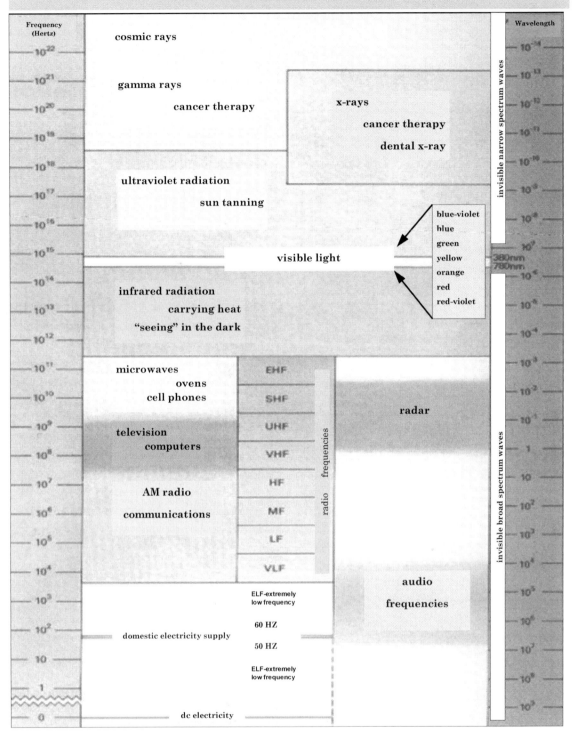

THE ELECTROMAGNETIC SPECTRUM

The electromagnetic spectrum depicts the hierarchy and the breakdown of radiation that exists as visible and invisible light radiation. These electromagnetic waves are electric and magnetic, which vibrate and oscillate together through space at 186,000 miles per second.

not be too much dismay; however, if the article of clothing was a museum quality heirloom or something that was prized or greatly needed, we may experience a relative increase in upset.

When the ability to perceive gravitational forces declines, the person most certainly begins to lose the ability to perceive losses that are vital to survival. Decisions on important matters may go unattended and more time is spent on activities that are not vital to survival. The person may be the type who does not mind the loss of his job, but gets very upset when losing fifty cents at a family card game.

The full spectrum of loss available in the environment, is based on the ability to perceive energies moving away from us. Other symptoms, which may indicate gravitational sense imbalances, are extreme sadness, fear of being left alone, exhaustion, tiredness, nausea, dizziness, unwanted sensations and a person who is easily moved to tears.

Sensory Channel 17
BIRTH
(starting new cycle)

The conception of the crystalline structure is part of an infinite idea that pervades the universe. For the realization of these entities, Thought must perceive its creation. The desire to make a crystal must come from a higher authority than the crystal itself, because the crystal is most certainly an effect of the desire for it to be.

We must consider that there are invisible forces more powerful than the objectivity, the material reality that is available to view in the environment. The Electromagnetic Spectrum (page 114) supports the fact that there is at least an 80 to 1 ratio of invisibility to visibility. And therefore, these energies are part of the creative birthing process. If an individual crystal desires to create one similar to itself, then it must have the preconception to accomplish this action. Without this preconception, the whole process is worthless.

SPECIAL NOTE: This is the actual working of the Z Process. Because this process itself was born of automaticity, confusion has resulted in its study. Human beings find it difficult to believe in the vast automaticity of life controlled by energies beyond their understanding. However, these energies are definable and discoverable.

The study of the human being directs a person's attention to the fact that the human race itself is predicated on the action of birth. Without birth, there would be no human race; however, without the ability to conceive of birth, to measure its ability to happen, the unpredictability of these phenomena would cause humankind to hesitate. Luckily, due to the fact that the sex act is a very pleasurable experience and the raising of children is a rewarding activity, the human race moves onward.

However, many individuals do not fully realize that the birth process, as a perception, is part of the creativity of life on all levels, and not just sex and bodies. There is the birth of new ideas and concepts, and the creation of structures of energies that advance mankind to higher

The symptoms of an imbalanced ability to perceive birth processes will be impotence on a sexual level and impotence on a creative level as well. The person may find it difficult to start new projects.

The realization of the individual's desire is that point when
Thought becomes Matter.

technologies and new and different forms of awareness. There is the birth of all the material reality (objects) in the environment under the control process of thought and creative motion.

The glands and organs of the body directly affecting the birth process are, of course, the sex organs, the adrenal glands, and the hypothalamus; however, there is a connection of energy in the body related to the mind and the spirit, which helps to direct energies for a constant, everyday creation.

This creative energy is needed to work on projects that must be born. Birth must be given to each and every idea during the course of the day. We need to start a new energy cycle for every activity in the environment, which might be as simple as turning on a radio, a light switch, making a phone call, making the bed, eating breakfast, lunch and dinner, talking with friends and neighbors, going to work, etc., all of these are birth processes, which require that we make decisions, either automatically or by more sophisticated evaluation processes involving the mind and the control centers of the body.

The symptoms of an imbalanced ability to perceive birth processes will be impotence on a sexual level and impotence on a creative level as well. The person may find it difficult to start new projects. There may be muscular troubles, twitches, ticks, convulsions and other situations that hamper the smooth activity or exchange of thought and desire into reality. The reason why a person may experience neurological symptoms is that the subtle exchange between the mind, brain and the body is corroded with unfin-

ished business. If the person were to go back over all of the projects and plans that have not come to fruition and methodically make them come to be, then much of the energy blockage taking place within the system could be freed up. The individual may find that he is more able to perform the activity of creation endowed into every living being in the universe.

Sensory Channel 18
GROWTH
(continuing of cycle, gain)

The first crystal formations on the planet developed a keen perception for those things that would aid or duplicate their existence. Growth is that period where a duplication process aids in repeating the same expression over and over again. This is, in a sense, the actual makeup of living objects. Living objects are merely a duplication of themselves and their initial ancestors. If a crystal desires to create a certain form in mass, then this formation of energy must be duplicated over and over again; so the perception for the ability to duplicate is extremely important when accessing changes necessary to create living objects in the environment.

The human body has devised an extremely intricate and powerful plan to duplicate itself. The study of the growth process is one that follows closely behind birth and is basically the realization of the individual's desire. It is that point when thought becomes matter.

After matter is reached, it is the task of the individual crystalline structure to duplicate itself. This is easily demonstrated by birth of a baby. On a cosmic level, in a perfect world, when a result of loving people, there are no accidental births. Following the initial format of developing energies between two people, a man and a woman, they can then duplicate their love. The energies, which they set forth in this endeavor, are part of the perceptive process that aids the body in its task of duplication. Once the connective process is made and there is an agreement of thought between the two, the birth and growth process can begin.

Symptoms that are noteworthy in those who have lost this ability to perceive growth are indicative of people who cannot carry projects through to their conclusions. They have difficulty in copying or in duplicating the habits and actions of others. They are slow learners. They cannot retain very much information when reading. There may be upsets and dysfunctions of the sexual glands, of the pineal gland and also of the mouth. The person may have difficulty expressing himself. He may stutter, stammer and not be able to choose words well. The organs involved are the adrenal glands, the hypothalamus and the sex glands. The pituitary gland, as well as all the gland functions may cause symptomatic patterns that will leave the person nervous and unsure of himself.

Sensory Channel 19
MATURITY
(stagnation, stuck-stopped)

The idea of maturity is easily perceived by the crystalline structure because it, in its actualized form, is in a state of maturity. This condition, maturity, is the action of the energy forces of growth and the energy forces of decay in complete equilibrium. In a sense, it is a stalemate of activities; it is the condition that gives the environment its appearance of motionlessness. A certain percent of energies increasing in force and a certain percentage of energies decreasing in force will provide the illusion of stillness.

The human body reaches maturity when it has fully actualized the genetic plan that had been blueprinted for it from the moment of conception and birth. At the point of conception, the genetic planning mechanism (GPM) takes over and fashions the organism so that it will be programmed or instilled with the data that will carry it through the rest of its life. However, at a certain point in the existence of the organism, in this case human beings, these energies, which have provided growth forces, are met with an equal number of decay forces present in the environment. All genetic programs are written toward a certain amount of immortality and a certain amount of mortality. In other words, parts of the body must die and be replaced. The body itself as a unit never actually needs to cease function. However, because humankind is not versed in the ability to activate certain portions of the genetic planning mechanism, the environment scrambles the immortality program in which a person has been instilled.

The environment, coupled with the adventures and misadventures of the spiritual guiding force (the spirit) of the human being, interferes with the primary program of survival and inputs data that is *non-sequitur* to its existence. The organs receiving much of the input from the environment are especially the hypothalamus and the senses (the eyes, ears, nose, mouth, skin), the adrenal glands, thyroid, and thymus. The brain also receives data from the environment but only after it has been filtered by the peripheral mechanisms such as the senses, which mine-sweep the environment for dangerous or poisonous substances that may do harm to the body.

So, there is an ever, non-ending battle going on between the individual and his environment. The environment is trying desperately to convert the human body into material to prolong its survival at the same time the body is trying to convert the environment into materials that will prolong its survival. In this case, we usually have a standoff where the environment is 50% strength and the human body is at 50% strength, both pitted against each other. However, at certain points, as will be discussed in the next energy channel #20, the environment be-

(below) The Life Cycle is a circuit. It designates a complete circle, energy in a ring. It begins in one place and by going through many changes will end up at the place of beginning, in order for the cycle to repeat. Everything on earth and this planetary system, everything mentioned in the Steps of the Z Process follow this same cycle.

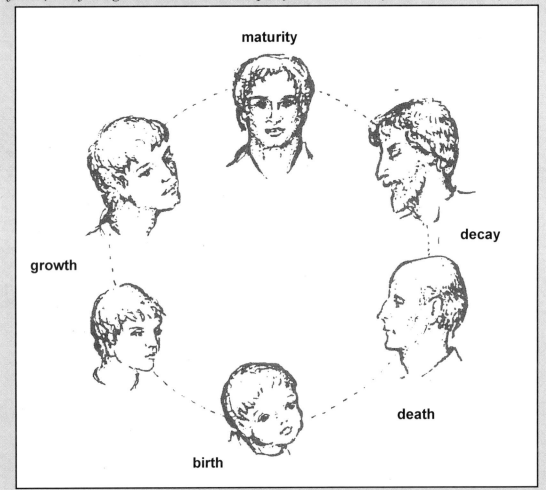

gins to win the game and the body starts to decay. It is not a readily noticeable phenomenon, but the person begins to lose the ability to confront the environment head on after about 18 years of age. Up until that point in time, the person is actually growing and is generally a winning force against the environment. The body is continually getting bigger and stronger. Many people have been able to extend this part of their process of living, but eventually the mysterious and invisible energies in the environment, which are many, invade the spaces that the body occupies and cause it to decay.

The final resting place for the human body is in the dirt or in the air (cremated), offering itself back to the environment from whence it came. It is a never-ending cycle of genetic change and lineage that energies from the environment will recycle and reshape themselves under the masterful control of, at times, the genetic planning mechanism and at other times the environment's planning mechanism.

The symptoms that we may begin to experience when perceiving the state of maturity are stagnation, being stuck or being stopped. There is a certain amount of boredom attached with maturity because the principle idea of maturity is not to either gain or lose but to conserve, to be conservative. Part of the reason that energy decays so rapidly in the body is that human beings resist this total complete boredom of suspension. If anything, the body, to a spirit or its guiding force, is a mechanism that is tempered by his desires. Because the present environment has become such a fast-paced, accelerated place, the body has had more demands placed on it by us to perform or even do ordinary things that would have seemed fantastic to our ancestors. Flying in airplanes, riding in cars, watching television, using computers and talking on the telephone air waves are some of the fantastic experiences that could alter the hormonal balance of a person. So the body must be constantly tuned and reprogrammed to be able to assist at the boring level of maturity without drifting into decay.

There are many scientists and great thinkers who believe that the body could continue to maintain its youthfulness if we would learn the science of vitamin supplementation, healthful food and exercise. However, until the great researchers of the earth discover the exact mechanisms that control the moment-to-moment existence and union of the body, mind and spirit, the environment will have the upper edge on the birth, growth, maturity, decay and death process.

Sensory Channel 20
DECAY (loss of cycle)

The early crystals were very sensitive to the energies in the surroundings that would pull vital forces away from them. This sensitivity was essential in order to prevent decay. However, the crystalline energies that existed prior to organized life and protein structures developed systems to monitor the amount of decay that was occurring. The cyclic energies causing the birth, growth, maturity, decay and the death of energies within the crystals themselves had to be closely monitored. In other words, energies, just as in the human body, must go into a decaying process when they are worn out, and then discarded. Even the tiniest of tiniest minute crystal goes through the same process via atomic and subatomic particles. This is the order of the universe.

Energy must go through certain positive and negative cycles to complete total existence. The reason why decay is so necessary is to eliminate the old and make room for new and better forms. Without the decay process, energies would stack up and block the progress of the genetic programming mechanism (GPM), for if it devises a better way to survive, and the entity, crystal or organism refuses to go into decay, then the new plan could not commence. Therefore, it requires a great deal of decay so that individuals may control its process and even enhance the action of it. The decay of disease, worn out cells, poisons and other vermin, which do not belong in the body, is an absolute necessity; yet if an individual is constantly preparing himself to prevent decay and fight it on all fronts, he may lose his immortality faster than he realizes. The environment, moving at such a rapid state of progress, demands that all organisms become more efficient. If the new plans and ideas are not laid into the genetic programming mechanism for their approval and their initiation, if an individual is somehow preventing or stagnating the decay process, then the individual himself will succumb to the environment's devious plan of absorbing energies.

This is the case with many of the drug products used, which are purported and seem to diminish pain and other unwanted conditions in the human body. When taking these drugs, prescription or over-the-counter medicines, the person may think that he has lost a poison (pain), but he has actually gained a misperception of buried, stagnated crystalline structures within his system.

The energies that communicate to the human mind and body that something is awry in the system can be squashed by prescription and over-the-counter medicines. Eventually, a human being who practices this "art of numbification" will find that his body, weighed down with stagnated matter within his frame, is becoming less able to survive due to the fact that the GPM cannot initiate new changes in cellular structure.

The reason why the GPM cannot make these changes is because its energies are frozen and stuck as well. Conglomerated masses from outside energies (drugs and other chemical frequencies) may lodge themselves in position between the genetic programming mechanism and the protein matrices, which control the framework of the body, and the GPM's energies cannot be transmitted properly to make the changes.

Persons who inadvertently convert themselves into coagulated masses of inert matter by ingesting concentrated poisons from the environment may be duped into believing that they are controlling energy signals in the body, when in actuality they are falling right into the hands of the poisoned environment. Eventually, at their burial, they are interred in a stone sarcophagus, which symbolizes their life and death; the person has methodically turned himself into stone in life and in death.

The organs that may give a hint that the person is losing his ability to perceive decay are the skin, the nerves, the brain and the liver. The colon is implicated as well, for it is an elimination system that signals the body when substances in the digestive tract have been left to putrefy and rot.

The skin is the first line of defense to alert the body that forces in the environ-

The energies that communicate to the human mind and body that something is awry in the system can be squashed by prescription and over-the-counter medicines. This is the practice of numbification. It will weigh down the body and the GPM will be frozen and stuck as well.

ment are attempting to erode the human being. These signals are relayed into the muscles and bones, which then contact the nervous system and the brain to coerce the GPM to create as quickly as possible a new program that will ensure that the person will be able to survive in an ever-changing atmosphere.

The liver works in a mysterious way to transmutate, degrade and digest energies from the environment. It is in the liver that many of the processes of decay are kept secret. The degradation of energies ingested into the body is part of the massive system called the reticuloendothelial system, which produces antibodies as chain-linked to the liver, thymus, tonsils, appendix, Peyer's patches, lymph nodes and all those systems that protect the body against degradation of energies within by environmental forces. However, the liver is the organ that stores and codes many of the substances that have been contacted by the body. The enzymes transferase and transaminase, which are housed along with thousands of other enzyme codifications, are logged into the liver so that the body and its GPM can tap the file system on energies that are similar to, exactly the same as, or different from the materials that a person contacts on a day-to-day basis.

The major symptom a person may experience when losing the ability to perceive decay is pain. Pain is a great signal, a loud signal alerting the individual that the decay process is in full swing. Cancers and other degenerative conditions that

exist today in epidemic proportions are the symptoms and the results of individuals losing the ability to perceive this most needed process. Degenerative conditions are a full-scale, hysterical retreat from the ability to control what is vitally needed to replace old, tired and worn-out programming with new and better ideas, which help to promote the organism into a more highly evolved state

Sensory Channel 21
DEATH (end of cycle, situation or events)

The early crystalline structures, which lined the ocean floors and began to promote life in the form of protein matrices, developed a great understanding for the perception of death. Death and maturity had a very similar look. However, with death, the cycles of energy that were in competition in maturity, the positive and negative forces which pitted themselves directly opposite each other and created a standstill, were at rest. In other words, the power of both forces ceased to be.

Death is the end of situations as they are and is the eradication of existing energies so that new and better-evolved forces, programs and energies can take their place. Without death, there could be no newness. And so the process of death is one that actually heralds the birth of the new.

The end of the genetic lines as such, however, were not the end of the genetic program. Even when lineage of a certain family was broken, the genetic programming or planning mechanisms were held intact. It is not fully understood, but it is postulated that the genetic program mechanisms (GPMs), which pervade the human body, are transferable not only by linking mother and father to son and daughter and to the children's children's children, but also by environmental contact. In other words, the GPMs can transfer from one organism to another via environmental contact. This means that genetic plans, programs and purposes can be borrowed without having to be of the bloodline of a certain family in order that many of the traits that are positive and pro-survival, whether in that genetic line or another, may be accepted. However, when a line dies out it is because of its inability to utilize the genetic plan laid in for them and it cannot continue survival on a wholesale basis.

The death of a genetic plan occurs because of its unworkability; it is important to eliminate the weakest forms to make way for the stronger ones. The environment, as it is structured, is set up on a very organized basis in this regard. The stronger will always survive because the GPM realizes that its main force of endeavor is pitted against the environment as such, and is not pitted against other human beings. Even though other human beings make up the environment, it is the genetic programming that postulates new and better survival programs for human beings to exist *ad infinitum*.

The organs of the body that are the main channels for the death perceptive process are the skin, lymph and the thymus. The skin is constantly recycling new cells through its pores; in fact, the body sheds all the skin cells that are used and worn out within one month's time. How-ever, the thymus, connected with the spleen, is most intuitive on the death process, for this system must recycle red blood cells by utilizing a specific cellular technique that engulfs and devours worn out, spent materials. These are then handed off through the liver and expelled through the urine or the colon.

All along this process, the organs within the body must have a perception as to just how alive or dead the cells are, for it does not want to unleash energies against cells that are still living. And so, the mechanism must be structured to perceive when the time has run out on certain structures of the body. It does this mainly by sensing the amount of pressure that exudes from certain locations in the body. Like radar, the thymus is able to scout the body and pick up areas where pressures have increased beyond the normal operating capacity of the body. These pressurized areas, as minute as the DNA-RNA molecules themselves, can be sensed and eradicated by the forces that are present in the body. This energy system is vital to maintain a homeostatic balance between those energies in the body that are just being born, those that are in a growth process, those that are mature, those that are in decay and those that are dead. Because the organism is structured to exist forever, this balance procedure is a must.

Sensory Channel 22
SKIN SENSITIVITY

Early crystalline structures that inhabited the planet developed a finely tuned sense for the perception of the division between themselves and the environment. The layers of electromagnetic charge, which made up the auras that surrounded the crystals, ultimately became a type of protective membrane. These structures, however, had no supple, elastic covering like the human body. They were mainly constructed of electrical bands of energy, which, at a certain point became solid, thus defining the periphery of the crystalline structure itself.

The human body has long since developed a sophisticated mechanism for controlling the influx of environmental activity around the body. In a very real sense, the skin must be able to filter poisons encountered in the environment. It must be able to allow helpful energies into the body and stop harmful ones from entering. It must be able to control the amount of energies contained within the structure so that it expels the harmful substances and contains the helpful ones inside the body. In all actuality, skin is an extremely powerful organ, which secretes substances that aid the immediate survival of the human being. Even though it is a highly reactive mechanism, the skin contains many electromagnetic programs to selectively act against viruses, toxins, poisons, vermin and other polluting frequencies. The body must make decisions on the acceptance of light and other energies in the surroundings, and the skin plays an extremely important role in this procedure.

The symptomatic patterns that develop on the skin give us a hint as to the activity occurring inside and around the body. The electromagnetic fields, invisibly anchored around the body, are also considered more intelligent and sophisticated "skins" that alert the visible mechanism to react in specific ways to facilitate this process of filtering poisons and allowing helpful energies to enter the body.

The reaction to poisonous plants, for instance, is one method in which the skin protects the body. If this poison were to move in toward the center of the body, it might disrupt the functions of the endocrine organs or the brain itself. It is extremely important, when contacting some type of poison in the environment, to aid the skin in its efforts to not only block the poison's path in toward the center of the system, but to expel it to the outer skin as well. (The outer skins are the electromagnetic force fields that extend one inch from the visible portion of the body to anywhere from 100 yards to 1,000 miles.) The ability of the skin to disrupt the invasion process of poisons into the body is directly related to the electromagnetic field that surrounds it. Within these fields, energies may be held in suspension. This means that poisons, vermin, toxins, pollution and even bad thoughts, anger, dissent and other invectives against the individual, may be held trapped somewhere in the layers of skins outside the body.

This is the most interesting study concerning the human body, for the process by which energies transform into the visible light spectrum begins somewhere outside the body on their way in and deep inside the body on their way out. The skin is such an imperative study because it is the point where the metamorphosis of light radiation moving inward and out-

The electromagnetic fields, invisibly anchored around the body, are also considered more intelligent and sophisticated "skins." This field helps to filter out the poisons and at the same time it aids the helpful energies to enter the body.

(above) Rhus Toxicodendron, also known as poison ivy, contains an oil that is irritating to the skin of most people who touch it. It is a climbing vine and or a shrub. "Rhus Tox" is an old-time homeopathic remedy used to reduce sensitivity and allergic response.

ward from the body becomes visible. The point is that the bones deep inside the body are actually invisible to the naked eye unless they are irradiated with x-rays. Only if a person loses the protective covering of the skin can anyone see or observe the bones within.

Symptomatic patterns that we observe on the skin in the form of pimples, warts and other encrusted areas are a warning that energies are held or trapped in suspension, either moving inwardly or outwardly from the body. The skin must consider that these energies are poisons; for once trapped on the surface they are visible and are an expression of other upsets connected to higher forms of energy.

As an example, a teenager may develop acne during puberty because of the extensive changes within the endocrine system. However, someone could also sustain this poisonous condition by continually having bad luck and traumas in life. We do not have to be a teenager to experience the condition of acne and it is the skin that gives us a signal that the activities in which we are partaking are not pro-survival. Rashes, birthmarks, cold sores and other conditions fall into the same category.

The nails and the hair on the body are an outgrowth of protein, which demonstrate the patterns of energy within the body. The DNA-RNA holds a specific coded plan for each body that is imprinted on the fingers and toes. This is traditionally known as the fingerprints and the footprints of the individual. However, the nails, being protein redistributed in the body in an effort to realign to the RNA messages, are the true read-out of the body's activities in accordance with this plan.

The fingernails and the toenails, when closely examined, will show particular patterns that can give a person the hint whether or not his physiological and psychological activities are in accordance with his own genetic plan.

Deep ridges crosswise on the nails indicate interference or a disruption in the program that has been designed for this individual's body.

Long cracks or furrows are indicative of someone who is infested with bacterial and fungal organisms.

White spots on the fingernails or toenails indicate that the person is beginning to lose calcium in the body.

Discolorations, thickening and other upsets are indications that the person is losing his ability to cope with his present

Fingerprints contain a certain coded plan for each unique body, an imprint.

surroundings. The random movement, the action in the present environment may be too much for the person to bear. The study of the nails can be long and deeply involved; however, the author has left that task up to another promising, young researcher who wishes to take it on.

Sores, blisters and calluses that won't heal are indicative that energies are in a crystalline state, being held in suspension, neither decaying nor increasing in activity.

Persons who have had calluses on their toes or fingers for a very, very long time have created a state of pressurization that is just enough to keep it in a constant state of maturity. If this person were to stop using a hammer or playing the sport causing these things to form, then the callous or the anomaly should disappear. However, if one were to stop the activity and the callous or anomaly remains, it is indicative of unresolved internal endocrine or nervous system problems.

The color of the skin is also a giveaway as to the activities taking place outside and inside the body. The color is indicative of the movement of crystalline structures, salts, proteins and metals.

Sensory Channel 23
PERCEPTION OF HUNGER

The early crystalline structures, desiring to exist forever, realized that there was a necessity to absorb energies from the environment, reconstruct them, and coordinate them into their own structure. In a sense, the act was one in which individual control centers created energy by effusion. (For our purposes, effusion is the act of atomic and other particles producing desire, the act of creating something from something.)

The human being, after millions of years, has developed a very fine perception of hunger to utilize energies from the environment. The hunger perception not only extends to food, but also to people, places and concepts as well. When an individual perceives his hunger for one of these particular manifestations of life energy, he contacts a combination of misalignments that are imbalances of pressure. In other words, his hunger is directly dependent on need created by either the environment or the genetic planning mechanism (GPM).

A person has certain pre-described hungers (needs) that he feels during the course of a lifetime. These hungers are intertwined into the hungers or needs of the spirit, of the mind, and of the body. In other words, a simultaneous existence of the GPM and the spirit causes an intertwining of desires, which may sometimes coincide and sometimes conflict.

For example, if an individual desires to have an ice cream cone and the GPM has not programmed itself to accept that configuration of fats, proteins, and carbohydrates, then there may be a minor conflict, a dietary conflict.

More major conflicts would affect patterns of sleep, growth, cellular repair and other automatic processes, which are the realm of the GPM. All too often, those who are ignorant of the mechanisms of the GPM, or of its methods, will wonder about, want, or desire activities and materials that are counter-opposed to the operation of the genetic plan in force at the present time.

The evaluation of hunger depends directly upon the joint desires of the GPM and the individual himself. In many instances, the GPM may signal automatically to the brain that it is time to eat, but if the person is working or playing at a game, or doing something that he feels is more important, he can automatically override this command from the GPM and push it off to another time.

These types of infractions are commonplace in today's society; however, since the GPM is a senior mechanism of the spirit and a junior to its desires, rather than counter-oppose the desires of the individual, it will effort to change the program. The real trouble occurs when the program cannot be altered because there are certain primary directives indicated by the structure of the body. For example, if a person wishes to maintain a visible organic structure (the body), then he must ingest certain quantities of material in order to be harmonious with the genetic plan. He must eat proteins, fats and a certain amount of starches to maintain the structure of the body. If he refuses to do so, then he must suffer the consequences of violating the basic blue-

A person has certain hungers (needs) during a lifetime, which includes hungers of the spirit, of the mind, as well as the body.

print of the organism. It works the same way as an automobile that requires certain maintenance procedures, oil and gas; when we refuse to supply these particular needs, the automobile will simply cease to serve us.

The sensing mechanisms that the genetic planning mechanisms employs to force the person into complying with the blueprint are those of pain and sensation. These are the feelings of gnawing pain, unwanted and unyielding sensations in certain parts of the body when the individual refuses to heed the prescribed messages of hunger.

The harmony between the sensing mechanisms and the individual is mandatory for living happily. The symptomatic patterns that are visible when the individual is ignoring the senses of hunger are: anxiety, nervousness, restlessness and general overall fatigue, which results from running against the grain of the person's own physical existence.

Sensory Channel 24
ENZYME ACTIVITY

The enzyme is the electrical activity of crystalline structures. It is the expression of the desire of the crystal to achieve some type of work. Enzymes can be molded into different types of workers, defenders and other entities, depending on the desires of the individual crystals.

Enzymes can work as splitters, which act as a cutting edge to break down or demolish other crystals.

Enzymes can behave as activators and in this sense are catalysts to other energies surrounding the crystal.

Enzymes can be adders, which help to create energy bonds within the system. Enzymes can aid digestion, block poisons from moving into the system, transfer energy from one crystal to another and destroy other crystals by decay.

Enzymes can also hold energies in suspension while also possessing the power to activate crystalline commands to create new energy. (see *The Promethion* for more on the types and actions of enzymes.)

The human body, having evolved over the millions of years, has developed some extremely sophisticated enzyme systems, as opposed to the early crystalline structures, which made some very sensible and simple electrical changes. To maintain its correct structure the human body now needs the activity of enzymes to carry out its most basic automatic desires of survival. The enzyme actions that are a part of creating the overall power and appearance of the body range in the tens of thousands. There is enzyme action occurring at the cellular level, so the transactions occurring during the day can reach into the trillions.

The perception of electrical balance develops due to the fact that the electrical transfer between enzymes can be clean, harmonious and efficient. It is the perception of enzyme activity that alerts the individual that the plans and projects of the genetic planning mechanism (GPM) are not being carried forth. Certain manifestations in the structure of the individual will present pictures of ugliness when striving for beauty. The structures themselves may become lopsided (one leg longer than the other), the face may be distorted, painful and most of all, the body will feel heavy, filled with weight and effort. Individuals who lack the perception for these anomalies will be underachievers. They will feel that their ener-

> An enzyme is a protein that produces chemical reactions in the metabolism of plants and animals.
>
> Michaelis Constant for Enzyme Reaction was proposed in 1913. It is used in a variety of biochemical situations, including antigen-antibody binding, DNA-DNA hybridization, and protein-protein interaction. It is also used to characterize a generic biochemical reaction.

gies are being constantly wasted and that they are not getting anywhere in life.

Without enzyme activity, the individual cannot experience the exhilaration of life because the energies within the body are all dependent on enzyme movement.

Seeing as how the enzyme is mainly an electrical phenomenon, the symptomatic patterns that present themselves will be similar to those of radiation poisoning. There may be skin lesions, scars, stretch marks and especially cellulite and fat deposits in areas of the body where enzymes are not working properly. Visually, the person may appear lethargic, tired; hair will be lusterless, nails dull and thickening, the body itself will be rigid and inflexible. Hardened, crusted forms will replace the normal suppleness of the system.

Finally, the individual may experience

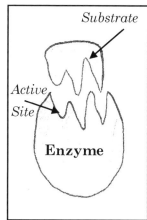

Enzymes are the electrical activity of crystalline structures.

Enzymes are highly selective and can be molded into different types of workers depending on the desires of the crystal.

degenerative or severe disease reactions, because enzymes are needed to combat and fend off diseases.

In essence, all disease activity depends on enzymes. So what is born is a war of enzymes between those of the body and those of the environment. When the environment is successful, the body will lose even more of the enzyme activity. And this is verifiable by examination of the equilibrium of the individual's mind, body and spirit.

Sensory Channel 25
VITAMIN ACTION

A vitamin is a group of complex organic substances required by an organism as a vital nutrient. Vitamins are closely associated with normal physiological and mental functions in man and other living beings, although the needs vary by species.

Vitamins, in a sense, are building blocks for enzyme activity. Vitamins are called co-enzymes for they work with the enzyme in the endeavor of creating electricity. When vitamins are missing, so are the integral parts of enzyme activity. In this situation, the enzymes never get the kind of electromotive force of which they are capable. For a comparative example, if we attempted to start the car without spark plugs, we would have no success even though we had plenty of gas and it was a brand new vehicle.

Those Who Lack Vitamin Power

The human body, devoid of vitamins, has much less response than someone who does possess them in proper amounts. However, the genetic programming mechanism (GPM) has rigged activities that the body performs to automati-cally generate vitamins. It is best to eat vitamin-rich foods, a balance of colorful foodstuffs, in order to ingest the entire spectrum of vitamin power. The act of eating and digesting food, breathing the air and drinking water provides the necessary components to develop vitamin and enzyme activity.

The genes themselves possess the automatic talent to direct electrical activity to carry out the precious plans of the GPM.

When we are in balance, the right and correct foods are chosen to consume for health and vitality. When the perception for vitamin activity is lost or we are unconscious to it, we are much less apt to gravitate to the best sources so that our body can glean the energies needed to recreate them. The early crystalline structures created co-enzyme activity by desire and the genetic structures consistently effort to utilize their endowment of vitamin energy very wisely. However, the system is in constant need of replenishment.

The natural vitamin, with all its complex of components, is found in foods, not in jars on the grocery shelf. Most of what is on the shelf is a chemical formula, said to "be the same thing" as nature, but remember that it has been chemically formulated.

Vitamin A
(Chemical title: Retinol, Retin-A)

Vitamin A, a fat-soluble vitamin, helps to maintain the immune system, teeth, bones, eyes, skin, hair and soft tissues. Carotenoids, such as beta-carotene, are turned into vitamin A by the body and promote good vision. As a major anti-oxidant, this vitamin helps protect the cells from free radicals.

When we are in balance, we naturally choose the correct foods we need for health and vitality.

The body has been designed to generate vitamins itself.

It is better to eat colorful, vitamin-rich foods for their vitality than to take vitamin pills off the store shelf.

Vitamin A is a primary co-enzyme made up of carbon-hydrogen atoms that can be either manufactured by the sun or the genetic planning mechanism (GPM).

In ancient Egypt those suffering from night blindness were fed liver, which is a great source. Vitamin A is found in fish liver oil, egg yolks and beef liver, and, as carotene, in the bright green and yellow fruits and vegetables – apricots, grapefruit, carrots, spinach, winter squashes, yams, sweet potatoes and beet greens. There are other sources of vitamin A, but in lesser concentrations than the above.

The individual with vitamin A deficiency will find parallels with radiation toxicity: rapid aging, and an increase of invader forces – more allergies and colds. The buildup of toxins, vermin, bacteria and other indicators point to the fact that the body cannot easily or consistently fight off poisons from the environment. This vitamin aids in the development of visual purple, which is necessary for night vision; therefore, a person deficient in vitamin A may find that he has night blindness. Persons who have developed allergies over the years may be consistently deficient in Vitamin A.

B-Complex

B-complex is comprised of several B vitamins and other substances closely related to the Bs, most of which are essential to health and help metabolization— all B vitamins convert food (carbohydrates) into fuel (glucose).

Generally, vitamins B-1, B-2, B-3, and B-7 (biotin) facilitate different aspects of energy production; vitamin B-6 is essential for amino acid metabolism; and vitamin B-12 and folic acid (B-9) aid cell division. Each of these vitamins has many additional functions listed on the following pages. (See also *The Threat of the Poison Reign* and the Radiation Cocktail of nutrients.)

The B-complex nutrients are found in whole unprocessed foods, nutritional and brewer's yeast, grains, liver and meat products. The B-complex affects the digestive tract, cell metabolism, the skin (pigmentation and vitiligo), eyes, hair and the liver.

A person with deficiencies of B-complex may notice development of digestive disturbances, cholesterol imbalances, chronic fatigue, inability to get proper sleep, ringing in the ears, constipation,

> *Due to research changes and discoveries, the vitamins and co-enzyme factors listed in this section have had differing names through the years.*
>
> *Vitamin research is still an open field, with some interesting discoveries being endorsed while others are being outlawed. Even though political organizations might only recognize 13 vitamins, there are many more co-enzyme factors, and others yet to be discovered.*

anemia and skin problems. Upsets of the heart rhythm, hyperactivity and weight problems are also attributed to displacement of B-complex. The complex has been useful for alcohol withdrawal, osteoporosis, wound healing, low stomach acidity, anxiety and pre-menstrual syndrome (PMS), as well as enhancing athletic performance.

In essence, the B-complex is a sophisticated electrical message, received and decoded by the genetic programming mechanism (GPM), which allows energies to be more coherent in the body in relation to the environment.

Vitamin B-1
(Chemical title: Thiamine)

B-1 was the first of the B vitamins discovered; originally called the "anti-beri factor" for its first use to combat the disease beriberi. This co-enzyme, water-soluble vitamin is essential for the breakdown of carbohydrates into energy. It is often called the "anti-stress" vitamin because it works to strengthen the immune system and combat stressful conditions. It is necessary to create adenosine triphosphate (ATP), which every cell in the body uses for energy.

Vitamin B-1 is found in rice bran, pork and organ meats, sunflower seeds, all nuts, legumes, brewer's yeast, enriched grains and brown rice, and black strap molasses.

Someone with deficiencies of B-1 may

notice numbness and tingling of the hands and feet, trouble breathing, eye movements (as with beriberi) and sensitivity to environmental stimuli, such as noise, confusion and loud talking. There may be pains in the heart, digestive disturbances, nausea, tiredness, shortness of breath, anemia, dementia, cataracts, and an inability to cope with stress. Alcoholics often display a deficiency. Diabetics have long been known to have low levels of B-1 in their systems due to the ability of this vitamin to aid digestion and metabolize carbohydrates into glucose (energy).

Vitamin B-2
(Chemical title: Riboflavin or Lactoflavin)

Vitamin B-2 is a co–enzyme that aids red blood cell production and causes the conversion of the amino acid tryptophan into nicotinic acid, which helps to rid the body of poisons. It works in concert with vitamin A.

Vitamin B-2 is found in eggs, yeasts and bran, nuts, seeds, whole grains, organ meats, black strap molasses, turnip greens, yogurt, milk, cheese, broccoli, asparagus and Brussels sprouts.

Those who are deficient in B-2 may experience slow growth, itching, red burning eyes, cracks and sores in the corners of the mouth, cataracts, dizziness, hair loss, chronic diarrhea, arthritis, "shark's skin" over the nose, and a red, sore tongue. There may be reactions or sensitivities to dim light. Vitamin B-2 contributes to the energy cycles that aid in the development of stored power in the body; and so the person who develops a deficiency in this necessary vitamin may continually experience feeling as though his energy were slowly draining from his body.

Vitamin B-3
(Chemical title: Niacin and niacinamide)

Vitamin B-3 is a co-enzyme used in the treatment of high cholesterol because it breaks down fat barriers. This breaking down of the fat barriers helps with the hallucinations due to drugs (which are stored in fat), Alzheimer's, dementia and age-related loss of thinking skills. Pellagra, depression, motion sickness, alcohol dependence, and fluid build up (edema) are also helped. It is effective against arthritis, circulation problems, and acne.

Vitamin B-3 is found in liver, chicken breast (especially the fat under the skin), yeast, veal, seafood, tuna, beans, cereal grains, and vegetables such as rhubarb and dandelion greens.

Individuals lacking in B-3 may have a higher incidence in the development of chancre sores, muscular weakness, nausea, headaches, insomnia, bad breath, high blood pressure, tooth decay, depression and pellagra. Niacin has been used to destroy energy barriers that have falsely developed under the instructions and the guidance of misinformed genetic systems. The use of niacin in the study of schizophrenia is one that helps the practitioner in understanding the development of elec-tromagnetic fields and energy barriers.

The final conclusion is that certain co-enzyme factors assist the development of energy abutments in the system and other specific co-enzyme factors aid the destruction of barriers that form. Niacin is most certainly the co-enzyme factor of choice when attempting to reduce the amount of electromagnetic barriers built up in the system (see *The Threat of the Poison Reign* and the Radiation Cocktail of nutrients, of which niacin is a mainstay.)

Vitamin B-5
(Chemical title: Pantothenic acid or panthenol)

B-5 is a co-enzyme factor called co-enzyme A; it is synthesized in the small intestine. This vitamin is electrically compatible with the adrenal glands and helps to smoothly make the transition of energy loss and gain with the system. It works with vitamins A and C to protect against infections.

Vitamin B-5 is found in whole grains, mushrooms, liver, brewer's yeast, eggs, legumes, salmon and saltwater fish.

Individuals who suspect a deficiency in B-5 will likely have symptoms of hypoglycemia, kidney trouble, respiratory infections, restlessness, nerve problems, sore feet, muscle camps, paresthesia, premature aging, vomiting, allergies, baldness, digestive disorders and tooth decay.

Vitamin B-6
(Chemical title: Pyridoxine)

Vitamin B-6 is a co-enzyme necessary for more than a hundred enzyme activi-

There are many ways to create co-enzyme forces (vitamins) between people by way of thought processes and electromagnetic radiation.

ties, principally protein metabolism, amino acid metabolism and thus, the biosynthesis of neurotransmitters, which aids in reducing depression and other maladies. Assisting the proper placement of protein matrices in the body, B-6 thus helps the development of the entire protein structure. B-6 helps reduce water retention in the joints and swelling from arthritis.

Vitamin B-6 is found in rice bran, chickpeas, beef liver and organ meats, tuna, salmon and poultry. Although available in fruits and vegetables, B-6 is found in lesser amounts: bananas, winter squash, nuts, raisins, oats, brown rice, wheat germ, green leafy vegetables, blackstrap molasses, whole grains and breakfast cereals (often fortified with B-6).

Persons deficient in B-6 may notice an increase in dizziness and disorientation, chronic irritability, convulsions, weakness, anemia, acne, extreme nervousness, overweight and photophobia. Low levels of B-6 are found in those with peripheral neuropathy, alcohol dependence, pregnant women, the obese and those with malabsorption syndromes.

Vitamin B-7
(Chemical title: Biotin)

As vitamin research continues, vitamin B-7 is found with various names: biotin, vitamin H, and Co-enzyme R. Vitamin B-7 is a co-enzyme factor involved in the synthesis of fatty acids and amino acids. It aids cell growth, digestion of fats, and maintains blood sugar levels. As vitamin H, studies show it strengthens hair and nails.

B-7 is synthesized in the body by intestinal bacteria and is found naturally in Swiss chard and green leafy vegetables, egg yolk, soybeans, yeast, mung bean sprouts, and legumes. It is a constituent of whole grains and organ meats such as liver.

Those found with low levels of B-7 are alcoholics, burn patients, the elderly and athletes. A person who suspects a deficiency of vitamin B-7 may experience insomnia, muscular pain, dry skin, tiredness, depression, dermatitis, poor appetite and metabolic disorders, and a peculiar discoloration of the skin causing it to exude a grayish hue.

Vitamin B-9
(Chemical title: Folic acid, folate)

Known in research as folic acid, and vitamin M, Vitamin B-9 is a co-enzyme factor essential for many body functions and reactions. It is a part of living vegetation and becomes coincident with animals and other organisms that partake and consume these materials. It is an extremely important substance in regulating the reproduction and repair of protein matrices (DNA) and also involves the cell division, growth and redistribution of red blood cells and the energy matrices, which are precursors to these. It is important for proper growth of fetus and newborn babies.

Folic acid is found in leafy greens such as spinach, lettuces, in asparagus and egg yolk, legumes, beans, peas and lentils, salmon, liver and kidney meats, vegetable juices.

Certain drug materials later in life create great reductions and imbalances of the available folic acid. Deficiencies are suspected with noticeable premature graying of the hair, digestive problems, retarded growth and anemia. There also may be loss of hair, stomach ulcers, mental illness, nerve damage, chronic diarrhea and an inability to cope with stress.

Vitamin B-12
(Chemical title: Cyanocobalamin)

Vitamin B-12 is a co-enzyme factor essential for red blood cell formation and DNA, RNA synthesis; it contains cobalt and assists in metabolism. This vitamin decreases with age so is used for the elderly for boosting the mood, increasing energy and memory, weak bones and skin infections.

Vitamin B-12 is found in protein foods – all fish, crab, herring, salmon, eggs, cottage cheese, all cheeses, milk, poultry and organ meats, especially liver.

Deficiencies of B-12 may present as anemia, allergies, hand/eye coordination difficulties, weakness in the legs and the thighs, general weakness and unsteady gait, shoulder problems, bone problems, bronchial asthma, weight loss, mood swings, dementia and an inability to cope with stress.

Vegetarians, the elderly and those with impaired gastric mucosa or lowered amounts of stomach hydrochloric acid (HCl) are often deficient in this vitamin. Supplementation of cyanocobalamin (pill, oral sublingual or by injection for severe depletion cases) is readily converted for use by the body.

Vitamin B-13
Chemical title: Orotic Acid

A co-enzyme factor, orotic acid is manufactured within the body by the intestinal flora. It is useful for the DNA, and is sometimes used after a heart attack and in such conditions as multiple sclerosis and chronic hepatitis.

Root vegetables, such as carrots and beets assist the intestinal flora in manufacturing orotic acid, as well as liquid whey.

Vitamin B-15
(Chemical title: Pangamic Acid, calcium pangamate)

Vitamin B-15 is a co-enzyme factor first promoted by the Russians. It is a derivative of the amino acid glycine, called dimethyl glycine (DMG) and B-15 may be produced in the body from this. Vitamin B-15 aids in oxygen utilization within the blood cells, helps the immune system, increases cell life, combats fatigue and helps regulate hormones.

This co-enzyme is found naturally in whole grains, organ meats, eggs, seeds, nuts, meat, yeast and brown rice.

An individual may be deficient in this co-enzyme if experiencing nervous and glandular disorders, premature aging, shortness of breath, and emphysema. The Russians and Europeans have done the most research and their findings show supplementation can reduce the buildup of lactic acid in athletes and so will lessen muscle fatigue and increase endurance. It is used in Russia for alcoholism, drug addiction; mental problems of aging and senility, autism, heart disease, high blood pressure, in some cases of childhood brain damage, schizophrenia, for skin diseases and liver disease and for chemical poisonings.

Vitamin B-15 (the chemical Pangamic acid) can be difficult to obtain in the USA depending upon political organizations.

Vitamin B-17
(Chemical title: Amygdalin, Laetrile)

Vitamin B-17 is from the ancient Greek word for almond—*amygdale*. It was isolated in 1830 and has been used in cancer treatments since that time. When synthesized in the laboratory, the chemical compound Laetrile results; Laetrile contains cyanide. Ernest Krebs conducted cancer research with amygdalin and Laetrile, which he called vitamin B-17.

Amygdalin is found in bitter almond pits, apricot pits, and the seeds of black cherry and apple.

The chemical version, Laetrile, was available in the USA until the 1970s when the FDA outlawed it.

Vitamin B-x
(Chemical title: PABA Para-AminoBenzoic Acid)

Vitamin B-x is a co-enzyme factor. PABA is closely aligned to the activities of radiation in the body. It is necessary to aid the protein structures of the glands, hair, and skin. It is used externally in sunscreen products.

PABA is found naturally in brewer's yeast, mushrooms, whole grains, wheat germ, blackstrap molasses and organ meats (liver and kidney).

Individuals who suspect that they are deficient in PABA may experience graying of the hair, infertility, over-active thyroid gland, depression, digestive disorders, chronic constipation, headaches and irritability.

Choline

A co-enzyme factor usually grouped with the B vitamins, choline is an essential nutrient – it must be ingested; it cannot be synthesized from other sources. Choline helps to build cell membranes, is a pre-cursor for neurotransmitters and thus improves memory, depression and muscle control. It is found in eggs and fatty meats, peanuts, beans, soybeans, fish, organ meats, butter, flax seeds, sesame seeds and soy lecithin.

A person who is deficient in choline may experience heart trouble, kidney dysfunction, high blood pressure, retarded growth, stomach trouble and an inability to digest fats. A deficiency may lead to hardening of the arteries, fatty liver, liver disease and a high incidence of dizziness, constipation and sensitivity to noise.

Vegetarians are often susceptible to choline deficiency, as are athletes and alcoholics.

Inositol

A co-enzyme factor, Inositol has properties similar to a sugar (sweet carbohydrate). It is an electrical factor that helps to prevent the dissolution of energies that maintain the proper balance of fat and protein within the body (a lipotrophic agent). It is extremely useful in aiding a person's ability to relax and face up to environmental pressures and stress; as such, it is often considered in the B complex of vitamins.

Inositol is found in muscle, meat, viscera and is supplemented in the diet with cantaloupes, oranges and citrus fruits, vegetables, nuts, molasses and lecithin, in which form it is readily available. The inositol in bran cereal and beans is not digestible by humans.

Individuals deficient in inositol may experience high levels of cholesterol, eye problems, hair loss, constipation and skin trouble. Over a long period of time they may also develop heart disease, chronic constipation and be overweight.

Vitamin C
(Chemical title: Ascorbic acid)

Vitamin C is a water-soluble, essential nutrient that must be supplied in the diet. It is a co-factor in many enzyme activities as an electron donor. It facilitates wound healing, lowers uric acid levels to improve gout, and reduces hypertension to improve cardiovascular disease. It is a natural antihistamine, aids the immune system, and helps to build collagen.

Vitamin C is abundant in acerola, lemons and all citrus fruits, rose hips, cantaloupe, red and green peppers, goji berries, parsley, kiwi, elderberry, strawberries, and tomatoes. Eaten raw is best because heat tends to lessen its availability.

Hints that there may be a deficiency in vitamin C are scurvy, bleeding gums, ruptures of capillary walls, poor wound healing and easy to bruise. There may also be a higher incidence of dental cavities, infections, poor digestion, nosebleeds, fatigue and anemia. Those most susceptible to deficiencies include smokers, those with malabsorption and kidney disease, and those with a mono-diet (limited variety of foods).

Vitamin C as a curative is extremely controversial because over the years, researchers have claimed miraculous cures involving the use of vitamin C with critically ill and cancer patients. High dose intravenous injections of vitamin C have shrunk tumors and kept vision problems (macular degeneration) from worsening. It is a powerful antioxidant.

Vitamin D
(Chemical title: Ergocalciferol, Cholecalciferol)

A vital co-enzyme factor, vitamin D is necessary for strong bone formation, blood clotting and proper skin respiration. It aids the absorption of calcium, helps the thyroid gland, the parathyroid, adrenal glands and is essential for the regulation of heart rhythm and the absorption and stabilization of the calcium/phosphorus balance in the body.

Vitamin D is a fat-soluble vitamin found in very few natural foods; the chemical formulation is added to milk, orange juice and breakfast cereals as so-called "fortified" foods. In nature, it is found in the flesh of fatty fish, fish liver oils, bone meal, egg yolks and mushrooms, if they have been exposed to ultraviolet light. Its principal source for humans is sunlight; vitamin D is generated naturally in the body when the sun and ultraviolet rays hit the surface of the skin, reacting with the body's cholesterol, which leads some researchers to consider it a hormone (a Greek word meaning "impetus").

Deficiency in vitamin D may lead to chronic diarrhea, nervousness, softening of the bones and teeth (rickets in children; osteomalacia in adults), osteoporosis, and burning sensations of the mouth and throat.

Vitamin E
(Chemical title: Tocopherol, Alpha-Tocopherol)

Fat-soluble, vitamin E is a co-enzyme factor that acts as an anti-oxidant; it has the ability to prevent oxidation of tissues and is the principle reason why it is excellent in retarding the aging process, protecting those exposed to tobacco smoke, air pollution and errant frequencies, and ultraviolet rays. It is useful in reducing cholesterol, assisting blood flow to the heart, strengthening the capillary walls, and protecting the lungs, muscles and nervous system. Vitamin E has been reportedly very beneficial for scars, warts, wrinkles and wounds.

Vitamin E is found in vegetable oils such as olive, wheat germ, safflower, corn and sunflower oils, eggs, dark green vegetables (spinach and broccoli), liver and organ meats. It is also found in oatmeal, nuts and seeds.

Deficiencies in vitamin E may cause difficulties in sexual performance, dull, gray or thinning hair, muscular atrophy, neuropathy, abnormal eye movements, impaired immune system and sterility.

Vitamin F

Essential Fatty Acids (EFA) or vitamin F as this was first called in 1923, are co–enzyme factors responsible for many functions in the body: from well-balanced hormone levels to normal growth and behavior. A balance between the omega-3s and omega-6s EFA is essential; but at present the omega 6 is far more prevalent in the American diet. When balanced, the EFAs build up the immune system to protect the body from radiation and x–ray damage, improvements are noted in the cardiovascular system by lowering cholesterol, as well as the blood vessels, adrenal and sex hormones, thyroid gland, healthy hair and skin, and cell membranes. Balanced EFA reduces edema and helps beneficial intestinal bacteria.

Essential fatty acids must be ingested, as they cannot be synthesized in the body.

These are found naturally in fish and meat, oils of grains, nuts and seeds, avocados, sunflower and flaxseed (linseed). Omega-9 is found in olive oil. Acquiring these by eating whole food is best.

Omega-3 EFA

Omega-3 is found in fatty fish, such as salmon, cod, sardines, herring, tuna and mackerel. Grass-fed animals are good sources; walnut, pecan and butternut oils, as well as flax seed, hemp seed and chia seed.

Omega-6 EFA

Omega-6, which can throw the balance off, are abundant in grain-fed meat, evening primrose and borage oils, vegetable oils and legumes. The American diet tends to be heavy on the omega 6 side, which has increased inflammation, arthritis, and cancer. Drugs used to control these conditions do so by inhibiting the omega-6 action.

An individual who is deficient in the balanced essential fatty acids may experience symptoms of hair loss, eczema or acne and other skin disorders, dry tear ducts, chronic diarrhea, kidney, heart and liver damage, gallstones, brittle hair and nails, varicose veins and be underweight or overweight (thyroid). There may be learning disabilities, inability to concentrate, depression or memory loss.

Vitamin K
(Chemical title: Phylloquinone)

A co-enzyme factor, vitamin K has been called the "coagulation vitamin" (first published in a German journal, as Koagulationvitamin, thus the "K"). It is a life-saving factor for hemophiliacs. Vitamin K aids bone metabolism and prevents bone loss and fractures due to the taking of steroids, osteoporosis, and cirrhosis.

Vitamin K is synthesized in the colon from food sources. Found in the green leaves of plants, green leafy vegetables, such as spinach, collards and kale, dandelion greens, asparagus, blackstrap molasses, olive and safflower oils, and especially in alfalfa and grains. Fruit sources include avocado, kiwi and grapes.

Deficiencies in vitamin K may cause the tendency to hemorrhage, diarrhea, nose bleeds, gallstones, menstrual problems in women and upsets of childbirth. Broad-spectrum antibiotics decrease the production of this vitamin in the intestines. The elderly and those who take blood thinners are advised by their doctors and pharmacists not to eat vitamin-K rich foods.

Vitamin P

Flavonoid and Bioflavonoid, Catechin and Quercetin are all names of vitamin P.

This co-enzyme factor is part of the C-complex and is a more recent discovery in vitamin research. Vitamin P has anti-allergic, anti-inflammatory, anti-microbial and anti-diarrhea properties. Studies show Flavonoids inhibit cancer and improve cardiovascular disease.

Flavonoids and Bioflavonoids are found in the skins and pulp of fruits, cherries, grapes, all citrus, plums and apricots.

Strawberries, dark cocoa, green, white and black tea, and red wine are good sources of Catechins, while beans, onions and apples supply Quercetin. Other sources are seabuckthorn and ginkgo biloba.

A person who is deficient in vitamin P may experience anemia, infections, dental

cavities and rupturing of the capillary walls. It can also cause bouts of dizziness, hemorrhoids, rheumatism, ulcers, colds and bleeding gums.

Vitamin T

Called "T" for Torulitine, vitamin T is water-soluble, and can be destroyed by alcohol. It is a growth factor and as such may improve memory and concentration. Little research has been conducted on T, and it is best found and used in the food sources listed. Vitamin T may be heard more often in some groups as a slang term for testosterone and/or tequila.

Vitamin T is found naturally in insects, egg yolks, sesame seeds, as well as sesame seed paste (Tahini). Because of this, vitamin T is known as the Sesame Seed Factor.

Although research continues about its health benefits, sources indicate vitamin T has been associated with strengthening red blood cells. By bolstering blood cells, the vitamin may be effective in blood cell related ailments, such as anemia and blood hemolysis.

Vitamin U

Vitamin U is a co-enzyme derived from S-Methylmethionine. It is found in raw cabbage juice, alfalfa sprouts, spinach, kale, parsley, celery, radishes, wheat and barley. Raw and fermented foods are the most effective sources.

Vitamin U is good for the liver and the intestinal mucosa, and has been used in the past for the healing of peptic ulcers and treating acid reflux.

It is found in several different types of food and is used by naturopaths and nutritionists to treat a variety of health issues.

****

According to the US government, there are currently only 13 vitamins. That being said, the vitamins and co-enzyme factors that have been recited above are a short list of the more common energies found in foods and other entities in the environment. There are other vitamin factors in foods and in the environment which, as of yet, have not been discovered. There are co—enzyme forces in almost everything that exists; some are created only once for a specific purpose and then are finished.

However, it is important to understand that there are many ways to create co-enzyme forces between people by way of thought processes, intention (Channel #114), and electromagnetic radiation (Channel #105). The perception of vitamin activity, is dependent upon the person's ability to understand and appreciate that the environment is structured to cause an interdependency between human beings. If we did not need outside forces to catalyze reactions within our own body; that is to say, if we could exist solely on our own without aid from the sun, plants, minerals, animals and humans, then we would not need co-enzyme factors or vitamins to exist.

Sensory Channel 26
DIGESTIVE ACTIVITY

The early crystalline structures, knowing that co-enzyme factors, enzyme action and hunger were part of their existence, had to develop more efficient methods of absorbing energies from the environment and converting these into structures coherent with their own purposes. In other words, the crystalline structures needed to absorb energies from the environment to make them part of their own structures.

The periods in the Earth's history that provide a fertile ground for the development of the digestive processes had to be in the era considered the Precambrian times that the crystalline structures most certainly develop the propensity to absorb energy and reconvert it into their own structures.

However, the entire system, the action of digestion, is one that was taught from the early moments of creation, for the sun's energy sprays into the environment and redistributes itself by being digested by its receipt points. The energies of the sun, filtering down through the atmosphere, are collected each step of the way by similar receptors needing particular electromagnetic radiation. In other words, the ultra-violet bands of light gravitate to those receptors of energy in the environment that utilize it more readily. The infrared bands, all the color bands, the x-ray, cosmic rays bands and all the other fields of electric radiation, which are sent forward from the sun to the planet Earth, are respectively swallowed by the receptors created here on Earth for just that purpose.

As an example, the skin absorbs ultra-violet light from the sun so that man can create hormone and enzyme action, which will aid the structure of his own body. The plants are doused with a broad spectrum of light, which, by photosynthesis, allows these rooted organisms to propagate themselves.

It is interesting to observe animals and people sunbathe. Curled up on the grass, stretched out on towels or lounge chairs, they are absorbing energies from the environment in order to make those

When there is the ingestion of some material, whether a mental thought or a physical item, the GPM will track and record whether or not the person was able to refine and understand it.

energies part of their own structures.

The perception of this digestive activity has been degraded into an action of digesting raw materials that may not be proper for the system. The act of digestion at this current and late date in history has become degenerated to an activity of swallowing articles that do not have specific receptor sites within the body. This means that energies ingested, just for the pleasure of tickling the palate of the individual, may find that there is no particular purpose within the body scheduled for its use. Individuals who swallow materials for which there are no receptor sites in the body, not in the stomach, liver, small intestines, bloodstream or any of the organs to include the receptor sites to the brain, will wind up having these ingested materials become inert deposits within the system.

The organs involved in the digestive process are the hypothalamus and the alimentary canal. However, the cells themselves possess digestive capabilities so that energies can move in toward the DNA-RNA and alert the genetic programming mechanism (GPM) as to the relative success of the digestive process.

Everything ingested in the body must be broken down by electrical entities, such as enzymes and co-enzyme factors, so that it can be reduced in particle size and analyzed by the GPM. The hypothalamus is that electrical receptor which analyzes light radiation via the eyes. It is the universal sensing mechanism that coordinates the activities of the senses and their channels of input, relaying them to the

brain for further evaluation. There the genetic programs may be altered, rewritten and redesigned so that the individual may better cope with his environment. On a grosser level, the hypothalamus demands a certain large conglomeration of energy particles, such as foods, to be digested and refined so that they are processed into light particles.

Individuals who have a reduced digestive sensibility will experience symptomatic patterns as a by-product of the inability to break down certain substances and decode them. In actuality, this is a lesson of confusion to which we can be exposed on any level. The confusions of the mind are very similar to the confusions of eating habits. As we are beset by problems in our environment that are insoluble, so, too, can the body be plagued by substances (chemicals, toxins, and poisons) which lodge in the body and are indiscernible by the GPM.

The digestive process is structured so that we may take in mass particles, energies and other phenomena in the environment and then break it down into known quantities. The action of taking in an unknown and making it into something known is the realm of digestive activity. When we absorb an unknown, dissolve it, digest it and understand it, it becomes part of our personality or physical structure.

If for any reason we take on a problem or ingest some material too hard or difficult for us to digest, then it is either expelled violently and rapidly, or it becomes lodged in the body. However, even those quantities of poisons that are expelled violently and rapidly leave a trace on the system. These traces are part of a memory that the GPM records to measure how well the system is doing against the environment. In a sense, this is another win-loss column for the organism. When there is the ingestion of some material, whether a mental thought or a physical item, the GPM will track and record whether or not the person was able to refine and understand it.

The symptom patterns that erupt in an individual who has lost the ability to digest properly are those of the average civilized man, for his digestion is most certainly off when living a life of over-consumption of inert thoughts and food-stuffs of no value.

Sensory Channel 27
MINERAL ACTION

The early crystals were themselves minerals, and even though today minerals are called co-enzymes like vitamins, the minerals maintain a more substantial stabilizing power than do the vitamins. The minerals are actually electromagnetic frequencies in the invisible infrared spectrum and the visible light spectrum. These are the energies that allow crystalline structures to communicate with one another. This communication is necessary for the survival of all organisms. Mineral action occurring in the body is part of a drama that has been played over and over again and is detailed in *The Promethion: A Comprehensive Study of the Principles of Life Energy*.

The mechanism of the human body has grown up around the action of minerals. Minerals, being one of the earlier levels of energy, are spawned by the power of the sun and radiation. The development of electric pressures in the body is directly responsible for the transmutation of light minerals to heavy minerals, and finally into radioactive minerals as was previously detailed. The perception of this process is all important to help maintain the human being's sanity during transactions between the minerals, because minerals have power to communicate very, very intense thoughts, which may disrupt the thought processes of the individual.

The awareness of mineral levels in the body is first and foremost for all human beings, for these levels aid the genetic planning mechanism (GPM) in structuring a program of strength, power and ability.

An individual who loses perception for mineral levels in the body will experience that phenomenon called "heavy metal war" as described in *The Promethion*. It is a time when elements veer out of control, transmutate very rapidly and haphazardly, and cause the bizarre afflictions of nervous disorders and mental confusion.

A greater study of mineral actions can be found in *The Promethion*; however, it can be stated here that the mastery of mineral levels, their actions, their movements and their control, is all that is necessary to uplift the mind, body and spirit to those heights at which they had originally been intended. The degradation of the human being occurs due to his own ignorance of mineral action in his body. Minerals, under his direction, can create any situation, condition or program that he so desires. The right mineral action in the body was the dream of the alchemist, who sought to understand mechanisms that had degraded his ancestors, affectionately called Adam and Eve.

Heavy Metal War occurs when the person has lost the perception for mineral levels. The elements veer out of control, transmutate very rapidly and haphazardly, and cause the bizarre afflictions of nervous disorders and mental confusion so prevalent in today's world.

From the early times on Earth, man has longed to know the secrets that have controlled the mineral levels of the body. Scientists, philosophers, and religious men alike have understood that the basic components of the body, mind and spirit, specifically electrical phenomena and the like, are controlled by certain qualities assigned to mineral action. In other words, it has always been known to man that energy movement, change, correction and renewal was possible instantaneously, with the correct knowledge of mineral activity.

Today, scientists and researchers treat disease and all the ramifications of life and living with the concoctions of minerals that their ancestors handed down to them. From the very beginning of history, man has been bequeathed with the secrets of the mineral levels. It is up to each of us individually to understand the principles of their control to aid our quest in reaching the highest states of awareness.

Sensory Channel 28
GLANDULAR
TRANSACTION (Hormonal)

The early crystalline structures, becoming more sophisticated in their behavior, started to develop automaticities, including the construction of sub-control centers or sub-brains within the crystalline structure itself. Essentially, the crystal, anchored in position, required certain

vortices of radio frequency, which converged and caused magnetic buckling, coincident to the angles of the crystal.

In other words, the facet, or the variations of light energy making up the crystal, made smaller crystalline structures within the crystal itself. As a result, there were created sub-existences of radiant energy within the organization of the crystal. These were the earliest times of pre-designated organization in which the structure was interdependent upon itself for survival. The development of this structure happened nearer to the creation of the planet some four billion years ago approximately, while the organization of life as it were, in cellular form, would not exist for another two billion years. Theoretically, it was at this point that the crystalline structures, supposedly devoid of life in an organic sense, began to develop some type of DNA-RNA structure, which allowed them to procreate and re-design their own structures.

The human body as is, with all its organisms maintaining cellular structure, has developed an intricate system of sub-mechanisms to carry out the intelligent planning of the genetic program mechanism steering their structures. Because larger and more powerful structures, such as animals and human beings, required the addition of trillions of crystalline substances making up trillions of cells, sub-energy systems or sub-brains had to be constructed to facilitate this very large endeavor. These sub-brains ultimately became what are known today as the glands and organs of the body. These glands and organs are outgrowths of brain transmission and reception sites, which have over the period of evolution, made many electrical transactions. In

Hierarchy of Glands & Organs

+1. Brain (32 sections dedicated to perceiving sensation or the loss of pressure)
+2. Eye
+3. Pineal
+4. Hypothalamus
+5. Posterior pituitary
+6. Anterior pituitary
+7. Thyroid
+8. Parathyroid
+9. Thymus
+10. Spleen
+11. Adrenal (left or right depending upon the sequence of energy used to develop the body)
+12. Kidney (left or right depending upon the sequence of energy used to develop the body)
+13. Sex organs (testes, ovary, mammary)
0 Bones—Muscles—Stomach
—13. Sex organs (testes-ovary-uterus-prostate-mammary)
—12. Kidneys
—11. Adrenal
—10. Liver
—9. Chest—Diaphragm
—8. Pleura
—7. Lungs
—6. Heart
—5. Throat
—4. Nose
—3. Hearing—Sensing Tactile
—2. Eye
—1 Brain (32 sections dedicated to perceiving pain or the build-up of pressure)

(For a greater understanding of the electromagnetic principles of glandular exchange, see: *The Promethion*.)

fact, so many transactions were made that crystalline structures, acting as residue to these cycles of energy, had to be compensated for in mass. The structures of the eyes, ears and the nose developed coincident with the amount of usage of those perceptions, especially those of seeing, hearing, and smelling.

To give an example, let's say a man developed a product line of clothing in a small town somewhere in the United States. If he had relatively few transactions, his small company would remain the same size. There would be no branching out because there would be no demand for his product in other regions. But if his transactions suddenly increased and he began to experience a tremendous demand for his product, it would almost be a necessity for him to branch out and create sub-brains or sub-distributors in the rest of the country. This would have to be done to facilitate the need for his products.

And so it happened that the body experienced the same type of phenomenon because the genetic planning mechanism (GPM) developed a structure that was very functional and easily adaptable. Eventually, all the organs that were developed out of the outgrowth of energies from the brain were endowed with electromagnetic frequentizing ability so they could exist as much as possible as independent entities. The glands have a certain amount of independent action and a certain amount of dependent nature, which make them an extremely cohesive force in the human body.

Referring to the **Hierarchy of Glands and Organs,** we see a rundown of glandular development and the preference of structure in the body. The electric development of the organs in proper se-

All the organs were endowed with electromagnetic frequentizing ability. The transactions made between the glands are postulated to be extremely harmonic and at this time are recognizable as a sophisticated system of laser-reflected light.

quence caused their position or pattern formation in the body. The organs that are situated the furthest from the brain are more fully developed at later stages of a woman' pregnancy. The core areas of the mid-brain, especially the thalamus, hypothalamus and the pituitary gland, are the organs given primary consideration in the early months of pregnancy. The reason for this is the fact that these primitive brains are the precursors of electromagnetic energy, which is communicated to the rest of the body in coded radio frequencies that turn protein structures, minerals, and water into sub-brain entities such as the liver, pancreas, stomach, spleen and sex organs.

A certain amount of electrical sending and receiving between the glands is perceptible by the human body. Each gland has a particular station, which makes it responsible for a product that benefits the whole organism. For example, the liver works on breaking down protein matrices to facilitate the structure of the entire body. The adrenal glands will process minerals, fats, carbohydrates and proteins to aid in the placement and digestion of these substances so the body can have more energy and integrity of structure.

The transactions made between the glands are postulated to be extremely harmonic and at this time are recognizable as a sophisticated system of laser-reflected light, demonstrable only by noting the principles of laser construction. All the glands have the necessary materials to construct laser stations for more instantaneous communication and more balanced energy transactions.

The garden variety laser is constructed by assembling a crystal, usually a ruby or a garnet, with a metallic rod positioned in the center of it. The ruby must be impregnated by a metallic rod, usually made of aluminum, yttrium or any other material as long as it is highly conductible and resistant to burnout. The ruby impregnated by the metal rod is in position between two mirrors, with one mirror being a certain percentage more reflective than the other. The weaker mirror will be the area from where the beam is fired. The action of the laser is principally that of charging the ruby with electricity and then allowing the light to bounce freely between the two mirrors very rapidly, until the light becomes so intense that it overwhelms the weaker mirror. At this point, red pulsations of light in harmonic fashion beam through the weak mirror. After the beam has left the primary chamber of the laser, it can be modified by magnifying glass or lenses and channeled through many different, interesting labyrinths of reflective material.

Laser Factories in the Body

The laser factories in the body, that is, the glands and organs themselves, contain all of the necessary components to easily construct laser-like communication systems in the body. Every gland has, for its basic operating construction, crystalline materials in the form of salts. These cellular salts can be and are easily im-

The hormonal system of the body involves a complex, electrical matrix that records transactions between the glands. In a sense, the hormone is merely a confirmation of a laser transaction. When glands want to interact, they do so with tremendously high-speed, harmonic messages, which are later confirmed by the hormone.

pregnated by the respective metals that work with the glands.

Magnesium, potassium, sodium and chlorine work with the pituitary and the hypothalamus to transmit messages throughout the body. The energies emitted by these glands help to balance elements in other parts of the body, particularly sulfur, bromine, calcium, selenium, iron, nickel, manganese, copper, chromium, zinc, aluminum, phosphorus, lithium, chlorine, rubidium and iodine and even such exotic metals as lead and gold.

The metals that pierce the crystals (salts) in the body are electrified by the nervous system and the brain. Once charged, the energies can bounce back and forth between other metals. (Mirrors are merely shiny metal, usually tin or steel.)

If we can imagine a highly developed and sophisticated laser system modified by the strategic placement of silica (a natural compound found in most of earth's rocks including quartz, and which bears the qualities of bending light), we can easily understand that the body can communicate its glandular transactions at such incredibly high speeds as to baffle the existing science on physiology and psychology of the mind and body.

For example, if we were driving in a car and suddenly an animal leaped out in front of the car, the reaction is almost instantaneous. The body may take 3 to 4 seconds to react; however, the mental image picture has already caused many, many glandular, laser-like energy trans-

actions to occur between the structures of the body. The reason why we take such a long time to react is because we have so much deflecting, reflecting and interfering energy qualities within our system. The toxins, poisons and cellular debris, which exist around the glands, do much to forestall the smooth transmission and electrical balance of glandular transaction by laser light.

Perhaps prototypes of the human body, being devoid of so much pollution and interfering material that we have today, were able to perform fantastic feats of transmutation and reconstruction instantaneously. Today, the mind and the body of man are so clogged that even the thought of having the reactive power of the laser at our command is absurd. The sluggish response, the weightiness and the doped-up, poisonous feeling that we experience from inhaling the smog, drinking the water, eating contaminated food, and being poisoned by drugs and other chemical frequencies has all but placed us in a chronic state of hopelessness.

The hormonal system of the body, only now beginning to be understood, involves a complex, electrical matrix that prints out "statements" after transactions have been made between the glands. In a sense, the hormone is merely a confirmation of a laser transaction that has already taken place. When glands want to interact, they do so with tremendously high-speed, harmonic messages, which are later confirmed by the hormone.

It is much the same if we were to pick

up the telephone, call a friend to see about a date for the movies. The transmission across the telephone lines or through the air waves allows us to communicate across great distances without actually having to be there in person. The action of going to the movies is finalized by a long process of preparation and energy movements allowing the two of us to meet one another.

If we try to imagine the liver ever traveling up through the body to meet the thyroid to relay a message, then it is easy to consider that energies, which would travel to and from the sub-brains of the body (the organs and glands), must be of a highly sophisticated nature. The capture and crystallization of the hormone structures is but a small step toward understanding the inner working mechanisms of the glands and organs.

Essentially, we need a clear image as to what each gland and organ does before we can maintain a certain amount of perception and understanding about them. Each gland has its own particular function (which will be discussed in later perception channels), and each of the glands is predisposed to occasionally taking over the duties or actions of one of its failing sister or brother glands.

The symptomatic patterns of individuals who've lost their perceptions for the glandular transactions in the body are also those that belie detection. The glandular structure, especially the endocrine glands, are too close to the person's own personality for him to accurately assess whether or not he is merely demonstrating some quirk of his personality, or actually suffering from a glandular malady. In gross dysfunction, of course, glands can disturb the sugar balancing metabolisms,

causing the person to demonstrate conditions of hypoglycemia or diabetes, in which the individual is predisposed to attacks of anxiety, apprehension, fear and other such symptoms.

Diabetes and hypoglycemia are two characteristic conditions that are created because of an imbalance in glandular structure. However, diabetes and hypoglycemia primarily show an inability of the glands to harmonize light radiation.

The earliest consideration of the human body is its maintenance of sugar, glucose ($C_2H_{12}O_6$). If this process goes awry, the individual then suffers the inability of not being able to smoothly and accurately carry out the genetic blueprints, which have been laid down by the GPMs within the body. Many times this is due to traumatic intervention or a gross conflict of desires within the human being. The mechanism that is set to run for certain types of people may be disrupted by someone who does not wish to live his life as ruggedly as the body prescribes.

For example, due to happenstance, someone may become an executive when his body is accustomed to being a hard physical worker. Because the executive gets little physical exercise and is subject to much more mental and emotional upheaval, the body may capriciously use sugar and cause this executive to experience hypoglycemic symptoms, which include dizziness, nervousness, forgetfulness and many of the symptom patterns that plague us today.

The sugar problems, which can quite easily be rectified by understanding and controlling the body mechanisms, have been severely dealt with by the medical communities. An all-out war against diabetes and hypoglycemia has been launched in the hopes of demonstrating man's mental superiority over the GPM. In actuality, if an individual would attempt to understand the sophisticated, synchronized, computer-like activity of the genetic programming mechanism, he would not have to go to such extremes to adjust the programs that exist within the body.

Sensory Channel 29
MAGNETIC POSITION
(8 Gyros, Internal balance)

The magnetic balance of the body originated with a great deal of study on the development of crystalline structures on the planet. The alignment of crystalline structures had maintained an exact balance of energy, which ultimately created the brain and the spinal cord. The positioning of the body, or its anchoring in space, is wholly dependent on the brain and the spinal cord's ability to transact business within itself at a given location. If there is a weakness within this system, the whole structure of the body begins to lose its ability to take up space; this means that the body begins to generate and lose its structural integrity, not only of the bones and muscles, but of the glands and organs as well.

The existence of the *gyros* (Greek for circle or spiral), which spin at certain speeds to maintain the electrical balance of the body, has been shrouded in mysticism for thousands of years. The term "chakras" (meaning wheel) has been loosely used to denote the location of gyroscopic entities within the body, which help stabilize or anchor the structure in space. Each gyro, which is wholly dependent upon the gyro preceding it, transmits cycles of energy applicable to the glands

The chakras are gyros or spirals of energy that create power and maintain the electrical balance of the body.

8—Enlightenment
7—Crown
6—Third Eye
5—Throat
4—Heart
3—Solar Plexus
2—Sacral
1—Base-Root
(Sitting or standing, this anchors to Earth)

and organs in its vicinity. If we can imagine a line being drawn down from the top of the head to the base of the spine and then to anchors on the ground, and eight energy transmission stations located along this corridor, then we can visualize the development of this sophisticated balancing mechanism.

The gyros create power. We define power as the ability to successfully com-

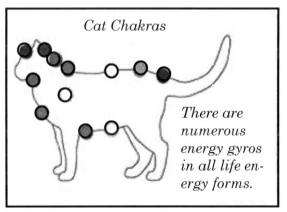

Cat Chakras

There are numerous energy gyros in all life energy forms.

Lapis lazuli and Peridot are considered by some to be the philosopher's stone of the alchemist. These have been used through the ages to open and energize the chakras.

plete energy cycles in sequence, so the gyro is necessary to take energy fed to it from above and convert it into a proper wavelength and frequency for redistribution to the glands and organs near it. The concept is more easily understood when comparing with electrical transformers. As a unit of energy passes from one electrical transformer to another, it is cleanly and efficiently converted into energies that can be used by the donor receptor sub-brains existing near it.

In the body, this acts much like an assembly line of power. As energy is transformed from desire or thought into physical manifestation, there is a gradual reduction in the wavelength and a corresponding proportionate increase in frequency so all of the functioning parts of the body receive the energies necessary for their operation.

The symptomatic patterns that erupt when an individual does not have an appreciation or sense perception for the magnetic position of the body are dizziness, confusion, disorientation and a feeling of "unrealness" causing the person to be disconnected from his own reality

.Sensory Channel 30
MAGNETIC REFERENCE 1
(ability to magnetically locate people)

The early crystalline structures had to develop a finely tuned, keen sense for similar structures that caused a transmission of power from one to the other. When opposites attempt to align in a circuit, a high rate of resistance occurs and the transmission of power is effectively reduced. The magnetic referencing ability of crystalline structures was developed very early, so that magnetic electrical structures could be developed to aid survival. Part of the individual crystal's ability is to be able to pick out other energies or entities in the environment that may act as reference points.

Today the human being has a very sophisticated reference ability, most of it done by way of electromagnetic transmission. The sight sense is very seldom used for referencing people, for the population has the ability to scatter itself quite easily across the countryside. Therefore, the magnetic referencing of people must take place on a subliminal level and involves the pituitary gland, the brain, and the spinal cord. What occurs is the ability to sense the exchange of energy and power between individuals, in different parts of the house, town, state, country and the world. In other words, we can easily reference ourselves in comparisons with other human beings, no matter what the distance or barrier may be.

The symptoms of imbalance alerting the individual that he is losing his ability to magnetically reference people, especially those he loves, but not discounting those he holds animosity toward, are: Dizziness, confusion and pressure about the head, face or chest.

The individual may also experience tingling and chills up the back and spine. These are warning signals that individuals who are believed to be in certain localities may be changing positions.

It is very important to the human being to know where his people are, mag-

My people, my tribe

netically and subliminally. If he loses that ability, he may fall into the anxieties and disillusionment that plagued his early ancestors when being separated from the tribes. Man basically finds comfort in existing in groups. This is why the great cities have been constructed all over the world. The ability to live together, work together and play together is dependent upon the harmonious connections of friends and family across some very esoteric and intangible fields of energy.

The magnetic reference maintains a controlling arm on the individual by feeding back "feelings". Our feelings are most certainly aligned to the magnetic referencing of people, for if we lose a partner, friend, or a relative, there is definite electrical magnetic phenomenon occurring within our body.

able to take up positions in the environment used by the Homo *sapien* as reference points. These locations in space are extremely important to the person's awareness. The existence of mountains, minerals, land and trees in certain combinations make up the positions of the earth and are used by people to connect themselves to a certain place on the planet.

When an individual loses the ability to locate himself on this planet, he also loses the ability to control energies in his own body, for the body is constructed of materials that belong to this earth.

It is necessary for us to maintain a certain amount of intellectual integrity as to our origin points so we can control the energies that have been grandfathered into the body by our forebears, our ancestors. Not knowing our origin points and the locations of energies within the body causes us to become sick, debilitated and degenerated.

The symptomatic patterns that encompass an individual who remains ignorant of his origins are the specific disease patterns endemic to civilized man.

Sensory Channel 31
MAGNETIC REFERENCE 2
(ability to locate place, origin points)

One of the more difficult perceptions to understand is intrinsic to the crystalline structures. Because crystals have an almost immortal existence compared to the human being, as such, they have been

Sensory Channel 32
MAGNETIC REFERENCE 3
(planetary scale)

Cellular structures have a specific relationship to energies within the solar system as well. The energies of the Earth are similar to but different from the energies of Mars, Saturn, Venus and the other planets in the solar system. It is a deep study. It is briefly mentioned here to give

You are here

It is important to know our location in the planetary system.

the reader the understanding that there are controlling factors involved in reference to energies outside the Earth's atmosphere. This was demonstrated and recorded by early homeopathic physicians who were able to develop radio frequencies around known earth substances, which converted them to energies that were more similar to substances, minerals, plants, etc. beyond Earth's atmosphere. This was accomplished by highly diluting the substances.

The symptomatic patterns of an individual losing his perception of the magnetic reference of the planet is imperceptible at this time, for humankind is so buried on other levels that it is difficult for one to imagine or be able to perceive this type of relationship with the planets.

Astrologers and those who are consid-

ered less than scientific use and understand information connected to the planetary cycles. The average person innately believes that there is something to these phenomena, but still has a very difficult time perceiving them.

The psychic or the person with great imagination is one of the few who have been able to channel their energies and abilities to achieve a greater appreciation for the incredible, marvelous universe that has been constructed for man to decipher.

Sensory Channel 33
PROTEIN, INTERNAL
(electric-micro wiring)

The early crystalline structures attempted to construct energies to propagate their species. It was necessary to develop a type of electrical similar, which would reproduce itself over and over again, millions, billions, and trillions of times, until it proliferated the environment. This is the basic concept of survival.

The idea that energies need to be reproduced over and over again to survive is a basic principle. Even those things that do not propagate themselves quite readily have protein matrices that will reproduce over and over again. As the environment moves from moment to moment through time, energies need to be replaced, even to maintain the status quo. This does not discount the idea of expansion; it only reiterates it.

There are many individuals, organisms and substances that do not noticeably proliferate themselves. However, upon closer examination we can see hundreds and thousands of sophisticated electrical cycles preceding these that have already made a constant recreation or duplication of the image that a crystal or a human body is trying to portray. It is these cycles, controlled jointly by the genetic programming mechanism (GPM), the mind and the spirit, that decided to launch a survival plan that efforts to duplicate energy.

Protein can form anything that it wants to form. It could be a kidney, nose, it could be a toenail, a finger or hair. It is the genes that decide what will be produced and where it will go. It is all figured out and we take it for granted.

The human body has specific plans and programs allowing it to produce energies needed to constantly rebuild and repair the system. The amount of protein in the body is second only in proportion to water. The structures of the hair, nails, skin, teeth, bones and muscles all have substantial amounts of protein invested in them.

Protein itself is an electric-carrying material that allows the easy transfer of laser-like messages from the glands and organs, between themselves and to the brain, mind and the other portions of the body. Whenever there is a breakdown in structure, the body is automatically planned and programmed to replace it. This is part of the program that is an ongoing endeavor to restore and rebuild energies in the body and procreate at the same time. A certain amount of precious proteinaceous substance goes into creating other human beings as well, via the sex process.

This perception track #33, Protein Internal, is the area where energies have begun to stabilize and allow transmissions to occur through them. This action is opposed to the substances such as carbohydrates and sugars, which cannot stand up to electric current. With a high amount of current in the system, sugars and carbohydrates begin to dissolve, whereas the proteins will maintain a certain amount of conductivity and remain unscathed. In essence, the protein structures are a more formidable form of energy and mass, which the body can use to carry out its genetic plans and programs.

The symptomatic patterns one may experience when losing the ability to perceive and control the protein matrices of the body are those that involve the degradation of protein structures. This could involve the development of gross anomalies, such as clubfeet, muscular problems, bone structure problems or anything involving the usage of protein that may become disturbed when the individual senses his need for the substances. Initially, the GPM may lose its control over the placement of proteins and not be able to displace worn out proteins, toxins, poisons, vermin and other invading pests with the protein structures that are used for defense. Certain immunoglobulins, constructed by the GPM in cooperation with the glands and organs of the body, normally seek to defend the structure from infiltration of the environment, but may allow certain poisons to infest the body and rot out its structures.

There may be a case of the system starving off proteins from the adrenal glands; the adrenals are denied needed proteins. These glands are in charge of our secondary sex characteristics (changes that occur in puberty), and our ability to change carbohydrates into energy. If not corrected, we could end up with immature sexual attributes and being hypoglycemic.

The whole idea of the aging process causes the individual to experience a certain timed program, which seems to be against the human body. As we grow older, our body ages and seems to relinquish the ability to repair itself. If we were able to tap into the GPM and reprogram it to have a more capable protein structure sensing ability, the body would effectively be immortal, for all we need in this life, besides a clear thinking mind, is the ability of the body to regenerate itself. Thus, existence could be carried on forever.

Sensory Channel 34
PROTEIN, EXTERNAL
(electro-micro wiring)

The early crystalline structures not only developed a sense for the duplicate development of powers within the structure itself, but also in structures outside

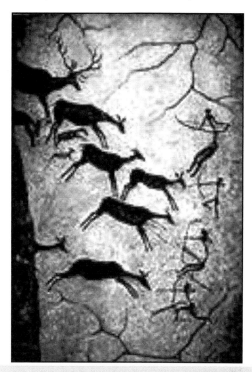

The perception for locating other animalities, other protein bodies (#34) meant survival in the days of Stone Age man. Cave painting, c. 15000 BC, Lascaux, France.

itself in the environment. This level of perception was necessary for early life's awareness of animalities in the environment.

Today, the perception of external protein is relegated to the task of helping us to select our meals, and also to pick up the relative sense of power among our peers. One of the greatest pastimes for those who wish to maintain a solid protein structure is weight lifting and bodybuilding. The development of muscle tissue and well-defined protein matrices is a serious activity dedicated to the idea that the display of muscle tissue will cause sensation in others in the environment, and well it does. Not only does well-developed muscular tissue excite interest in the opposite sex, but it also provokes fear and respect from other people, including males. The main reasons why a person would want to build up muscular tissue in such a fashion is to show greater survival potential and gain muscular confidence when being in the company of others.

There is a subliminal fight occurring between the protein structures of every person's body. The energies that exist to survive must necessarily have a perception for the dangers in the environment.

All through man's evolution and the history of life on this planet, there has been a constant undercurrent of courageousness and fear brought to bear by the desire of other moving animalities to consume protein. This is easily demonstrated by watching the statistical charts on the consumption of meat in the United States. In fact, in all parts of the world the consumption of protein is a controversy. While some people and groups say that it is mandatory to have at least a pound of good animal protein per day to maintain energy, the vegetarian societies claim this is untrue. It will always be a very hotly contested subject because people have an extremely acute perception of protein externally, as well as protein internally.

Whether it is protein for consumption or protein for show, there is a high intensity of awareness in operation, which measures the amount of pressure that protein substances follow or track. For example, when driving the car if we suddenly have a near miss with another car, the energy output coming from the an-

Protein bodies carry potent electric charge. The GPM maintains surveillance on the size, shape, weight and intensity of other bodies close by.

gered, other driver has a curious effect. The electric pressure that builds up in the protein matrices of a person who is fearful will register a certain amount of intensity on the genetic planning mechanism (GPM), which has a watchful eye on the intensity of protein in the vicinity of the body. This type of attention is dissimilar to the type of attention that the GPM spends on large objects of a mineral configuration, such as mountains, boulders, buildings, etc. This is also a dissimilar perception from the one the GPMs use when analyzing vegetable matter, such as trees, plants, flowers, and other carbohydrate substances.

The protein forces that carry an extremely potent electric charge are important to the GPM so they can measure the survival ability of the body that it has programmed. In confrontations with other people, the GPM will always maintain surveillance on the size, shape, weight and intensity of the other bodies that confront it.

The reason for this is simple. Throughout the evolution of man, there have been many, many confrontations with other animals. The body is fraught with traumas involving mishaps with other protein bodies. In many cases, the genetic line, which the GPM is using to base its memory bank, is filled with instances where vicious animals and powerful human beings have unleashed energies at the body, causing great pain, unconsciousness or even death. Because the GPMs have access to all these instances and keep them on file as a reference, then they will constantly need to create a level of confidence within the body so that it can comfortably exist among other protein bodies. If an individual has a difficult time being around other people, it may be because the GPM is erroneously triggered into believing that one of these other bodies is going to do its host bodily harm.

Therefore, the symptomatic pattern we detect when examining this phenomenon is fearfulness. The body has a keen sense of awareness when it comes to surveying activities, objects, people or even places that may be detrimental to its survival. Because protein carries such a formidable electric change, it is much easier to detect its presence. The body itself, being made of a protein very similar to other protein bodies, ensures the person will have an extremely well developed sense perception of danger.

In many cases this sense perception may be on full stimulation, alert to a danger memory, and cause a chronic, hysterical fear, which could lead to difficulties being with other people. In this situation, the person may also become chronically ill, jaundiced and show signs of anemia.

Sensory Channel 35
FAT INSULATION
(Stage 1, oils)

The development of the earth required that a tremendous amount of energy be released without very much resistance. However, over a course of time when energies escaping into the atmosphere were on the rampage, materials had to be developed to protect and insulate the planet. A gradual development of fat (which will be discussed further in Sensory Channels 36-42) is an interesting step in the Z Process, and is actually a resting phase for movement of energy.

Fat is the greatest insulator there is against protein and water. It stops elec-

Oils and fat are essential for the proper working of the human system. These insulate us from errant frequencies of all types, whatever radiates toward us that is harmful on body, mind, or spirit levels. (See the list on page 49.)

tric flow and its judicious arrangement reroutes the course of life energy within all human bodies.

The perception of development of fat within the body is coincident to perceiving traumas present in the environment. When a person experiences a certain degree of upset or trauma, then fat begins to solidify or congeal around the trauma to prevent it from overloading the circuits in the body. However, on this sensing level, the genetic planning mechanism (GPM) has an acute awareness of the lubrication of the mucous membranes and those areas of the body requiring a movable liquid insulation. In other words, oils are lubricating, protective substances that can be changed over. The type of suspension created with an oil is one that is highly beneficial to the body.

Individuals who lack oil in the body are missing that protective substance. They will most probably be vitamin deficient or underweight, and experience burning sensations in the mouth and throat, diarrhea, have eye troubles, softening of the bones and teeth, nervousness, poor metabolism, allergies, skin problems, nail problems, an increased tendency to hemorrhage, nose bleeds, miscarriages and susceptibility to infections, especially of the sinuses and respiratory tract.

Sensory Channel 36
FAT INSULATION
(Stage 2, emergency)

The early crystalline structures had to develop systems to barricade or buffer energies so that there could no longer be any impression, depression, or suppression by outside forces. Thus, the evolution of the crystal brought forth the concept of fat. Fat is considered an important breakthrough on the evolutionary scale because it is the substance that allows organisms to remain cordoned off from other organisms.

If energies were made strictly of protein, rather than also including thought processes, energy transactions would not be confined to one individual organism. It would be so highly electrically-charged that energies would pass between two or more entities so rapidly that there would be no way to actually discern which organism was doing what process. In other words, if human beings were built totally of protein, they would have no secrets, no boundaries. However, this would create a

When we have an infected sore, parasites and bacteria, which are airborne, will automatically gravitate to those areas to get to work and break it up. That is their purpose, their creation impulse.

The best way to alleviate fat is to alleviate the trauma that caused it.

very boring state of affairs because it would be difficult to have any private conversation; and after a while the need for individual organization would decrease and the human body would not survive. So the genetic planning mechanisms of a particular body must have a very good perception of the fat barriers within the body. Fat is essential for the life of the organism. It is a protector.

On Sensory Channel #36, the second stage emergency fat situation involves the creation of pus and mucus to inhibit traumas, both nutritional and environmental traumas, and to prevent upsets of metabolism from overriding the protein structures within the body, which would cause them to transmit erroneous data and ultimately destroy the body. Infections, diseases, viruses, poisons, toxins, environmental pollution, radiation, and all those frequencies and materials that are part of a hostile environment, can be smothered in pus and mucus to temporarily inhibit their advancement against the core of the body. Without this emergency fat, the person would surely succumb.

However, it is extremely important for the GPMs to be able to control the DNA-RNA, the emergency pus and mucus, so these will recede after the job has been completed. Often the body will sit within a re-stimulated trauma, the faded or obscured memory of a trauma, and will not allow the mucus and pus to recede. For some reason, the GPM in this case has decided, through data and information present in the environment, that it would be a bad maneuver to draw back or expel mucus and pus from the system. Conditions such as pneumonia, bronchitis, si-nusitis, sinus infection, bowel dysfunc-tion, colitis and other diseases all involve chronic mucus buildup. Generally, in these cases, there is a subliminal, trau-matic experience that has not been re-solved within the system. This could be of mental, spiritual or physical origin. Once the trauma is removed from the system, the emergency fats dissolve or are ex-pelled.

The problematic situation that arises is that in emergencies, fats and pus for-mations, by nature, attract, or call in parasites and other vermin by their chemical configuration (frequency). Es-sentially, the environment is built on a situation requiring that communication breakthroughs be made in those areas where fat has been assembled for too long. If a person has a sore that is festered or areas in the body filled with mucus, then parasites and bacteria, which are air-borne, will automatically gravitate to those areas to get to work and break it up. In a sense, the addition of antibiotics is merely a hedge against the breakdown of mucus by outside forces in the environ-ment. In the sense that antibiotics take away the bacteria and leave the trauma, they are inefficient. To present another viewpoint, the antibiotic is doing a great service; the antibiotic allows the person to live, in order that someday he will figure out his traumatic connection with his en-vironment. However, the positives not-withstanding, the chronic, constant use of antibiotics is always a detrimental situa-tion.

The symptomatic patterns of an indi-vidual who has lost the ability to control or perceive these second stage fat barriers are chronic sickness, asthma, pneumonia,

mucus or pus buildups in any area of the body, especially the colon, the sinuses, the ears and other body cavities. There may be felons (infection on the tip of the fin-ger), abscesses, boils, wens and other pus-like formations in separate parts of the body, especially the feet, hands, back and face. Acne and other pustular eruptions on the face, back, feet, legs and hands is a sign that the individual has broken down his ability to confront certain influxes of electric pressures, whether these are hor-monal or accidental.

Sensory Channel 37
FAT INSULATION
(Stage 3, hardened)

The development of fat barriers, mak-ing a breakthrough from a period when prolific duplication was rampant in the environment, became itself an over-whelming activity.

The third stage fat barrier is a con-figuration of traumatic experience that becomes walled into the body and is probably there to stay. It is the dangerous and risky attempt on the body's part to build up barriers to prevent an influx of energy on or in a particular part of the organism. What has happened here is that the combined efforts of the genetic planning mechanism (GPM), the spirit, the mind and the body, have not been able to cope with a particular trauma that has been harassing the organism. There-fore, a joint decision has been made to continually barricade those areas of the body with fat, indeed, so much fat that it begins to collect minerals, calcium and other metals and creates a sophisticated impediment to energies that may be at-tempting to enter the body.

The human being has learned to live

with fat. In many ways, it is disgusting to him; however, since the fat itself is due to the development of unconsciousness and trauma, it has almost become a national pastime to try and get rid of it. It is difficult to assess the amount of effort going into regulating fat metabolism because each individual suffers from his very own particular, personal, traumatic experiences. Since the traumatic experience is the impetus for the development of the fat, the elimination of fat lends itself to a great deal of confusion as evidenced by the potpourri of advice from so many different types of weight loss characters and experts, plus ads and charts promoted by the government and others on low fat products. Guests on television and news shows, authors of weight loss and diet books, and inventors of fat-dissolving machines and devices all preach about their methodologies and proclaim the best way to reshape the human body.

The best way to alleviate fat is to <u>alleviate the trauma</u> that caused it. The only way that this can be done is by instilling knowledge of the cause, creation and control of the trauma itself. This takes a sophisticated amount of programming and understanding of the genetic planning mechanism and its relationship to the mind and the spirit or guiding force of the individual. The types of fat that a person will find on or in his body are particular to his own structure, and this lands and settles in those areas where the most stress and trauma occur. The saddleback fat, love handles, double chins, cellulite and fatty lumps and bumps in all those places that a person has the most difficulty getting rid of, paint a telltale picture of the person's inabilities to confront simple but powerful poisons, toxins, errant

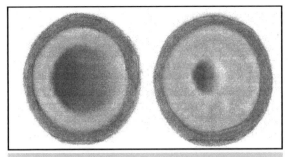

Interior of artery. On left, an artery that allows blood flow; on right, a narrowed artery clogged with fatty deposits, a good example of Stage 4 fat deposits.

frequencies and traumas, which confront him in his everyday environment.

The symptomatic pattern of a person who has lost the perception for the third stage fat barrier also includes the probable disability of not being able to come to any conclusions on life's little ordeals. The individual who works at a job that he doesn't really like; the person who has a weekly blowup with his or her spouse; the chronic beer drinker; a secretary who types eight hours a day; a jackhammer operator who puts his machine under his belly to give it more back pressure, are all such examples.

Sensory Channel 38
FAT INSULATION
(Stage 4, extremely hard)

The development of fat is limited to a certain amount of degradation. In other words, a trauma can only cause so much of a barrier to build up until the individual is completely encased in a solid, congealed mass of protection. Fat can only get so hard before the whole area is choked off.

In the fourth stage fat barrier, the individual has created a barrier that is so formidable that it causes energies in the system to totally reroute to other areas. This is the hardened, calcified fat that is as formidable, in some cases, as tempered steel. This is the material that the individual fears greatly. It causes heart disease, arteriosclerosis, atherosclerosis and other such maladies, which eventually choke the life from his body.

The origin of this state of fat insulation is the inability of a person to cope with his environment while still suffering the throes of attempting to decipher it. The energies that combine in an environment, namely the poisons, toxins, pollutions and all the bizarre chemical frequencies that are found in the atmosphere today, present such a disturbing and unintelligent picture to the genetic planning mechanism (GPM) that many times these subtle structures grudgingly call for <u>more fat protection</u> within the body, all in an effort to prevent the person from succumbing to the volatile poisons surrounding him. However, over a long period of time, the chronic positioning of fat in certain areas of the body may turn the person into a veritable pillar of stone.

The symptomatic patterns that someone may experience when loaded with heavy, hardened fat barriers are primarily dizziness, heart palpitations, and pains. These hardened areas most certainly choke off the cardiovascular system and cause anxiety attacks and great fear that something bad may happen. The in-

The presence of fat and oils in and on another person indicate that person has been inundated with traumas and confusing ideas. Fat helps to thwart the influx of damaging situations so is seen as a pro-survival mechanism.

dividual is subliminally aware that there is a device working inside the body that may ultimately do him in.

This strategy by the GPM, to keep certain poisons away from the body, has a disheartening effect on the mind and the spirit. In this case, a person is ultimately, physically crippled to the point where he is unable to climb or descend steps and must nurse conditions within the body that predispose him to heart failure and unpleasant conditions, such as stroke and the evidence of ever-present thrombi, or blood clots. The removal of hardened fat by surgery in some cases is the only alternative; however, it does no good for the mental and spiritual aspects of the development of fat, namely, the hidden trauma or errant frequency that caused it. In most cases, individuals who have had heart bypass surgery and other sophisticated operations to remove this powerful barrier fall right back into the same pattern of metabolic existence, which demands that they again wall themselves into this tomb of organic energy so marvelously created by GPMs as a protection.

Sensory Channel 39
FAT EXTERNAL
(Stage 1, oil)

After reading about fat as insulation against traumas, we can understand that it is much easier to associate with human beings, animals and other living objects that have not been overly traumatized. The presence of oil in the system (as opposed to hardened fat) shows that the person has a freer ability to communicate. They are more changeable, however, and may be indecisive.

The GPM can always observe and discern whether an individual is stable or

When the perception of external fat begins to wane, the individual may choose situations and conditions in his environment that may be detrimental, even toxic, to his survival.

itinerant, wandering. There is a sophisticated measuring mechanism for the amount of fats, whether hardened or simple fats, and this type of situation is an aid in the attractiveness of one body to another. Individuals who are fraught with hardened fat barriers are displeasing to the eye. They are not only sick and immobile, but are also filled with confusing thoughts and ideas.

The symptomatic patterns of an individual who has lost his perception for simple fats and oils are those that are closely aligned to a loss of internal perception of simple fats and oils; however, a person may more strongly gravitate to situations that may do him harm. When the perception of external fat begins to wane, the individual may choose situations and conditions in his environment that may be detrimental to his survival. He may join organizations, teams, and groups of people who do not have his best interests in mind.

The fluidity that accompanies simple oils is sometimes lost in perceptibility to the human being and he may choose traumas and conditions that are not easy for him to figure out. Therefore, such a person may always find himself in situations that are nightmarish. Teaming up with other people who are a poison or toxic to a person's existence is due to faults in electric perception and GPMs.

Essentially, all individuals like to gravitate to others who can do them the most good. It is important for the existence of the living creation that we align ourselves to agencies, groups and other people with whom we are most compatible. The divorce rate in the United States and the world is soaring because the GPMs have not been able to cope with the amount of trauma unleashed on it within the past century. The ability to select comfortable mates is a very important subject, and has significant influence on the perception of simple oils.

The electrical resistance presented in all organisms is detectable by the GPM and measured directly by the ability of the body to resist electrical flow. For example, when speaking to another person, the amount of confusion and trauma increases, even in a simple conversation, and this will cause fat barriers to build as a means of protection. During the conversation, the level of simple oils and simple fats will remain high in the person who is comprehending, while the level of hardened fat barriers will be low. Conversely, a person who experiences misunderstanding and confusion in the environment, even in simple conversation, will experience a very high level of hardened fat and a very low level of liquid fat.

If we can imagine this spectrum of variable structure from liquid oily fat to gross granite-like structures of fat, then we can understand that the intensity of life and living can be directly proportionate to the existence of liquid and rock-hard fat.

The GPM does not have to experience the trauma within its own structure. It can communicate with other GPMs in other bodies and observe and learn from the traumas found there.

Sensory Channel 40
FAT EXTERNAL
(Stage 2)

If we were to witness a terrible and very large accident on the highway, where cars are piled one on top of another and tractor-trailers were jack-knifing, we would automatically pull to the safe side of the road and stop the car. Experience tells us that these situations are detrimental to the human body; stopping is a definite, pro-survival reaction. This reaction is also relegated to the GPM so that it can easily and simply discern the type of company that the body should keep. In many cases, the poisons that exist as traumatic experiences in other living beings become the lessons for specific genetic plans within the host body. This means that the GPM does not have to experience the trauma within its own structure. It can communicate with other GPMs in other bodies and observe and learn from the traumas found there. Obviously, this is the most advantageous way to exist; it is not necessary to destroy one's own structure in order to learn about the dangers of the environment.

The symptomatic patterns one may experience when realizing defects of the emergency fat levels of his body will include upsets and poisons within his own system. Many times, this apparatus causes a psychic phenomenon to result. A person may experience or sympathize with poisons in the other person and tap into and pick up their traumatic experiences, or find that he is acting out or dramatizing the confusions of the other person. This often occurs with husbands

Imaginary ills are just as painful as real ones.

and wives who are closely aligned in life. Sympathy pains and other sensations occur in the host body because the GPM is constantly scanning and attempting to discern the relative, traumatic experiences of the closely connected significant other. This explains the incidence that a man may have severe gastroenteritis when his pregnant wife goes into labor.

The pitfalls of having mechanisms that use radiant energy for scanning, such as the GPMs, are that they can easily and subliminally connect with other electric beings or entities in the environment, such as human beings, animals and plants, and become ensnared in the confusions of the others.

The main remedy for this effect is to be cognizant of this fact and learn to disentangle these energies just by noting which poisons belong to which person. Imaginary ills are just as painful as real ones.

Sensory Channel 41
FAT EXTERNAL
(Stage 3, hard)

The genetic planning mechanism (GPM) has the propensity to observe the third stage fat barriers in other individuals as well, and this, of course, keys into the aesthetic mechanisms of the mind and the spirit. When selecting bodies, however, the genetic planning mechanisms will ultimately get together and make a composite of the amount of fats versus trauma within the other's system and the two systems collectively. In other words, when two people join forces as a husband and wife, their energies are collected and put into the same bin, so to speak. Just as when two people get married, their fortunes are united, as well as their misfor-

Egyptian coffin. Our time of earthly departure can be sensed by the GPM and we can be alerted (Stage 4).

The GPM is logical and practical; it assesses the relative disease state of the other person in the hopes of preventing its own demise.

tunes, so, too, are their traumas and fat barriers collectively analyzed. "The two shall become one."

Unfortunately, because the GPM is being inundated with insoluble problems, such as how to arrange a plan or program for the individual body to survive forever, the selection of a mate may be relegated to the mental capacity or the spiritual capacity only. Even though the physical appearance is important to the GPM, it is not as important as the person's survivability. It is the GPM, and not the mind or the spirit that is able to pick up the other person's survivability. The GPM does not want to align with another body (and its own GPM) that is unable to cope with the environment. Often when people marry, their minds and their spirits are willing, but their GPMs are not. Because the mind and the spirit can override the GPM to a certain extent, many times the genetic mechanism loses the right to veto a potential mate. The only reason why it would do this is because the host body may be loaded down with traumas, poisons, toxins, vermin and other pests and parasites with which the body cannot easily cope in a lifetime. On the other hand, the GPMs will often aid in the selection of a mate, because the prospective mate is filled with desirable electrical powers of a free-flowing nature and is not encased in too many hardened fat barriers. If the GPMs could be tapped into easily, it should be consulted in all partnership formations of this nature.

The symptomatic patterns that may be experienced when the third stage fat barriers of one person are triggering upsets of the host's GPM are: hypoglycemia, dizziness, nausea, vomiting, gnawing sensations in the stomach, feelings of unreality, nervousness, fear of being left alone and other numerous sensations particular to each individual's conditions.

Sensory Channel 42
FAT EXTERNAL
(Stage 4)

The genetic planning mechanism (GPM) is also able to detect the presence of disease in another living being. Sensing the presence of the walled-in confusions and traumas of another individual is an important perception in order to prevent the alignment of the host's body with another's traumatized system. There is really no profit, according to the GPM, to align with another body that is about to expire. The sense perception of the GPM in its ability to perceive the timetable of death in another person is uncanny, and has been relegated to mysticism, occultism and other forms of science because this is so abhorrent to our aesthetic sense. In other words, the communication between human beings is devoid of predicting when another person will die. However, the GPM is a very logical, practical and sensible device. It will assess the relative disease state of the other person in the hopes of preventing its own demise, and feed back this information to the genetic blueprints.

The mind and the spirit are inextricably attached to this communication channel and can tap into it at any time. However, there is an unwritten code that people will avoid or ignore this very sophisticated sense perception and leave the time of earthly departures up to the angels, saints in heaven and God.

The symptomatic patterns that may be experienced in disruptions of this sense perception are nervousness, lethargy, impotence and hopelessness. The individual may experience development of poisonous situations in the body, which cause him to repel and reject another person. This may be the underlying reason why many couples fight and argue: their traumas are not soluble by their union.

The incompatibility and misunderstandings that exist between many married couples occur because their collected, free-flowing energies are not enough to overcome their collected traumatic experiences.

The GPM is aware of this fact and constantly feeds back information to both systems, causing the people to argue and repel one another. The idea that arguments begin over extremely simple confusions is evidence that there are basic and unobtainable traumas encased in hardened fat, secretly stored away within each person.

The only way to be able to detect such trauma at this stage, without going to the GPMs and perceiving it outright, is to analyze the physical diseased state of the people involved. Diabetics, arthritics, those with cancer, and people who are prone to other degenerative conditions are more than likely harboring some type of extremely unsolvable conundrum (problem), which perhaps an army of physicians in all their wisdom could not unravel. So, in these cases it would seem that the odds against the two individuals remaining together might be extremely high. However, with the dawning of a new type of processing utilizing the "Z" method, and increasing the awareness of these sensing tracks, individuals may experience a greater ability to dislodge poisonous situations within their own systems and conquer them.

Sensory Channel 43
SUGAR (spark)

The predevelopment of crystalline structures depended on the constructions of captured radiant particles. This was previously discussed earlier in Step Five, Simple and Complex Sugars; however, it is important to note that the genetic planning mechanisms (GPMs) developed the perception of sugar mainly to meter out its own ability to change, for sugar is that spark of energy that causes the processes and plans of the GPMs, the mind and the spirit to come to fruition.

There are many types of sugars of various origin that are sought by humans: malt and milk sugar, maple, birch, ash and beech tree sugars, beet, corn and cane sugars from plants, and sugar from fruits.

(left) Sugar crystals. Sugar is that spark of energy that causes the processes and plans of the GPMs, the mind and the spirit to come to fruition.

Sugar, as glucose, is the most unrestrained energy that exists. It is the pure energy needed by the body to produce energy and power. However, when in an unbalanced state, it causes rapid aging.

The perception of sugar and its disturbances causes symptomatic patterns that are most closely akin to energy usage and problems, such diabetes, hypoglycemia and the energy anomalies that were listed previously in Step Five.

Sensory Channel 44
CARBOHYDRATES
(stored spark)

A carbohydrate is, of course, a more complex sugar and a more slowly burning material that is readily available for usage. It is also a precursor of the crystalline structure, but is itself more crystalline than sugar. The idea that carbohydrates can extract crystals from sugar is evidence that carbohydrates are successors to sugar structures.

The genetic planning mechanism (GPM) is highly perceptive of its intake of complex carbohydrates due to the fact that the body does not possess many substantial enzyme systems for breaking down the carbohydrate structures. A carbohydrate is scheduled for reduction as soon as it enters by phosphoric compounds, which will cause energies to explode and ignite in much the same manner as sugar. However, the fuel will be burning much more slowly than sugar molecules.

The GPM's perception of the amount of carbohydrates being used is extremely important, for just as it does with sugar, the carbohydrate situation can cause a chain reaction of explosive force within the system that may do damage to the cellular structure and the tissues. The carbohydrate molecule lands in the muscles and around the bones, and expresses itself very slowly. For this reason, the GPM is extremely cognizant or aware of the fact that too many carbohydrates can ultimately clog the system. This clogging is directly responsible for the development of fats because the stress and trauma of having to cope with an electrical explosive force stored in a carbohydrate configuration causes fat to build up. For this reason, those consuming large amounts of starches may at some point develop fat deposits in the body.

The ingestion of complex carbohydrates sometimes has a very judicious action, especially at those periods when the person is devoid of solvable problems. Complex carbohydrates help to prevent the sense of loss, such as when loved ones have been lost in the family, or there has been a divorce or a separation. However, at other times, when the person is more closely connected to trauma, more protein is needed.

When a person is connected to energies that are loaded with activity, it is not a good idea to absorb or eat carbohydrates of a complex nature. Someone who works in the office of a large company, or even a small company that has many problems, will not function very well with complex carbohydrates. It would be better to eat proteins in this circumstance.

If the person has just suffered a divorce and cannot find a job, then it would be more advantageous to partake of complex carbohydrate substances, for the carbohydrates will sustain the energy activity within the body. The person who has enough sustaining energy in the environment surrounding him does not need more starches and complex carbohydrates to facilitate this matter.

It is important that we know our own situation well, and that we maintain a balance between the complex carbohydrates, proteins, fats, sugars and water in the system.

The Macrobiotic Society and other groups have attempted to cross-correlate the exact times, seasons and years to ingest proteins, carbohydrates, etc., which will best facilitate the individual. However, the GPM is a much more sophisticated program and needs an even more precise type of menu planning as befits each person.

The symptomatic patterns experienced with carbohydrate-sensing difficulties would include diabetes, hypoglycemia, arteriosclerosis, atherosclerosis and many of the diseases of civilization that are byproducts of stress. When we begin to experience upsets in the environment that are reducing pressures, then the advantage would be to consume carbohydrates.

When in our work or daily activities we begin to experience high pressures, the type of pressures that cause constriction and pain, then it would be more advantageous for us to utilize more fats and protein.

The example of the executive and the person out of work, as relayed above, provides us with a measure as to which type of foods to eat.

Sensory Channel 45
PAIN

The early crystalline structures developed a signaling mechanism to alert the internal structures that controlled them that deterioration or destruction was imminent. The dangers in the environment surrounding the development of the Precambrian Era and primordial crystalline structures were such that high heat, pressures, and other condensing factors would cause instantaneous evaporation or evisceration of the structures as they existed.

The action of pain as a signal is used as a survival mechanism. Without pain, an individual would have difficulty knowing when dangerous electrochemical conditions existed in the environment that could cause him the loss of his entire organism.

The genetic mechanism is tuned to pain. Pains received are perceptions of various increases in pressure, which make many characteristic sensations in various ways. Pains can be extremely descriptive as noted in the homeopathic repertoires, and their format depends on the area of the body being assaulted by environmental pressures. The imagination of the individual plays a large part in the

Pain is a signal to heed; it is a survival mechanism.

Our electrical structure changes in accordance with the electromagnetic commands of the sun to the earth. The distance of the sun from Earth, approximately ninety-three million miles, is proportionate to the distance of atomic particles in the body. If these are aligned properly there will be comfortable pressure and space = no pain, no sensation.

type of pain signal generated. People are in a constant battle with the environment to avoid collisions with objects and people that may cause them the pain signal.

The avoidance of pain has created a large market for painkillers and relievers. Present day society uses aspirin, codeine, morphine, narcotics, analgesics and all manner of numbing agents to relieve the pressure.

Alcoholism is one of the greatest problems from which human beings suffer because alcohol is one of the best pain relievers. Alcohol has properties that alleviate or ameliorate the pressure buildups that lead to pain, and so executives who've built up an intolerable amount of stress and electrical pressure during a workday will find themselves struggling to keep from being addicted to this readily available substance that seems to shut it off.

On a late night talk show, a guest claimed to not feel any pain whatsoever. This was such an anomaly; the entire audience envied him. They all believed that this would be the most optimum state of being, the inability to feel any pain. However, when the man began to describe his tale of horror, of existing in a constant state of fear that he might run into or contact something very dangerous and detrimental to his body, such as stepping on a nail and not know it, not feel it, the audience began to appreciate the sense perception of pain.

Neuropathy of the feet, where there is little or no feeling at all, is a case in point. Fire-walkers, who walk on hot coals and may seem to be more evolved and advanced, have de-sensitized themselves to the point of numbness. It is difficult to assess a value on the ability to feel pain, because pain is often the mechanism in an individual's life that will save him from ultimate destruction.

The brain, the nervous system, and the hypothalamus are the primary sensing organs involved in the perception of pain.

Pain is a most basic signal. The electrical structure of the body, being tuned to the spatial alignment of the planet in its relationship with the sun, causes an electromagnetic network to be developed within the body. Any area in the body, or around the body, can sense pain.

Pain is a violation of the comfortable alignment of pressure and space within the system.

As the seasons pass, the months change, and the weeks, days, hours and minutes revolve around the clock, our electrical structure changes in accordance with the electromagnetic commands of the sun to the earth. The distance of the sun, approximately ninety-three million miles from Earth, is proportionate to the distance of atomic particles in the body. Scientists who use a sophisticated infrared apparatus to measure the density of the body believe that the atomic structure of the body is approximately .93 microns wavelength and frequency. In other words, the subatomic and atomic particles of the body replicate the exact distance from the sun to the earth at all moments in time.

This means that in the springtime in the northern hemisphere, when the sun commands the earth to move closer in orbit toward it, when the sun is pulling the earth towards its center, the subatomic particles, and likewise the atomic particles in the body, will be pulling energies closer together.

In the autumn of the year in the northern hemisphere, when the earth is moving further away from the sun, so, too, should the particles move in the body. Each hour, minute and second as the sun is changing position moment to moment and the earth is realizing a specific distance away from the sun, the body should, in direct proportion to this phenomenon, align its spaces and particles to exist in comfortable pressure and space.

If the body does not do these things, or if there is some internal or external agency preventing the subatomic and atomic particles of the body from aligning themselves with the proper electromagnetic commands of the sun, then the individual begins to violate the laws of comfortable pressure and space.

The genetic planning mechanism (GPM) can easily sense the variations of pressure and space within the body, and the warning signals of these variations are either pains or sensations, depending on whether or not there is a violation of high pressure (pains) or low pressure (sensations). This situation develops an easy electromagnetic grid, which acts much like a cobweb to a fly, as it captures any extra pressure that is felt by the body. When this pressure builds up, there is a definite sensing of pressure in the form of pain. If we were to drop a bowling ball on our foot, the gravity and weight of the ball would cause a signal to travel rapidly via the nervous system to the brain. The signal was developed because crushing pressures provided enough compacted energy to send a rippling wave effect up the body to the brain. That would be a loud, broad pain; we could also demonstrate pain by sticking a needle into the skin, a more pinpoint and sharp pain. Both types of pain are registered by character in the body.

The body will pick up pressures and demonstrate the pain to the brain by sensing the configuration of the pressure. The bowling ball, for example, has more curvature than the pin and so the characteristic of pain will vary greatly from one object to the other. In essence, the body will measure pain by the shape, size and the power of the objects that bump into it.

In the case of pain received on emotional bands, the person is being impressed by energies that are of an electromagnetic nature. The body and the mind already have an ability to perceive almost any type of physical, mental and spiritual phenomena.

The symptomatic patterns experienced when the sensing mechanisms of pain begin to fail are numbness, unconsciousness, dullness, inappropriate emotion, visual dimness, hearing difficulties and an overall sense of degeneration.

The reason we fail in our ability to perceive pain is likely because we have had an overabundance of pains in our life-

When pain is received on emotional bands, the person is being impressed by energies that are of an electromagnetic nature.

time. In this case, after a while, the magnetic netting of the body becomes tremendously clogged with pressure, like a trash compactor filled with so much garbage that it can no longer compact any more trash. The body begins to backup pressures, concentrated inert materials, toxins, poisons, bacteria, vermin, viruses and many other types of garbage that do not belong in the body so that these materials begin to create a sensing cushion that filters pain.

It is interesting to note that when a person decides to clear himself on body, mind and spiritual levels, the poisons leaving allow the person to perceive, for the first time, pains he didn't know or realize he had! This may lead him to believe that he is getting worse when he is actually improving. When the cotton is taken out of someone's ears, so to speak, he is able to hear things that may not be very pleasant at first.

The intensity of pressure in the environment may be difficult to get used to for some time; however, to save a body from being turned into a garbage dump for every environmental poison, errant frequency, pollution and trauma, we need to launch a campaign of first detoxifying the body, mind and spirit in total, and second, learning to cope with stresses, pressures, traumas, injuries and impacts which are assuredly part of the everyday environment of modern man.

Sensory Channel 46
SENSATION

After the perception of pain, the early crystalline structures then developed a fine sense perception for that condition when pressure was lost, which is defined as a sensation. The definite and decisive connection needed by energy to its environment dictates the need to know when one is truly plugged into his surroundings.

The individual may find himself experiencing other stimulated sensations due to the fact that the environment is loaded with materials that can cause him to lose precious body parts. When ionized electrical forces enter the body, these damage, destroy and literally vaporize energies. This action creates sensations, because sensation is a signal to the brain that something is being lost. People who lose anything in their lives will experience the disconcerting feeling of energies moving too far out and away from their bodies. They may experience dizziness, exhaustion, and other types of phenomena causing them to be out of comfortable pressure and space.

As was mentioned in Channel #45, pain is caused by violation of the alignment of subatomic and atomic particles, which mimic the relationship of the earth and the sun. As the calendar progresses and the seasons change, so must the changing of the electromagnetic particles in the body. In cases where the subatomic and atomic particles of the body do not become closer together during seasons when energies should be moving closer together, especially in the spring and the summer, the individual may feel bizarre sensations which really are the effort of energy within the body to close the gap. In this case, particles are too spaced out for comfort.

The present nutritional genre has dubbed the sensation "hypoglycemia", but it is really just the inability of the body to stay in tune with the electromagnetic commands of the sun. The reason for this

The genetic planning mechanism (GPM) wants to experience the pleasure of balance. If the only available model for a person who has lost is the individual who has hurt him or caused the loss, then the hurt person, the loser, is definitely going to copy the "winner", even if the winner is a louse!

is, of course, the toxins and frequencies in the environment, coupled with traumas that the individual received during his misadventures with his fellow man.

This Channel #46, Sensation, deals specifically with losses. The symptomatic patterns that accrue when sensation is the culprit are in direct proportion to the amount of loss experienced. Someone who is ill but does not feel pain will probably have a very interesting and convoluted history of losses. Businessmen, housewives, athletes, and anyone who participates in life to gain in understanding and material possessions, will certainly have periods in their existence when he or she has lost a most sought after situation, be it a marriage, material goods or even spiritual awareness and consciousness.

The times when the person experiences losses create a situation in the body that is unresolved.

There is a gap.

There is something missing. It feels that way, too. It feels as if it is all emptied out, hollow. His head may feel wooden and his brain is missing. His stomach, diaphragm, and heart may also feel empty. The individual may be easily moved to tears, prone to needing sympathy and may feel that the only way he or she could ever get ahead is to lie, cheat and steal from his fellow human beings.

The reason a person feels this way is because other people, who have done a similar action, have hurt him. If he feels wronged, then he may feel justified in taking possessions away from another, and justified in causing losses to other people. The contagion of this type of thinking occurs because the genetic planning mechanism (GPM) wants to experience the pleasure of balance. If the only available model for a person who has lost is the individual who has hurt him or caused the loss, then the hurt person, the loser, is definitely going to copy the winner, even if the winner is a louse! It is often the case that a person who wrongs someone else is actually mimicking the dirty dealings done to them in the past. The loser is then going to perpetrate the crime done to him, onto others.

This is the proliferation of sin; a transgression occurs because the GPM accepted the programming of loss. It improvises and causes the person to behave in a pattern that could salvage their life. The theory is that if a host can be hurt or damaged by another, then that other person must have programming superior to the host. Therefore, many genetic plans and programs are borrowed from one body to another, depending upon who wins the girl, the fight, the job or the money.

Examples abound in sports. In the city championship basketball game, the home team is blown away by the visitors, 10-34, and the next season, the losing team begins by playing in the style of last season's winning team. By accident or design, consciously or unconsciously, the losing team will mimic or copy the winners. This is true in any situation of competition. Liability on the part of the winners is the fact that all of the material,

We can transcend the pattern of perpetrating our losses onto others and end a genetic cycle of abuse through intense mental and spiritual processing (SAF®).

ideas, athletic prowess and whatever was used to do the winning, will be borrowed, copied and reprogrammed by the loser, so that someday the loser may come back and whip the tar out of the winner with his own methods. This is basically how the environment has been "balanced" for so long.

This is most certainly the philosophy of fear and pain. It seeks to rectify damages by causing the person to accept or absorb the ideas of the people who hurt him. Therefore, if the winners in life are unethical, then eventually the whole planet will be an unethical mess. Conversely, if the winners in life are ethical, clean, and upright, then eventually the whole planet will be forthright and just. It is definitely a characteristic verifiable by periods of history when leaders have varied in time from evil, wicked men to honest and forthright leaders and patriots.

In the time before and during World War II, there was such a phenomenon. Honest men accepted the ways and ideas of Adolf Hitler and atrocities were perpetrated. These conditions and practices were rampant in Germany due to the fact that the primary opinion leader, the "winner" (Adolf Hitler who promised retribution and a better economy while blaming others), was copied and duplicated over and over. In a sense, there were thousands of Hitlers running loose who, as ordinary citizens, had absorbed the genetic planning and programming commands of Hitler.

In times when sane, ethical and organized human beings run the planet, everyone will mimic their examples and eventually the planet will be a sane, ethical and safe place to live.

Other sensation symptom patterns would include a general sense of loss and disconnection, which makes the muscles weak, tingling and ineffectual. The person has a lost, empty feeling inside. The pressure is reduced on the system; however, it is a reduction of pressure that is unwanted. The person may experience the movement or replacement and restructuring of salts, water and protein within the body, which cause the bizarre sensation of emptiness that he may experience.

In cases where energies have been stolen or lost, the GPM immediately signals the DNA-RNA to make changes in the system. This change and the symptoms that follow can be very disconcerting to the human being.

Through the self awareness process, we can transcend the pattern of perpetrating our losses onto others and end a genetic cycle of abuse by complete recognition, which allows the pattern to release.

Sensory Channel 47
UNCONSCIOUS PAIN

The early crystalline structures, knowing that pains and pressures could build up to the extent of going beyond the first line sensing mechanism that signal the control centers, developed a sense mechanism to alert the control center that there was pain that could not be felt. This is basically a perception of unconsciousness, that area where the individual is not aware of certain pressure buildup.

In the development of the planet, energies became backed up and so pressurized that crystalline structures needed a means of being able to perceive exactly what level of pain was being expressed. As history progressed, several new levels of pain were introduced. That is to say, as the planet matured, pains became more and more sophisticated. In the early days, when the planet was young, the gaseousness of the sphere made the planet light and almost buoyant, but as time progressed, the orb became condensed and heavier.

In today's world, we experience different levels of pain that are available to our senses. However, there are many other levels of pain beyond our conscious grasp. These are pressures that have built up, possibly genetically, over centuries and are yet to be released. These pains and upsets, once contacted and relieved, will catapult us into greater heights of understanding about our origins. However, most of these unconscious pains are those received when we were under the influence of some type of anesthetizing drug or a very traumatic situation. With a high degree of impact, we could have been traumatized to the point of being rendered unconscious; these periods in our history exist as super-pressurized moments in time that can develop into quirks of personality. (QUIRK: Questions Understood by Intersecting Retrievable Knowledge).

It is a QUIRK because when we are contacting the mechanism of pain installed by the traumatic incident, we cannot perceive it. For example, let's say at some point we had fallen down and hit our head hard and for fifteen minutes did not know where we were. Twenty-five years later we try to remember that very same incident and still cannot recall

A QUIRK is defined in SAF® work as Questions Understood by Intersecting Retrievable Knowledge.

QUIRK was one of the first SAF® computing programs that sequenced the weaknesses and strengths of organs and glands.

Love *represented a buildup of energy in thyroid and the heart (10-2)*

Loss of Love *degraded energy as heart to thyroid. (2-10)*

Loss of Zest for Living: *adrenal to endocrine/hormone system. (13-17/18)*

Lying *sequence: thymus to bones and muscles. (1-9)*

The Self Awareness Formulas (SAF®) is the method used to decipher the conundrums and unknowns on body, mind and spirit levels. These quirks are a part of the chain sequence work with SAF® Online.

where we were.

In essence, that area of the memory, that part of the body that was traumatized, became so super-pressurized that we cannot perceive or mentally recontact the unconscious pain that exists there. However, if for some reason, by some agency or process, we were able to remember exactly what happened, the unconscious pain would then release into a conscious pain. At this moment, of course, we could reprogram our sensing mechanism by understanding exactly what occurred in what sequence to hurt us. It is the <u>understanding</u> that releases the pain, because pain and pressure can only exist by misunderstanding, trauma, accident and injury.

The quirk can only operate in a band of pressure beyond or outside the awareness of the individual. When one becomes aware of it, a certain amount of pressure has been discharged, thus eliminating the power of the quirk.

The symptomatic patterns of an individual who is deficient in the ability to perceive unconscious pain are recognizable primarily by unrelenting fatigue. One of the ways an individual is programmed to release pressures, especially unconscious pains and super-pressurized areas of the body, is through sleep. People who are narcoleptic, catatonic, in a coma, or constantly overtired are being plagued by conditions out of their conscious grasp.

The super-pressurized area of the body, mind or spirit, which has been conditioned by traumas, impacts, injuries, operations, drug taking of all sorts, and occlusion, and the subliminal effects of radiation, pollution and other environmental poisons and frequencies, show themselves by causing the person to be dull and appear stupid. Persons who for no other reason constantly nod off and yawn at the slightest provocation are demonstrating the fact that energies in their bodies are pressurized enough to cause them to drift in and out of consciousness. When a person is chronically yawning and tired, it is for a good reason; however, the reason is not very detectable at first glance.

An individual must deal with the inner workings of the genetic planning mechanism, the mind, and the spirit to understand exactly how moments in time can serve as "knock-out drops" for an individual. These are replays of the traumatic incident. Anyone who cannot perceive those times in his history when his body was super-pressurized, will be prone to inadvertently and at the most inopportune times replay or relive those instances. Because the instance is beyond his awareness, he will dramatize or un-

consciously act out part of the experience.

The primary signal that a person is acting out something unconscious is a deviation of his behavior. Yawning or tiredness is but one deviation; however, if the person is alive and awake one minute and falling asleep the next, then that is a sure sign. A person may also be prone to shifting in moods and intelligence as well. He may be happy one moment and angry and sad the next. He may be busily working on a project, studying or creating some new idea, and then suddenly be unable to confront it anymore, or worse, remain in bed or on the sofa, too tired to move.

Many of the projects and plans that are left unfinished by individuals are due to the fact that certain quirks in the system (super-pressurized, unconscious areas of pain and sensation) are in full restimulation; an individual loaded with quirks will be changing moods and tempos quite frequently. He will also be privy to the plot of confusion in his mind. It is this secret information that he needs to unravel. It is like a riddle which, when deciphered, releases the individual from the control of the quirk.

The quirk is a program. It acts like a sophisticated computer command to cause the individual to behave in a certain pattern or to show certain symptoms, whether visible or invisible. The quirk is

The quirk, the pain is a riddle that needs to be accessed and deciphered. It is the <u>conscious understanding</u> that releases the pain that was once unconscious. It then becomes an illusion.

created by super-pressurization into unconscious pain or sensation. It is itself a riddle or a question which can be understood by using a person's previously known data about the situation and intersecting it with what he does not know about the situation. Quirk in this sense refers to the SAF® questionnaires that take known data and create a sequence of numbers that puts the spotlight on unknown situations. Because the SAF® system is so personalized, quirk became a catchy title for being able to find our "quirks," our personal peculiarities and syndromes related to particular subjects.

It is important to be able to retrieve the information lodged within the quirk. Just as one would try to debug a computer program, so does an individual attempt to find the quirk first and then understand its workings and mechanisms. Once the equation or the computation is understood and deciphered, then the electrical phenomena holding the quirk together is discharged.

By definition, the quirk can only operate in a band of pressure beyond or outside the awareness of the individual. When one becomes aware of it, a certain amount of pressure has been discharged, thus eliminating the power of the quirk.

Once the quirk can be sensed, or is realized, and becomes conscious to the owner, it then is merely an illusion or a picture that loses its force in reality.

The most advantageous situation to all humankind is the elimination of all quirks. This would be the eradication of all genetic programs and plans that were inadvertently or accidentally programmed into the mechanism and this would eliminate all the poisons, toxins and debris in the system that did not belong there.

Sensory Channel 48
UNCONSCIOUS SENSATION

The early crystalline structures, while developing a strict sense for super-pressurized pains, also had to develop a sensing system for super depressurized losses. As it became evident that energies would be lost in the system, there developed a hierarchy of significance of loss. An example of this hierarchy would be if we were to lose a one-dollar bill as compared to having our house burn down.

Human beings experience super depressurization when losing the companionship of a loved one. Of course, the degree of loss is always measured by the amount of significance the person has in the life of the person. A dearly loved one causes a more severe depressurization than one who is an acquaintance, whether family or friend, so the losses that a person accrues in a lifetime can be graded in importance.

However, the losses that become culprits or the quirks (Questions Understood by Intersecting Retrievable Knowledge) in a person's existence are those that leave a lasting imprint and are indecipherable. Human beings have based their existence on possession. The mad rush to own as much material wealth as possible, plus the need to have companionship of people who help a person reach his goal set up a game of energy roulette. When an individual loses the person he regards as a highly significant character in his plans to survive on this earth, he loses part of himself as well.

When we lose a person we regard as highly significant, we lose a part of our selves as well. Losses that leave a lasting imprint are considered indecipherable.

The symptomatic patterns of a person who experiences a super depressurization or heavy loss is demonstrable by the existence of inabilities to cope with certain conditions in the environment. A person may express the fact that he does not wish to be married again or he decidedly does not want to associate with people. He may become very distrustful of relationships. He may decide to give up on the idea that anyone could be honest and businesslike. In short, the individual loses not only the object of his affection and admiration, but he also loses his ability to love. This causes him to recede deeper within himself as a protective mechanism. A withdrawn person who refuses to get involved or the hesitant individual who wants to get involved, but for some odd reason cannot, is a person who has experienced super depressurization and is now being controlled by a quirk.

If the quirk could be reached and dismantled, and its program could be understood, rerouted and the inner energy discharged, the person could do all of the things that would make up a full life.

Sensory Channel 49
DEATH FROM PAIN

The development of crystalline structures on the planet experienced an even greater phase of pressurization, which caused the ultimate death of not only individual crystals, but also certain lines and species of crystals. This was a third gradation of super-pressurization even beyond that of unconsciousness discussed in the previous sections. It marked the end of the idea that certain crystalline structures would be immortal. Inasmuch as conditions are constantly changing in the environment, the action of super pressurization became necessary to eliminate the old style crystals and make way for the new.

Today, one of the most often discussed subjects amongst human beings is death. It is a powerful subject because it possesses the super pressurization of three distinct levels of energy. It is not enough that unconsciousness blocks the memory of the individual; death erases the being as well. The subject of death is completely abhorrent to many of us because of this great power. However, when analyzing the subject, we find that death can be caused only by a specific amount of pressure buildup, which goes beyond unconsciousness.

In essence, death is a collection of these various unconsciousnesses. The misunderstandings that surround death are questions or quirks (Questions Understood by Intersecting Retrievable Knowledge) in which human beings find themselves. We ask, "What will happen after death?" or "Where will I go?" Entire organizations, religions and other collected groups of human beings have assigned themselves to answer these riddles. Over the course of centuries, much of the effort of humankind to understand death has been relegated to these large-scale societies. The answers that have arisen so far are those that are steering the course of history.

In this text, there is no attempt made to define or condemn any religious activity for its solutions to the death question; it is only a guide to allow the individual to further understand the mechanisms of death. Where or what will happen to an individual is up to his or her own religious belief. How it happens is very obvious. If an individual wishes to kill a certain body

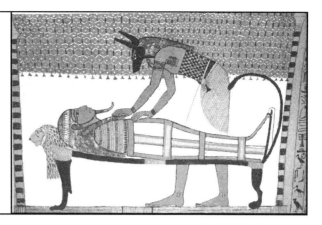

(right) Anubis, the jackal, was originally the Egyptian God of Smell, an herbal healer, and later was in charge of embalming with sweet smelling herbs and oils to prepare the body for burial. The Egyptians had elaborate funeral rituals, with the pyramids being the most highly regarded and sacred of burial sites.

or collection of cells and tissues, all he need do is super pressurize that area with a sharp or blunt instrument. A bullet, a knife, an explosion, all the weapons that man has become very adept at constructing, can demonstrate the death process very easily.

The accruement of pain unconsciousness, super pressurized to a point where the individual's systems are blocked or collapsed in some way, causes the final outcome. However, over long periods of time when an individual hasn't been unexpectedly shot or run over by a large vehicle, there are degenerative conditions which may predispose a person to a certain amount of unconsciousness which may abruptly and quite unexpectedly end his life in mystery.

This has been the constant and chronic upset of mankind. Humans find it difficult to rationalize the sequence of death. Even with those deaths that are quite understandable, such as those that are precipitated by accident and other known traumas, the individual's relatives, friends, and the people who knew the deceased well are all still at a loss to explain how and why the person could have gotten himself into a situation in which he would be killed or murdered.

If a researcher were to trace back the origins of a person's death, whether accidental or degenerative, we would see that all conditions begin with certain amounts of pain and anguish developing from concussions and impacts with the environment and other people. In other words, even the accidental deaths created by collision, such as in car accidents and airplane crashes, are caused by an accruement of earlier times of unconsciousness. Essentially, the person has to have had many prior minor impacts and traumas to super pressurize his system into enough numbness and stupor to make him so accident prone he drives the car into a brick wall or dies of arthritis, cancer or any of the other named diseases. Such diseases are simply terms for quirks that have become super pressurized in the system.

The symptomatic pattern of an individual who has lost the perception of super pressurization, which may ultimately turn into his death knell, is not easily detectable. The current status of human beings, in comparison with the God-like creatures who once roamed the earth (this is alluded to parenthetically in a better explanation of the story of Adam and Eve in the Garden of Eden, as well as the early men mentioned in the Book of Genesis), gives us a clue that people who do not attempt to dislodge or disconnect from their quirks are on a collision course with death every moment of their lives. Those who are constantly researching, studying and attempting to understand the mechanisms, which collectively have enough power to eradicate their existence, will enjoy a certain quality of life and be free from the handwringing that plagues the average person on the street on the subject of death.

The recognizable symptoms of confusion, disillusionment, worry, upset, fear for the future, anxieties, nervousness, apprehension, neurosis and psychosis, which emerge from the inability to properly access the value of life, are patterns we can easily observe. It is obvious from the viewpoint of sanctity and perfection that someone who disregards his own wholesomeness, who daily plummets headlong toward that time when he must tally his wins and losses and meet his own image of the creative force that put him here, in the process will show many signs of confusion and sickness. In essence, any disease is a warning signal that the individual and any one he can solicit to help him, must immediately start plans and operations to eradicate that quirk. If he does not heed the warning signals, then he will find himself in a greater danger later on in his life.

Anyone seeking to "live forever" must heed the warning signals of every quirk. Any quirks that are avoided may fester in an unconscious area, and may not be available to study. It is difficult enough to decipher the known problems of an individual, much less those that submerge below his consciousness. Therefore, it is important to handle all those conditions that present themselves to the consciousness of the person. All symptoms, such as colds, fevers, rashes, boils, and other physical phenomena, including all known emotional issues of pain and sensation, must be approached, analyzed, and deciphered whether these are part of a more chronic degenerative process or a simple transitory condition.

The prevention of death is the prevention of the accruement of unconsciousness, which predisposed the individual to his own mortality. It is as if the person were commanded by a higher authority to keep his garbage orderly at first, and then dispose of it when the time is right.

It is not enough to just be aware of one's condition, it is important to be able to understand and eradicate its influence.

Sensory Channel 50
DEATH FROM SENSATION

The perception of loss becomes extremely devolved in cases where losses are propounded by many losses. Individuals who are "losers" have had earlier losses, which are buried deep beneath their consciousness and direct their activities in erroneous patterns, thus making them "loss prone". The early crystalline structures had become extremely depressurized at certain points in time and lost so much energy that they vanished. This is a recording that is imprinted on the genetic planning mechanism (GPM) and part of the 128 sensing channels. It is part of the sensibility of protein to be able to perceive points of time when energies are so thoroughly depleted that the organism can no longer continue.

The human being today, with his sophisticated electronic network of energy, is extremely cognizant of losses of energies within the system. However, the deep-set losses of energy, which accrue over a

Loss is actually an illusion. If the person who has lost someone or something can be convinced that he did not actually "lose" anything, he will be able to have energy and will feel connected again.

period of time, accumulate and cause a condition very dangerous to the overall mechanism.

If a person chronically exhausts himself and continually loses energy in a certain way, he may cause the death of certain organs, cells and tissues within the body.

If we abuse our liver, pancreas and heart, eventually those areas will fail us with the loss of energy. However, it is more easily understood by observing the person who continually loses at the game of life. The energies that are necessary for everyday functioning power, when depleted, cause a condition of super depressurization, which freezes reactive materials in the body. This frozen state disconnects the individual's energy channels and he ceases to be.

Newspapers printed an article not so long ago about a pet dog that was left at home while the family went on vacation. When they returned after several days, the dog had died, not from lack of food or water for that had been provided, but from fear that the family he had loved so dearly had left him alone for good. The absence of the love and tenderness, which the dog desired or actually needed to sustain his life, caused a condition of super depressurization which took away his life. The dog died very dramatically of a broken heart.

Human beings have the same frailty to a certain extent. When energies are lost from the body, these must not only be replaced, but the quirk (Questions Understood by Intersecting Retrievable Knowl-edge) allowing energy to be drained, must be found and deprogrammed so that it does not create that situation again. Obviously, the dog could have lived for years if there weren't some program or quirk within his system that dictated that he needed the daily energies from his human beings to live. In reality, he did not, but the programmed mechanisms of his body, which were most certainly connected to his vital life support systems, computed the fact that the energy of human beings was necessary for existence.

Those who suffer depressurization following the loss of a great love, such as a wife, husband, child, mother, father, sister or brother, overtakes them. They must find and deprogram that part of the GPM holding memory traces of early crystalline experiences on this planet. These quirks are powerful programs causing an individual tremendously profound levels of grief from which they sometimes cannot recover.

The symptomatic patterns of an individual who has lost the perception of death from sensation include a spaced out look; the person is "not there", not present or fully alive in his own form. His mind will seem tuned out and away from the present time environment. His attention would be on concepts and ideas that are lost to him, and so he will exude an expression of emptiness. In a symptomatic sense, the individual may experience this emptiness in his stomach, his legs, especially in the thighs, his brain and his heart. He may have the shakes, tremors and deliriums. However, most of these conditions, as noxious as they sound, may be unknown to the person, and may be triggered by the smallest upset.

For example, the person may have a slight disagreement with someone and then go off in a corner and sulk for days. This is due to the fact that there are other unknown losses buried deep within the system that the person has not yet been able to uncover. The incident that triggers the upsets within the GPM, or the conditions allowing quirks to operate on the mind of the individual, are incidental to the actual programming that exists deep inside of the person.

The elimination of the quirk in the overall genetic mechanisms is of the utmost importance and is the premier project of all scientists and researchers on planet Earth. If we could eliminate the controlling "gene chip," which promotes the illusion in the individual that he is actually losing something, then it would be impossible to make a human being sick.

Losing energy is an illusion that is promoted by this particular gene chip. As long as the individual feels that he is well connected and has a sustenance of energy from his surroundings, he can always maneuver himself in a position of being fed with energy. Therefore, in a sense, he could never die from sensation.

Sensory Channel 51
Z REACTION FROM PAIN
(positive, pressure)

Early crystalline structures developed the ability to track complex diagrams of energy to respond to their survival needs and reactions. This mechanism came about after a good deal of pressure and application by the outside environment,

and here is where automaticity is programmed into the crystal itself. It is at this point that the crystal has been bombarded with enough pressure and pain and traumatized to the point where the recording of information will last in perpetuity.

Human beings rely on this ability to create their normal everyday automaticities and response mechanisms for survival. For example, a weight lifter uses this action to program his muscles to automatically respond to intense situations.

The Z reaction from pain mechanism is also part of the program instilled in an individual during a traumatic event, which often becomes erroneously programmed and causes that person to behave in bizarre patterns.

The problem that has been plaguing humanity is that the programs from pain and trauma become confused and a person responds in erroneous ways:

- By using the wrong response mechanism for the wrong situation
- By using the right response mechanism for the wrong situation
- By using the wrong response mechanism in the right situation

Basically what happens is that the human being does not behave properly and will ultimately fall into patterns that can be likened to or are labeled "bad luck". The person begins to lose his program. His programmed automaticities are not in sync with the current operation of his mind, body and spirit. Therefore, he is operating on stale information. Furthermore, much of the information coming from the program is in reaction to survival situations programmed for the individual only. Often times when the individ-

The primary mechanism of loss through the eons was being eaten. Individuals lost their position and their integrity because bigger, more powerful energies in the environment devoured them and sought to make them a part of the overall structure of the other's energy.

ual responds to this information, he appears selfish and self-centered.

As an example, in situations where the person feels he will be thwarted in some type of business transaction, he may carry on and complain that everyone is constantly trying to cheat him. He would be so fearful of this event that he may be completely useless in business. His talents and abilities are squashed by his anxieties about losing money. The gene chip at work here is coming from a similar trauma in the past in which he *was* the loser. Therefore, these programs are constantly appearing and displaying information to the person, but they are basically diagrammed in a losing situation.

Sensory Channel 52
Z REACTION FROM
SENSATION (negative, loss)

Conversely to the previous perception channel, a person, when creating Z reactions in the system, can do so by a traumatic loss. This has been explained time and again throughout this text and does not need further explanation, except to say that when someone has a painful loss, the experience will certainly lodge and install this information into his genetic program banks.

Early crystalline structures developed this system basically because energies were being lost to other individual structures in the environment. The primary mechanism of this loss was being eaten. Individuals lost their position and their

integrity because bigger, more powerful energies in the environment devoured them and sought to make them a part of the overall structure of the other's energy. Ultimately, a person who follows this pattern of crystalline information is extremely apprehensive about anyone communicating with him on any subject.

If we peruse through our own mind to times when we have been taken advantage of in some way, we will find that we have a subconscious, automatic reaction, which tries to protect us from further degradation. Often, we cannot completely understand what this reaction is, but we can sense its importance. The body's symptomatic patterns will react by causing tingling sensations throughout the nervous system and definite pains and sensations, which act as signals to warn us that we are encroaching on an area of activity that may be detrimental to us.

Sensory Channel 53
RADIATIONAL FORCES
(especially male)

The early crystalline structures, that is, those energies that existed on the planet before any other life form, did not actually have male and female designations. The primary substance of measurement (at that time and today) is water (H_2O). Any crystal with electric charges making it heavier or more dense than water is considered male, and all those crystals with an absence of electric charge and less dense than water are considered female. In fact, it is the parity and equilib-

(left) Yin-Yang symbol expresses the Chinese philosophy of the duality of energy: Two qualities, ever changing, negative (female) and positive (male), one becoming the other achieves balance.

yin	*yang*
female	*male*
dark	*light*
night	*day*
cold	*hot*
wet	*dry*
winter	*summer*
soft	*hard*
pulling	*pushing*

rium of the universe that designates male and female status.

The male body definitely holds a greater amount of electric charge and potential than the female body. However, the female is the one who magnetically coerces this male energy to move toward her. This relentless activity is based on a simple theme: Return to a rest or balanced state. Any energy out of balance will seek one that has an opposite charge to assist it in rebalancing itself. Therefore, males on this planet have been assigned the task of rebalancing themselves by aligning their energies with females.

A radiational force is an energy that pushes outward. Males have that intrinsic energy which thrusts itself outward, evidenced by the fact that the male genitalia are external to the body. This occurs because the male body has been developed with an excess of charge. It seeks to rebalance itself by finding the correct female with the correct aesthetic frequency to assist in the rebalancing process. The perpetuation of the system is experienced through children. Each child has his own charge, positive or negative, male or female.

The built-in process of being able to sense or perceive radiational characteristics is something of which all of society is aware. The male aggressiveness or energetic status assigned to men is easily recognizable. They are on the attack constantly and are looking for a mate with whom they can balance themselves.

In modern times, of course, this statement does not always correspond to reality. If we were able to observe Stone Age people for a time, we would most likely see this phenomenon repeat over and over again, but in today's society, individuals begin to lose their male and female characteristics, and their roles begin to shift. Many women now work outside the home in "the man's world." There are many men today who are not very aggressive. It is partly the hormonal balance of a person that causes him to have the aggressiveness that will label him male or positively charged, and part of a female's nature to be recessive or negatively charged; however, as was previously stated, in today's society the energies that are constantly

(right) Alchemic illustration, male and female principles have been known since antiquity. These principles are evident in many sciences, philosophies and religious practices: physics, electricity, gravitation, radiation, electrochemistry, magnetism, meteorology, sun—space, aggressive—receptive, and in the precepts of Asian and Chinese philosophies (yin—yang).

exchanging to and fro become confused, and the role of dominator and dominatee often switches.

Sensory Channel 54
GRAVITATIONAL FORCES
(especially female)

The early crystalline structures, through constant pressure in the environment also necessarily develop the talent for being able to perceive recessive traits. The mechanism causing the desire to rebalance oneself allows an individual crystal to perceive another's lack or need for energy. These crystalline structures began the present day Asian medical concept of yin and yang; that is, negative and positive charges, and female and male relationships.

This concept is important to our understanding that physical bodies and minds are often assigned male and female characteristics. We find that in different languages around the world, the perpetrators of these diagrams of communication assign male and female principles to inanimate objects.

For example, in Italian: la casa (home = female); il tavalo (table = male).

This primarily depends on the fact that certain objects are deemed to have aggressiveness (positive charge) and certain objects have for their sake and usage recessiveness (negative charge). In other words, there is always a dominator and a dominatee in this environment.

One might think that in all relationships people can have an equal partnership and be able to express themselves in whatever way they see fit. It seems that the more balanced individuals are able to retain both male and female traits, even though they have a particular positive or negative designation (have a male or female body). There are many such individuals who have found ways of equalizing their aggressive qualities with an ability to also be recessive and receptive.

Sensory Channels 55-68
COLOR & SOUND

In the following 14 channels, we enter extremely important perception levels. It is a point of harmony in this entire program that separates the raw or overt perceptions from those of a more profound

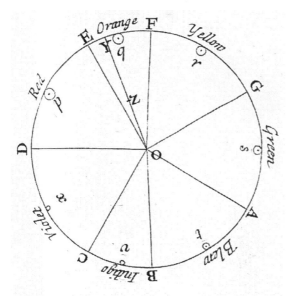

Newton's Opticks (published in 1704) contained drawings with the 5 colors Newton refracted from sunlight with a prism—red, yellow, green, blue, and violet. Later he added orange and indigo to match the number of 7 known celestial bodies and 7 notes in the major music scale. (above).

Many species can see light in frequencies beyond human ability.

Plants that depend on insect pollination owe reproductive success to being able to broadcast in the ultra-violet band.

Bees and other insects detect ultraviolet light, which helps them to find nectar and pollen (see chart page 105).

Birds, animals and fish that can see in the ultraviolet range cannot see the red or infrared wavelengths.

nature. It is here that the latter half of the crystal's and the human body's abilities of perception become more sensitive.

These sensing channels are some of the most powerful levels presented in this book. It must not be studied lightly but

with great intensity, for if we can address this zone of understanding with the right attitude, we could catapult into a higher realm of well-being.

The harmonics of color and sound begin to reproduce themselves and the individual has a greater ability to understand the finer details of life and living. The Greek word *syntony* means being in harmony.

Visible light, we know it as color, is a very narrow band of the Electromagnetic Spectrum (see page 114) nestled between the infrared band (discovered by Herschel in 1800) and the ultraviolet band (discovered by Ritter in 1801). The visible color spectrum was officially designated in 1802 by Thomas Young, a natural philosopher, with his idea that color was a response to different vibrations of light.

The early Greeks had noted similarities between sound and color, with Aristotle noting there were 7 major colors. In about 1670, Sir Isaac Newton used a prism to disperse sunlight into 5 colors (the optical spectrum, a rainbow), and later the poet Goethe noted the physiological effects of color on the human. Color was noted by Wilhelm Ostwald to be a sensation, for which he received a Nobel Prize in chemistry in 1909.

But this may be the first publication that identifies the exact correlation process in the human perception bands between color and sound, the connection of color and sound vibrations of crystalline structures and their relationship to humankind.

When we are in balance, we are able to accept and take in the color wavelengths we need from sunlight. Through the ages, light and color have been used as therapy and healing.

Light is perceived as pressure waves, but only in the visible color spectrum. We cannot distinguish pressures of light that are beyond the visible, in the infrared or ultraviolet bands. Light waves beyond the red pressure levels have too much space between objects. Conversely, waves of light in the ultra-violet band have too much pressure between objects to be visible to the human sight sense. When we visually travel the rainbow from red-violet to blue-violet, more and more pressure is encountered, with less and less space. The particles and waves moving closer together or farther apart create the changes of color that we see.

However, no matter how invisible these areas of light are, they can still be perceived by "feelings" and be understood by man. These can be tapped into by the Expanded Tactile Sense, what humans sometimes call the sixth sense or extra-sensory perception (ESP). Sensory Channels 55 to 68 expand and enhance Touch (Sensory Channel 1).

Sensory Channel 55
THE COLOR RED-VIOLET

The color Red-Violet is an area of vibration or zone of operation for crystalline structures and is of great interest to practitioners and those studying the forms of life energy, their diagrams and blueprints. Through the use of infrared detecting devices, these particular wave patterns of information are available to those who venture into this territory for exploration.

The Red-Violet band is considered the infrared band and the edge of the infrared band, which is just beyond the red band. All individuals and crystals are seething with this energy. (see chart page 114)

The patterns of infrared or Red-Violet energy can be used to detect the metabolism of energy within the system, which gives practitioners a hint of not only the past or present patterns of energy in the body, but also the future patterns.

Sensory Channel 56
THE COLOR RED

Early crystalline structures perceived that they needed to separate energies and be able to use different elements and materials at their discretion. As the function and power of automaticities began to build after the development of the Z reaction process, it became necessary to become more definitive, for a Z portends a conglomeration or disunity of energy, or a total unity of mass. The crystals that were developed on this planet needed the innate intelligence or guidance from some source of intellectual involvement to be able to discern one piece of energy or matter from another. It is color, and the variation of color, that accomplish this task. As we perceive differences between mere shades of gray and hues of stark color, we begin to realize that the variations of excitability of vibration in the environment are vast.

The color Red governs the wavelengths and frequencies for those elements in the body that are necessary for tranquilization and relaxation, such as sodium and potassium. The red area is a zone that is important for the intrinsic function of the light elements. These elements control the nervous system and nervous response reactions and are neces-

The Morning Star is like a Man; he is painted Red all over; that is the color of Life."   *—Pawnee Indian chant*

sary to the overall balance of electrical function.

Sensory Channel 57
THE COLOR ORANGE

To the ancient Egyptians, Orange and Gold symbolized divinity—the sun, God and creation.

As the structures went through further stages of development on this planet, they moved through the processes of creating different levels of vibration. Orange was that color that governed elements such as aluminum and all elements in the radiational bands. Orange has a more positive bent and is considered part of the wavebands that govern alkaline, earth-forming elements. Orange is the energy that is the signifier of radiation.

The sun itself is an orangey color and as it radiates its energy toward the earth, it is translated to other forms.

All those elements that have a factor of three within their orbital shells most definitely belong to this vibrational level.

Sensory Channel 58
THE COLOR YELLOW

The color Yellow became the designator of heavy metals. When we study the gradations of energy in this text, we immediately see the pattern of colors relating to the development of energies from radiation down to the heavy metals. On the fourth level of color, Yellow, we note that the heavy metal structures themselves are intimated to have a connection with the color Yellow. Metals such as copper, zinc, manganese, iron, etc. are con-

"The sun shines not on us but in us."
--John Muir

nected to this wave vibration.

When trying to understand more about the human body, we see that many of these heavy metals are vital to the function of the human body. For example, if a person lacks the metal zinc, then he will have difficulty healing wounds and in controlling his metabolism. If someone lacks copper, he may have liver troubles and lack the ability to defend himself from the invasion of toxins, poisons, viruses and bacteria.

The heavy metals in general, that is, those that fall in the color bands, or are perceived as color, are connected to a very important process of perception in the body. The person studying this program must realize that by gaining a perception of these particular metals, he not only understands their individual behavior but also the symptomatic patterns that they can create when toxic or deficient in the body. If he were ever able to control these particular levels, then it would be totally impossible for him to ever feel pain or sensation without his consent. The programs and protocols that have been created to gain a better perception for these particular levels of metal function in the body are paramount in study.

The Promethion was written primarily to study and express this particular phenomenon. By looking through *The Promethion*, the reader can see that the colors and the metals have been juxtaposed to show the high level of perception in this area.

This perceptibility factor should be in the middle range of the overall abilities of humankind, but nonetheless, is far above those of the average human being.

A person could easily extend his energy and his longevity were he to gain an

All of the elements, metals and gases have characteristic colors. For help in understanding and balancing these, see The Promethion.

interest in and control of these particular mechanisms of energy.

Sensory Channel 59
THE COLOR GREEN

Early crystalline structures needed a response mechanism to show the opposite effect of radiation in the system. The characteristic color Green, which is displayed on all foliage on the planet, is the response mechanism of crystals to the radiational flow of the sun. This is a basic mechanism, but also involves some specific elements that can be perceived by the individual. The element phosphorus, especially, is part of this energy transition process.

In human beings, the element phosphorus is extremely important. It controls our sense of reality and sanity. It keeps us connected with the actual exchange processes going on between the sun and the earth. If we can but coordinate this particular level, we would have sanity forever and ever.

The proof of this, many times, is to take a person who is overwrought by conditions around him in his environment, especially a city dweller, and take him out to the country for a day or two. Have him roam around the woods, wander through the pastures and the grassy knolls, and after a while he begins to regain his sanity.

"I go to nature to be soothed and healed, and to have my senses put in tune once more"
—*John Burroughs 1837-1921*

The relationship of these particular colors is extremely important to the survival of mankind and all other life forms as well.

Sensory Channel 60
THE COLOR BLUE

As early crystalline structures began to progress through programs of energy that were necessary for their own survival, they needed to develop a level of energy that was far above and beyond all other levels. This was primarily to extend the existence past the point of being able to merely transmutate radiation into an opposite color.

The Blue area is a cleansing one. The color Blue has an affinity with elements such as sulfur, and the specific monovalent negatively-charged elements such as fluorine, chlorine, and bromine, which are well-known cleansers.

Those who are familiar with these elements realize that sulfur is contained in many of the protein matrices of the body. It is an intrinsic part of the nature of the human because it is connected to the hair, nails, and many of the proteins that actually form the shape of the individual. It is part of the electromagnetic and electroplasmic haze that surrounds the person's aura and gives him a feeling of wholesomeness.

Hot sulfur springs have been meccas of healing and cleansing since the earliest of times.

If an individual begins to lose his perception for the color Blue, or if he has a definite deficiency and toxicity of elements that are involved with this particular range of electric equilibrium, he will find himself becoming dirty and unkempt. He may feel himself loaded with errant electric charge and becomes a magnet for additional poisons surrounding him.

Sensory Channel 61
THE COLOR BLUE-VIOLET

Again, the crystalline structures needed to reach for a higher level and at this point they pushed themselves beyond the color spectrum in answer to the opposite infrared band. This is commonly called the ultra-violet band or the Blue-Violet band of energy. The halogens and areas below the light spectrum would be included in this level. It is the perception of this level of energy, which gives one the ability to "see" bacteria, fungus, and other subcreatures that have taken energy from the environment and exist on a lower level.

In humankind, the observation of the Blue-Violet level, or the level of electric pressure that is near that band, is intrinsic for survival because it is an indicator of those areas that have been infiltrated by toxins, poisons, worms, parasites, warts, moles and all of the degraded processes of the cells and tissues, known and unknown.

Sensory Channels 62-68
SOUND

For sound to travel, there must be mass dense enough for molecules and at-

Synesthesia, from the Greek "syn" = together and "aesthesis" = perception.

This describes those who have "colored hearing", or seeing of color when a sound is played.

Pythagoras considered this to be a great philosophical gift and spiritual achievement.

oms to clash, collide and bounce. Objects moving swiftly together and then apart create distinctive pitches and tones. These sounds carry through the environment as shock waves, frequencies. This has been known since ancient times. The sensing of energies crashing in the environment is an art.

Many spiritual traditions put forth the idea that sound was responsible for creating the universe.

"In the beginning was the WORD and the WORD was of God, and the WORD was God."
—-The Gospel of St. John 1:1

The power, the radiation of God is absolute: He merely utters a frequency (sound) and mighty things are created.

The Egyptian Universal Mother Goddess Isis sang special words of power (frequencies) to heal the sick and raise her husband Osiris from the dead.

According to historians, the aborigines of Australia have used sounds and frequencies for healing for 40,000 years. Paleolithic caves in Europe have revealed flutes made from animal bones, aged circa 30,000 years old, so music and sound were important to Stone Age man on all continents.

The "chromatic music scale" comes from the Greek word *chroma*, meaning color and as mentioned there have been strong connections through the ages between sound and color.

The current system of musical notes, called solmization (from sol-mi), or the solfeggio frequencies assigns a syllable for each tone of a major scale. This system originated with the Arabic system. The Vedic texts, Indian, and Byzantine music all used scales with different names, yet

The syllables for the modern solfeggio sounds were written in an 8th century Latin hymn or chant honoring John the Baptist, in wide use by the 10th century.

The beginning of each line contains the named syllables, highlighted in bold.

> **Ut** *queant laxis*
> **re**sonare fibris,
> **Mi**ra gestorum
> **fa**muli tuorum,
> **Sol**ve polluti
> **la**bii reatum,
> **S**ancte **I**ohannes.

The hymn is translated: "So that your servants can sing with their voice your wonderful feats, clear their lips that are stained with guilt, oh Saint John!"

UT has been changed to DO; SI is now called TI.

similar tones.

English and Dutch languages use the Latin alphabet: C, D, E, F, G, A, and B, while the rest of the world uses the syllables: Do-Re-Mi-Fa-Sol-La-Si (Ti).

Sensory Channel 62
THE SOUND DO

The first of the syllables is the sound DO, formerly called UT but changed in the 1600s, and refers to the tone C.

The sound DO relates to the color Red-Violet. All those energies that vibrate within that spectrum are connected and therefore, relate to one another and can be interchanged.

(See Sensory Channel #55, Red-Violet)

The sound DO and the Red-Violet band are considered in or on the edges of the infrared band. All individuals and crystals are seething with this energy. The patterns of Red-Violet energy and the sound DO can be used to detect the metabolism of energy within the system, which gives practitioners a hint of not only the past or present patterns of energy in the body, but also the future patterns.

Sensory Channel 63
THE SOUND RE

The second of the syllables RE refers to the tone D.

This particular sound, RE, relates to the color Red. All those energies and spectrums of activity that involve Red will also apply to the sound RE. (See Sensory Channel #56, Red)

The sound RE and the color Red govern the wavelengths and frequencies for those elements in the body that are necessary for tranquilization and relaxation, such as sodium and potassium.

This sound (and the color Red) is important for the intrinsic function of the light elements. These elements control the nervous system and nervous response reactions and are necessary to the overall balance of electrical function.

Sensory Channel 64
THE SOUND MI

The third of the syllables is the sound MI and refers to the tone E.

The sound MI relates to the color Orange. All those energies that vibrate within that spectrum are connected therein, and therefore relate to one another and can be interchanged. (See Sensory Channel #57, Orange)

The sound MI and the color Orange govern elements such as aluminum and

all elements in the radiational bands. Orange and the sound MI have a positive bent and are considered part of the wavebands that govern alkaline, earth-forming elements. This level is the energy that is the signifier of radiation.

Sensory Channel 65
THE SOUND FA

The fourth of the syllables is FA, and refers to the tone F.

The sound FA relates to the color Yellow. All those energies and spectrums of activity that involve Yellow will also apply to the sound FA. (See Sensory Channel #58, Yellow.)

The sound FA and the color Yellow are the designators of heavy metals. When we study the gradations of energy in this text, we immediately see the pattern of colors relating to the development of energies from radiation down to the heavy metals. Metals such as copper, zinc, manganese, iron, etc. are connected to this wave vibration FA or the tone F.

When trying to understand more about the human body, we see that many of these heavy metals are vital to the function of the human body. For example, if a person lacks the metal zinc, then he will have difficulty healing wounds and in controlling his metabolism. If someone lacks copper, he may have liver troubles and lack the ability to defend himself from the invasion of toxins, poisons, viruses and bacteria.

The sound FA and the heavy metals are connected to a very important process of perception in the body. The person studying this must realize that by gaining a perception of these particular metals, he not only understands their individual behavior but also the symptomatic patterns that these can create in the body when toxic or deficient. If we were ever able to control these particular levels, then it would be totally impossible for us to ever feel pain or sensation without our consent.

The programs and protocols that have been created to gain a better perception of these particular levels of metal function in the body are paramount in study. *The Promethion* was written primarily to study and express this particular phenomenon; when examined, the reader can better understand the high level of perception in this area.

Sensory Channel 66
THE SOUND SO (SOL)

The fifth of the syllables is SO (SOL) and refers to the tone G. The sound SO relates to the color Green. All those energies that vibrate within that spectrum are connected, and therefore relate to one another and can be interchanged. (See Sensory Channel #59, Green)

The sound SO and the color Green have the opposite effect of radiation in the system. The characteristic color Green, which is displayed on all foliage on the planet, is the response mechanism of crystals to the radiational flow of the sun. This is a basic mechanism, but also involves some specific elements, for example, the element phosphorus is part of this energy transition process.

In human beings, the element phosphorus controls our sense of reality and sanity. It keeps us connected with the actual exchange processes going on between the sun and the earth. If we can but coordinate this particular level, we would have sanity forever and ever. The proof of this, many times, is to take a person who is overwrought by conditions around him in his atmosphere, especially a city dweller, and take him out to the country for a day or two. Have him roam around the woods and after a while he begins to regain his sanity.

The relationship of the sound SO and the color Green is extremely important to the survival of mankind.

Sensory Channel 67
THE SOUND LA

The sixth of the syllables is LA, and the tone is A. The sound LA relates to the color Blue. All those energies and spectrums of activity that involve Blue will also apply to the sound LA. (See Sensory Channel #60, Blue)

The Blue area, as well as the sound LA, is a cleansing level. The sound LA and the color Blue have affinity with elements such as sulfur, and also the specific mono-valent negatively-charged elements fluorine, chlorine, and bromine, which are well-known cleansers.

Those who are familiar with these elements realizes that sulfur is contained in many of the protein matrices of the body. It is an intrinsic part of the nature of the human because it is connected to the hair, nails, and many of the proteins that actually form the shape of the person. It is part of the electromagnetic and electroplasmic haze that surrounds the person's aura and gives him a feeling of wholesomeness.

Hot sulfur springs have been meccas of healing since the earliest of times.

If we begin to lose our perception for the sound LA or the color Blue, or if there is a deficiency and toxicity of elements that are involved with this particular range of electric equilibrium, we will find our self becoming dirty and unkempt. We may feel we are loaded with errant electric charge and may become a magnet for additional poisons surrounding us.

Sensory Channel 68
THE SOUND TI

The seventh of the syllables is TI, and refers to the tone B. For centuries, this sound was called SI but changed in the 1800s by music educator, Sarah Glover of England, to TI.

The sound TI relates to the color Blue-Violet. All those energies that vibrate within that spectrum are connected, and therefore relate to one another and can be interchanged. (See Sensory Channel #61, Blue-Violet).

The halogens and areas beyond the light spectrum are included in this level. It is the perception of this energy, the sound TI and the color Blue-Violet that gives us the ability to "see" bacteria, fungus, and other subcreatures that have taken energy from the environment and exist on a lower level.

In humankind, the observation of the sound TI and the Blue-Violet level, as well as the level of electric pressure that is near that band, is intrinsic for survival because it is an indicator of those areas that have been infiltrated by toxins, poisons, worms, parasites, warts, moles and all of the degraded processes of the cells and tissues, known and unknown.

Sensory Channel 69
ELECTRICITY KNOWN
(Concept Understanding)

Early crystalline structures had to develop an ability to perceive energies and to understand their existences, and whether or not they were friend or foe. Understanding in itself is a survival activity, and the mechanism of understanding is extremely important. Created step-by-step by the crystalline structures, it is a mechanism that can be stored.

This is not to infer that the spirit source does not have the ability to understand and must rely on crystals for understanding. The spirit has its own power to understand or perceive environmental situations, but the crystalline structures that were granted automaticity developed their own understanding capabilities.

The development of understanding is an extremely important process; understanding is the ability that separates the intelligent individual from the misinformed. The early crystalline structures developed the process of being able to definitively describe the entire package of information necessary for complete understanding, which is a six-part mechanism. To visualize this process more easily, a hexagram, a benzene ring with six sides is used. This shape is also the Seal of Solomon—Star of David, two pyramids within it (outlined with dotted lines).

At the top left is the word "where"; for complete understanding, it is important to know <u>where</u> something happens.

Top right corner is "when"; a crystal needed to know in what sequence (<u>when</u>) this action occurred, the

(left) Six-sided benzene ring, a hexagram. Illustration of complete understanding: **Electricity Known.**

When we finally and fully understand something, the energy, the electricity flows in, we light up!

chronological order of events.

In the lower left, "who" will define and explain the perpetrator of any activity; it is the perpetrator who houses a bank of information that coerces him to behave the way he does.

On the lower right is the "what." This is the exact diagram or blueprint of the motions or energies that were employed to perpetrate the action. We can easily understand what something is from observing its outline and form.

At the uppermost point is "why" and at the lowest point we find "how". These two descriptors encompass the overall picture of understanding. If an individual knows how and why something occurred, then he can fully understand it, but to know how and why, he must know the where, the when, the who, and the what.

Sensory Channel 70
ELECTRICITY UNKNOWN
(Concept Misunderstanding)

The primal structures of crystals, which existed on planet Earth in the beginning, needed to develop the perception of being able to see whether or not a moment or a circumstance was understood. As was previously described in Sensory Channel #69, the process of understanding is quite definite. It involves the intricate workings of the process of who, what, where and when perpetrated this particular scenario. How and why complete the total understanding of this structure.

To cause misunderstanding then, we would simply leave out any ONE of these factors. It was the early crystalline structures that programmed in that unique innate perception of knowing and sensing when one of these mechanisms and descriptors was missing.

The crystals themselves, as the basic memory traces that exist in all humankind, allow an individual to perceive the uncomfortable feeling, the darkness and the dreariness, the lowered awareness and lack of energy, which is a part of the signal of "misunderstanding". When an individual misunderstands, he means that he "does not get the picture"; he is in the dark. When understanding floods in, pictures and images turn on in the person's mind and he has encapsulated the scenario into a bubble he can easily read.

The processes and programs that are necessary to release the barriers to understanding involve the application of the science of understanding. If we want to be completely informed on the subject, we must study the four corners of that double pyramid (who, what, where when) and we will ultimately have our how and why for any subject.

Sensory Channel 71
MAGNETIC SITUATIONS
KNOWN (Crystalline Matter)

It is enough to understand a moment in time to get along in life, but the primordial energy factors, which ultimately developed into crystalline structures bent on survival, needed to have a greater capability of recognition. Instead of understanding bits and pieces of ideas, they needed to develop the ability to discern whole situations at once, in relaxed states, and be able to act upon this information to guarantee survival.

When we observe a mass or an object, our perception of this item or condition relays back to similar information in our mind so that we can compare the two and come up with an answer. This association process is different from definitive understanding. The association process can be confusing but ultimately is the same process that allows us to persist in the environment without having to get overly involved with every object that comes down the pike.

For example, if we wanted to survive well around certain objects, we would not necessarily need to know the total who, what, where and when of these particular objects. We would merely reflect the object back to a similar form in our mind bank, compare it with our other information, and then make the decision as to whether or not this object was dangerous.

For illustration purposes, let's say a person is running along a highway and happens to observe a truck moving toward him. He does not necessarily know who is driving the truck or where it's going; he is more connected with the understanding of what it is and when it will be closer. He does not know exactly how this object was created. He views the truck, compares it with other forms in his memory banks to ascertain whether or not this mass of metal, steel and rubber tires is dangerous or safe. The mechanisms that allow him to proceed without fear that this object will encroach upon his space are the experience banks of understanding that have been logged by crystalline structures over the years.

The runner recognizes this object. He knows it is a truck; he knows what it is for. Some pieces of information are missing (but in an understanding of this situation would not be a detriment).

In other words, an individual can exist quite easily without full understanding. However, it would be more to his liking to have complete control and perception of all objects around him, to be certain that they cannot harm him.

Sensory Channel 72
MAGNETIC SITUATIONS UNKNOWN
(Crystal-Matter, Pressure and Space, Reality)

Following the association process defined in Channel #71 for Known Magnetic Situations, if the magnetic situation is unknown, this causes the confusion or darkness of information connected to the human mind. If a person cannot find a mental template for something that is in the environment, then he must get the closest one that fits, so that he does not feel he is losing touch with reality.

This may be the perception point that requires the most work for human beings, because we can be so easily fooled. By presenting an object that looks similar to something that is in the mind banks, hu-

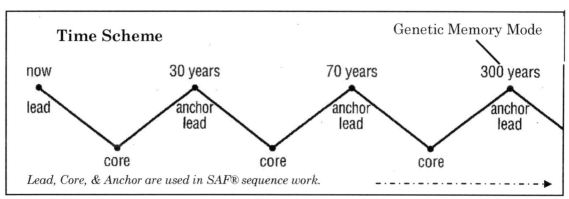

Lead, Core, & Anchor are used in SAF® sequence work.

mans are easily led astray and may behave in very erratic patterns.

For example, if a person who wore horn-rimmed glasses had harmed us in some way, then each time we see someone wearing horn-rimmed glasses, or even an object that vaguely resembles horn-rimmed glasses, we may automatically assume or associate that these two objects (people) are identical and we expect harm to befall us.

If unknown items *seem* identical to something in the mind bank, then our protective mechanisms, that is, the energies within our autoimmune system for body, mind and spirit, will thrust us into a protective stance, even if it is unnecessary.

Sensory Channel 73
SENSE OF SEQUENCE— TIME

Early crystalline structures needed to have the expression of a moment-to-moment catalog or record so that they could perceive sequences of events. This is the part of the human being that understands that traversing or traveling through time is just like unlocking so many doors and crossing a few thresholds in succession. We cannot unlock the door of our apartment if we have not first passed through the main gate. This particular sequence is necessary to accomplish the final goal: to get inside our apartment.

When we lose our ability to sense sequences, we are apt to make many kinds of mistakes. Common examples would be locking the car doors, then seeing our keys dangling in the ignition, or we put the car in drive mode to move forward, and we haven't turned on the engine. In different scenarios, if a surgeon mistakenly leaves instruments or sponges in the abdomen of his surgical patient and proceeds with the sutures, or a pilot attempts to fly an airplane with the wings still firmly tied down on the tarmac.

In Ode to the West Wind, by Percy Bysshe Shelley, we see a time sequence of the seasons.

"O Wind,
If Winter comes,
can Spring be far behind?"

These are minor examples compared to working in sequences for time-track

(left and below) **Time Scheme** *gives an example of the time and sequence work that is possible with SAF® chain work. Although written in linear fashion, the sequence of numbers is three dimensional and alive with energy.*

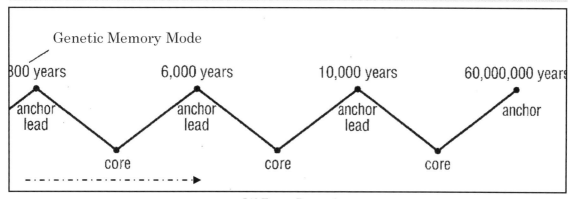

Genetic Memory Mode

| 300 years | 6,000 years | 10,000 years | 60,000,000 years |

anchor lead   core   anchor lead   core   anchor lead   core   anchor

memory events. An understanding of sequence will greatly help us when deciphering time sequences in our memories and past events.

What happened first?

The fact of the matter is that perception of time and sequence of events is essential for existence.

It is important to note that time (as we think of it) is not linear. We live in a time continuum; time repeats, our patterns repeat! This is reflected in the SAF® chain, which is both linear and a circular helix.

When viewing our situation in terms of emotions, as with the SAF® process, we can learn and understand how to follow our patterns through time in order to achieve resolution. (see *SAF Simplified*.)

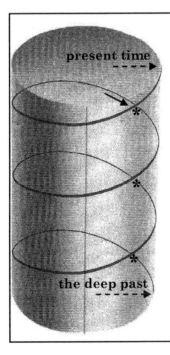

The SAF® sequence of numbers forms a circular cylinder through time. The present time bends to meet the past (*), where it connects to an earlier sequence (*), then to an even earlier one (*), and thus forms a circular helix.

Sensory Channel 74
ENDOCRINE SENSE CHANNELS (Emotions)

This sensory channel was developed by early crystalline structures to warn themselves of overloads of particular activities against them. It is here that the perceptibility tracks and channels of sensation are at their greatest height.

The development of the Self Awareness Formulas (SAF®) has come directly from this particular phenomenon of crystalline structures. The Endocrine Sense Channels chart is the language of SAF®.

The activities of a crystal in its own survival pattern mirror all the activities of humankind. This has already been proved. However, the sequence of activity and the promotion of energy around the system form a definite structure.

By observing the structure, the student can see that his energies may be in jeopardy if he overloads one of the functions. For example, if we overload the function of eating, digestion, and absorption, we may become fat and overweight, and this phenomenon clogs all the other channels of the body so as to prevent or hinder the functions of running and operating the body smoothly.

The human being possesses twelve pairs of cranial nerves emanating from the brain stem and cortical areas in order to regulate information flowing toward the structure of the body. We have developed a sense perception line for all of these functions and primarily have divided them up into categories so that we can provide ourselves with the mechanisms of survival.

The cranial nerves have allowed the development and further impingement of information from crystalline structures

Endocrine Sense Channels

(also known as The SAF® Operative Chart)

SAF #	Action	Condition	Organ/Gland	Emotion	LowEmotion	HighEmotion
1	Against	Protection	Thymus	Aggression	Reaction	Action
2	Run	Synchronize	Heart	Love	Deny	Accept
3	Contain	Detoxify	Colon	Hate	Failed	Achieve
4	Dissolve	Digestion	Stomach	Happy	Eaten	Assimilate
5	Direct	Coordinate	Anterior Pituitary	Observant	Controlled	Master
6	Keep	Transmutate	Liver	Sadness	Aged	Rejuvenate
7	Exchange	Vaporization	Lungs	Monotony	Stifled	Refresh
8	Attract	Reproduce	Sex organ	Apathy	Separated	Create
9	Hold	Locomotion	Bones/muscles	Pain	Blamed	Respond
10	Action	Metabolization	Thyroid	Anxiety	Criminal	Justice
11	Move	Circulation	Vein/arteries	Resentment	Gravity	Games
12	Time	Electricity	Brain/nervous system	Nervous	Complicated	Simplify
13	Pressure	Capacitance	Adrenal glands	Courage	Shame	Pride
14	Space	Analyze	Mind	Wonder	Unknown	Serenity
15	Result	Evaluation	Hypothalamus/Senses	Attention	Inhibited	Communicate
16	Refuse	Filtration	Kidneys/bladder	Fear	Poisoned	Purify
17/18	Coordinate	Equalize	Endocrine System	Conservative	Perverted	Balance
19	Push	Demarcate	Skin	Boredom	Lost	Win
20	Quality	Location	Pancreas/solar plexus	Laughter	Suppressed	Express
21	Quantity	Hydrolyze	Posterior Pituitary	Grief	Stuck	Free
22	Have	Experience	Parathyroid	Anger	Solid	Dissect
23	Do	Rejection	Spleen	Antagonize	Regret	Appreciate
24	Be	Accept	Lymph	Enthusiasm	Mystery	Understanding

(the genetic gene chips), which have been passed down through hundreds of millions of years. Both sensory and motor impulses are transmitted, in afferent and efferent mode.

The cranial nerves express energy from the mind via the brain to the organ systems in particular patterns. These patterns are part of the sensory channels being used by the various cataloged SAF® programs of the Life Energy System to help students of life search and discover energy from crystals and their relationship to human beings.

This channel #74, the endocrine sense channels, is a very important conduit, for it allows the individual to perceive when his body has become imbalanced in its activities. As we can see on the illustration of the Endocrine Sense Channels chart on the previous page, certain formats of activity in the body relate to formats of emotion. There are some basic actions and conditions that are necessary to be performed by the endocrine system, and these have a definite correlation to the emotional structure. If a person becomes jammed or inhibited on one of these channels, he may have a quirk in the ability to perform this level of activity.

Conversely, if there is too much energy flowing on one of these levels, he may have a hyper reaction and overload his system with that same condition or activity. The idea of jammed energy versus a flow of energy that is too fast is akin to the precepts of Chinese medicine and Asian protocols in meridian work.

The following perception channels 75-104 are extremely important to study, for these embody the system that is used by Life Energy Research and its SAF® (Self Awareness Formulas) programs for understanding of our system, and to make corrections in genetic functioning. These corrections are made with the basic premise that the body, mind and spirit are part of a very extensive and sophisticated computerized system. By approaching the human body as a computer, and using computers and computerized programs, students can hope to make the correct adjustments in his or her own system. And when we learn enough about the SAF® technique and method, we will be able to make various changes in the bodies and minds of other individuals as well.

Note: On Perception Channels 75-104, we find further information on the scope of the SAF® Computing system and how each of these sensing channels, each organ and gland system, relates to and augments the others and the composite whole that is the sentient human being.

Sensory Channel 75
THYMUS ACTIVITY

The early crystalline structures, in the next order of existence, produced a gland look-alike very similar to the operation of

References are made throughout this book to the SAF® sequence. By going to the website: www.LifeEnergyResearch.com, free questionnaires allow you to create your own SAF® chain of numbers. The numbers relate to specific organ and gland systems. Then, with chain in hand, the reader may compare with the Endocrine Sense Channels Chart (page 193), read about the numbers and meanings in the companion book, SAF Simplified, *or find an SAF® practitioner to work with on personal issues.*

the thymus gland. The crystal itself had an area and diagram of electric motion etched into it that eventually became the thymus gland. The reason why the thymus or the thymic pattern was developed first is because it is the primal order of protection and survival for the individual. The crystalline structures went through all forms of discovery to understand finally, at Level 75, that protection was the most necessary function of the body.

The earthly period of time that is most likened to this thymic expression is the Middle Cambrian, when crustaceans developed. Ages before this, it was deemed by crystalline structures that protection was essential; however, this came into full bloom with a tremendous increase in creatures in the Middle Cambrian, when large-scale action of survival allowed structures of a toothed-like nature to extrude from the surfaces of certain animals to protect them from marauding creatures that could easily devour them. Crustaceans, such as crabs and barnacles, are noted for their horned-like appendages, the better to ward off predators. Because the entire earth process involves eating and recycling of energy, the structures wanted to be preserved for as long as possible. Aggression is the emotion.

It is impossible for any mechanism to escape the ultimate—being devoured by another substance of greater energy—but the main purpose was to prolong existence for as long as possible.

The thymus in human beings has a similar protective function. Its radiational sensing and protection acts much like a horned-like structure of a crustacean, but as a sensor, it works on an invisible band to help the human being survive. In essence, it is an invisible shield. In newborn

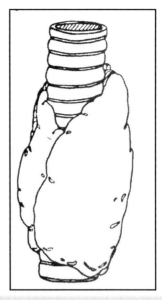

THYMUS (above) and immune system is part of a massive protective system, our first line of defense against invaders. This system includes the tonsils, appendix, Peyer's patches, and Protective Systems, Stages 1 to 3.

babies, the thymus gland is fairly large but with age and being bombarded daily by the electric pressures of pollution and toxicity its size, protective mode and effectiveness is greatly reduced.

In maintaining the balance of electric pressures, the thymus utilizes the electromagnetic power of the body to resist the infiltration of unwanted substances. Along with the thyroid, the thymus monitors the wavelength and frequency of the harmonic structure of the body and any dissimilar vibrations are dealt with rapidly. (See: Thymus and Defense Mechanism, page 240-241).

The SAF® program (which will be discussed throughout the endocrine portion on Channels 75-104) has designated the thymus as being first on the list of organs and glands that are besieged. Throughout man's history, infection, inflammation and toxicity, which are normally alerted and handled by the thymus gland or are part of its intrinsic pattern or diagram of operation, have been the scourge of humanity. All diseases that encroach on the human being can be considered in this first file. The SAF® programming, which has reduced all functions to a mathematical system, has designated the thymus with the number 1 and as such indicates the first place or the first activity to fall prey to environmental hindrances and attacks.

The actions and hindrances that are perpetrated after this first grouping against the individual will be less severe in the descending order.

The thymus attempts to shield human beings from the utmost degradation and the most fervent and insidious attacks. In all programs that are run in the SAF® procedures, whenever a number 1 appears, it indicates that the individual has the greatest amount of pressure on him that is possible.

Sensory Channel 76
TONSIL ACTIVITY

The tonsils are also a mechanism of protection. It may seem that there is an overabundance of attention being paid by the crystal to the idea and process of protection, but in the final analysis, existence for whatever reason needs to be sheltered and saved from outside intervention. Many times the individual will find, when doing programs to ameliorate or save himself from disease, that the disease itself has the capability to tap in on the effort and mechanism of crystals to survive in the body and uses this talent for itself. In other words, the disease entity has an ability to survive on its own, just as an

individual or a crystal would, and by tapping into the effort, the energy, some of the host's energy, is siphoned by the disease.

The tonsils, in SAF® programming, are considered to be in the same section as the thymus, number 1. In reality, the work of the tonsils is similar to that of the thymus; both help to control the actions of poisons and errant energies against the body. The tonsils can be considered a satellite operation, which exists in closer proximity to the thymus gland than the remaining divisions, the appendix and the Peyer's patches.

Sensory Channel 77
APPENDIX ACTIVITY

Long thought obsolete or of no value by many doctors and researchers, the appendix is, in reality, an extension of that same protective mechanism's diagram used by the thymus and the tonsils. The appendix is part of a crystalline reflex that indicates that all fronts should be protected. The tonsils are situated in the northernmost area, the thymus controls the center, the appendix is located in the southern arena, and the Peyer's patches, situated in the gastrointestinal tract, handle the east and west frontiers. These specific glands mentioned monitor the inner perimeter, while the outer perimeter is overseen by the lymph system. It is an extremely sophisticated protective system that has been developed over years and years of pressurization and interaction with the environment.

Protection is a major part of the game of life on this planet. We must have a sophisticated protective system, and when we study this and understand more about how the crystals protect themselves, we can align ourselves with that type of operation and will have a better sense of security and well being.

In SAF® programming, when the number 1 appears in the chain, the appendix would be included with the other alert and protection systems already mentioned.

Sensory Channel 78
PEYER'S PATCHES

Peyer's patches are groups of lymphoid tissue located in the ileum of the small intestine. As was mentioned in the previous channel #77, the Peyer's patches monitor the east and west or side-to-side defense. They control the inside defense at the same time the lymph system takes care of the outside defense.

The major understanding for the Peyer's patches is that early crystalline structures, in their effort to digest the energies of other structures, realized that care needed to be taken in what was swallowed. Protective mechanisms, which coordinate themselves in the body, will do well to keep all poisons filtered out.

Peyer's patches, in SAF programming, are also considered as being in the first line of defense, number 1.

Sensory Channel 79
PROTECTIVE SYSTEMS
(STAGE 1)

Again, the crystalline structures spent energies in protecting themselves. It seems that when developing any process, a good deal of time should be spent in the aspects of safety and protection. Through hundreds of millions of years, the crystalline structures have found it necessary, as a number one goal, to protect themselves

Cave drawing of crab and crab–like creatures. Protection in the way of spikes and an exoskeleton acts much like the human protective systems.

at all costs. Protection is the bottom line of all survival. With the right protective measures, one could conceivably exist forever, but with a careless and haphazard existence, a person is soon put out of his misery.

The protective system used in Sensory Channel #79, Stage One, developed the ability of the crystalline structures, and human beings as well, to be able to sense danger at a distance. In all forms of existence, human beings are capable of having an unlimited ability to perceive. Without limit. It is our own nature that causes us to limit our abilities to perceive our own survival. In an extreme example, those with psychic abilities can project a beam of understanding throughout the future and see the elements of nature coming into play that will cause a person's downfall or good fortune.

The activities of all human beings on this planet are focused very directly on

> *The entire earth process involves eating, being eaten, and the recycling of energy. The crystalline structures were prepared to be preserved for as long as possible through various levels of protection. Aggression is the emotion.*

the protective system of stage one. Humans constantly theorize and prognosticate for the future. Weather reports, stock exchange, business reports and constant speculation on whether or not an individual will do what he has promised to do are all part of the mechanisms that are related to this crystalline sense channel.

Sensory Channel 80
PROTECTIVE SYSTEM
(STAGE 2)

As a person puts his energies on the line, so to speak, he is primarily interested in protecting his body at all costs. The protective mechanisms involved in the endocrine system that will follow, are part of the chapter written into the sensory channels from 80 and above. The individual crystal has developed all forms of elaborate mechanisms to prevent itself from overheating (pressure) or losing too much energy (sensation).

Protective systems, Stages 1 and 2, are listed in SAF® programming as subsections of number 1. This means that the thymus, tonsils, appendix, Peyer's patches, and protective systems of the mind and body (Stages 1 and 2), are listed under the first category of the SAF® numbering system.

It is important in a study of symptomatology to understand this direct sequence of information; SAF® is a system by which we can break into these perception channels of crystalline structures and

read them with impunity. The endocrine sense channels *is* the language of SAF®: it is how we can understand what our body, mind and spirit are trying to tell us through symptoms; our pains and sensations are messages.

The readouts forthcoming from this project are tantamount to the answers for all life energy because they provide the ability to not only understand our system's messages, but also to deprogram and delete information that is detrimental to us and all human beings.

All of the poisons, Z reactions, and phenomena of automaticity that have been inherited through the crystalline structures can be accessed and addressed by using the SAF® system.

Sensory Channel 81
PROTECTIVE SYSTEMS
(STAGE 3)
(danger imminent)

The perception of extreme danger is important to the individual in situations that encourage the person to use not just discretion in behavior, but exemplary valor. Channel #81 is a perception of the true test of a person's ability to save himself from imminent disaster. While the other protective levels are more consistent monitors of energy throughout the day, this channel involves the level of energy that coordinates the actions and involvements of the individual with his environment on an imminent basis—right now!

Sensory Channel 82
HEART ACTIVITY
(love)

With the protective stages intact, early crystalline structures then moved

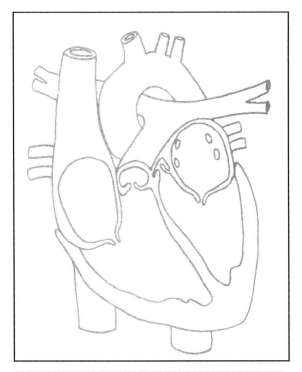

The HEART and cardiovascular system in SAF® work is the number 2.

other substance or entity that possesses similar energies, so that these energies can be shared and enjoyed.

In SAF® programming, love comprises group number 2. In all of the mathematical equations written about the endocrine system, the emotions, and the symptoms of an individual where the number 2 appears, the expression is concerned basically with troubles of the heart. This follows the complete gamut of energy from the mind and body to the spirit. It therefore involves not only the functionality of the heart and the ability of the heart rhythms to synchronize the activities of the whole physical body, but also the relationships from one human being to another, or one human to a beloved pet.

Love is involved as a synchronizing action in the schema of SAF®.

Sensory Channel 83
COLON ACTIVITY
(hate)

By following the crystalline structures and their formats, it is seen that the energy attempting to protect an individual had evolved into a form of affinity, which had magnetic, attractive powers. This affinity still pulls energies toward it so that similars will be near a similar form or entity, so that one crystal can be near another crystal of the same configuration, so that one atom can be near another atom of the same form, so that one molecule can be near a similar molecule and so that one human being can be near another human being who is like him.

As the forms of energy move throughout the crystal to aid the protection, and protection begins to split into pieces to make more definition to its protection, the

beyond the period of great need for protection, which then split into finer parts. The harmonics of protection split in the same way the color harmonics split up at Sensory Channel # 55.

In essence, the action of protection transmutates into a feeling of love. As a person consistently, overtly and covertly protects another individual, he changes, even obscures his sense of love. The question is, Is this love a form of protection? Or is it an intrinsic or innate love of affinity? Affinity is an attraction to or a like pulling towards a like. When a human needs some energy to exist, he necessarily protects it, and he can misconstrue this protective mode as a form of love.

In actuality, love is its own mechanism. It can either be an action of protection or an action that resembles any other level. It is simply the need to be near an-

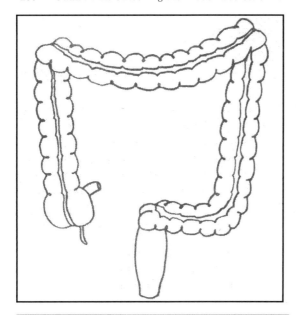

The COLON and elimination system are listed as number 3 in SAF®.

attractive affinity ratio moves into an energy of rejection, pushing out and away. Repelling another crystal, atom, molecule, or human being is part of a diagramed effect, which is intrinsic to the nature of all living things. The mechanisms of the environment must be able to select which materials they choose to be near. Without this ability, there would be no real meaning to the word love, for there would be no such thing as rejection. When one pulls another closer to him, he is in effect saying that he rejects all others.

In the SAF® programming and number system, the colon and elimination system comprises number 3. In effect, it is a brand new, different transmutation of the energies of protection. The individual is now protecting himself by rejecting energies away from him. That is, he protected himself by not loving someone. This feeling of hate or unlove involves pushing the energies out and away from him. The sequence 2-3 in SAF® is a love-hate relationship, once a strong bond.

Sensory Channel 84
STOMACH ACTIVITY
(assimilation)

As we move to this Sensory Channel #84, the stomach and digestive system, the changes that are made in the crystal are evident. At this channel, the crystal has learned to be selective about its energies, choosing those energies that it likes and pushing away those energies it dislikes. The stomach and digestive mode of all life energy forms in the environment is specific to the idea that the entity has a choice and can make a selection. The entire process of digestion is the ability of the body to select the nutrients that it desires and to absorb them and use them, while casting away the items it does not want. Those who have indigestion have definitely been exposed to some substance, or even a thought or concept, which it does not find palatable. The food, thought or concept is not digestible.

In the SAF® numbering system, the stomach holds position number 4. The protective mechanisms of the crystalline

The STOMACH and digestive system are number 4 in SAF® work.

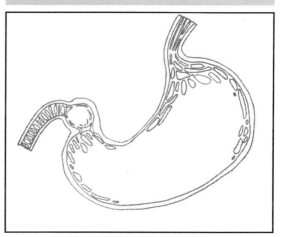

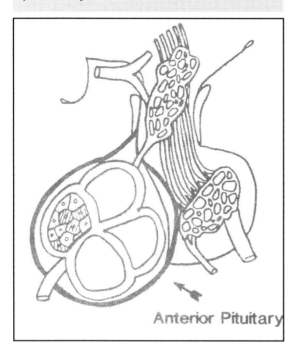

Anterior Pituitary

structures have now refined themselves even further. The two previous subsections of protection, love and hate, were on a very grand level, but the stomach is more refined and definitive in its ability to be able to evaluate and discern whether or not it chooses to accept something or reject it.

The symptoms examined on the SAF® programming involving the stomach and digestive system is directly assessing the ability of the individual to protect himself through this digestive organ and system. The stomach is a system of much upset for mankind because it involves an intrinsic process to the human mechanism. All human beings must be able to select the right pathways for themselves.

When we can do this, we are "happy", the emotion of the stomach and digestion.

Sensory Channel 85
SINUSES & ANTERIOR PITUITARY (gases vs. solids)

On a macro level, the crystals had to have the ability to perceive the density of matter and energy. This is one of the ways a crystal can discern whether or not other materials are compatible with its systems. An early warning mechanism was developed that correlates to the sinuses of a human being. This mechanism finds the correct density of material so that the crystal can align itself to it, rejecting materials that are too thick, too thin, too dense or too porous. As a structure it has the capability of observing the pH in chemistry, the acid/basic balance.

The sinuses and the related structures, the anterior pituitary, are associated with SAF® programming in position number 5. In all SAF® work where the number 5 appears, it indicates the sinuses and the anterior pituitary. Symptoms that the average human being expresses, such as common colds, sinus infections and drainages, uncoordination, dizziness, vertigo, etc. involve the inability to perceive or observe the proper pH in the system and will be relegated to number 5 on all programs.

Sensory Channel 86
LIVER & GALL BLADDER ACTIVITY (transmutation)

The next phase of protection necessary for a crystal was to be able to accept materials and energies given to it and then transform these into materials and energies that could be utilized by the crystal itself. This may be the first time that manufacturing came into being. The individual crystal took raw materials and con-

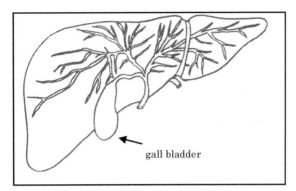

(above) The LIVER and GALL BLADDER are number 6 in SAF® work.

verted these into substances and subordinate particles, which could then again be remolded into products to help sustain its activities.

In the human life situation, the person finds himself encased in the necessary format of having to take objects in the environment and convert them into other particles of energy that can be reused. For example, a person works at a job because he'd like to have a nice car, but he must first get a paycheck and convert that money through a banking system into the necessary liquid assets, which will allow him to afford the machine of his dreams.

In SAF® programming, the liver is positioned as number 6. The gall bladder is included because the liver uses it to store necessary materials. If the gall bladder ceases to function, the liver will take on those duties.

Where the number 6 appears in the SAF chain sequence, the person has some involvement with liver upset and the ability or lack of ability to change things in the environment and keep them. People who are sad, depressed or morose are having a difficult time changing or transmutating something in the environment into what they'd like to see or have. If a person has a certain condition or unpleasant situation, if he wants to feel rejuvenated and yet feels hopeless about changing it, then number 6 is involved. The sequence 5-6 means plans and dreams are being thwarted.

Sensory Channel 87
LUNG ACTIVITY
(breathing)

The protective mechanisms of crystalline structures moved themselves into a new transitory period in which they aligned with a system for taking in energies and then, after exchanging the proper materials for use, released them. This process corresponds to the lungs and follows directly after the liver in that it, too, is part of the transmutation processes needed for protection.

The system protects itself because it has taken materials from the environ-

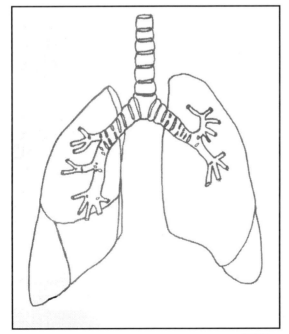

(left) The LUNGS, respiratory system and bronchi are listed in SAF® as number 7. Monotony is the emotion.

ment that are hazardous, and changed them into materials useful for the crystal itself. This is a primordial form of digestion. The individual needs to have these energies, but he must process them first before they are usable by his system. In other words, in the section that involves the stomach (Channel 84), the person merely took energies that he liked and discarded the ones that he didn't like. As we move through from the sinuses (#85), which is a collection and evaluation process, to the liver (#86), we find that the system is taking in more and more raw material for processing.

Reviewing the beginning phases of energy for the crystal, we find that in the phases of protection, the crystal was merely bent on keeping everything that wasn't his out of his area. Then, ultimately, this changed into a feeling of love or connection with certain items in the environment. After that, rejection occurred on a gross level via the colon. The next channel (stomach and digestion) showed that the crystal was able to pull in materials and make a more fine-tuned evaluation as to whether or not they were friend or foe. This idea is expanded at the 5th number with the sinuses and anterior pituitary. And then in the 6th group, a break occurs. The liver promotes the idea that it will take raw materials in and translate them into usable items. It may even have the idea that it could take everything in and fix it to suit.

As we reach the channel that is being studied now, the lungs, the individual crystalline program indicates that this exchange process, taking in raw materials and trading them for used-up energies, can be put into a full moment-to-moment reaction. The action of breathing is con-

sistent and effortless to the human being: it is monotonous; it is automatic.

In SAF® work, the number 7 is the designator for the lungs and respiratory system; and whenever it appears in an SAF® sequence of numbers, it indicates disturbances on that particular channel of exchange.

Sensory Channel 88
BRONCHI
(capturing breath and holding)

The trachea or windpipe splits into two forked branches, the bronchi; each leads to the lungs and are considered in SAF® programming to occupy the same group, number 7. The bronchi act as a sub-section to the lungs, and so will refer to many of the same symptomatic patterns that occur with Sensory Channel #87.

As a sense perception, this channel continues to define the role of the lungs by being the conduit for taking in vapors, holding these, and then releasing the spent materials. This track holds the promise of being able to refresh.

Sensory Channel 89
SEX ORGANS

This channel 89 is part of the perceptibility of crystalline structures that had now evolved to the point of being able to reproduce and propagate the species.

It is the intrinsic nature of energies on the planet to be able to join together and produce the object or the next generation of balance. In other words, the baseline action of crystalline structures and coincidentally, the genetic programming, which has been handed down to human beings throughout millions of years, has been to

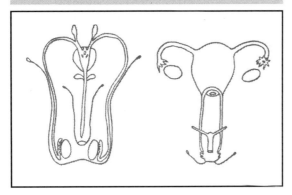

have energies in the environment come together and share their imbalances, in the hopes of creating balance. Finding balance is the nature of this universe

It is the abundance of one (male, positive) and the absence or lack of energy of another (female, negative) that attempts to resolve itself. It seems that this equation can never be completely resolved and thus, what is created is the progeny that contains an even greater balance.

The fault in the system many times comes about from matching the wrong terminals. If by some quirk of nature, two individuals get together who do not belong together, in other words, the balance of their energies is not a match, and yet they produce offspring, then the product of this union will not be able to afford greater balance for them. But if two right parties meet each other and share imbalances, so that there *is* balance, then the subsequent result would be creating a new human being with greater capabilities. These examples present the two di-

rections offered on this planet: chaos and cosmos, as exemplified by the above situations.

In SAF® programming, the number 8 signifies the sex organs and creation. It is considered the eighth form of transmutation of protection. The protective structures supporting an individual in the eighth group of SAF® programming are the efforts on the part of two individuals to survive through their children. Having children is a form of protection. By producing offspring, a family bond is produced, a bond of balance. A family can maintain its connection with creations and with location, as well.

Sensory Channel 90
BONES AND MUSCLES
(experience stored as crystals vs. activity limitations)

Early crystalline structures were directly concerned with the maintenance of their overall structure, and the forms and structure of each particular crystal insured its own protection. It was much easier for crystals to discern whether or not they belonged to other crystal families by their forms alone. Thus was created a most infinite array of shapes and sizes

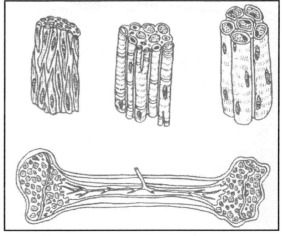

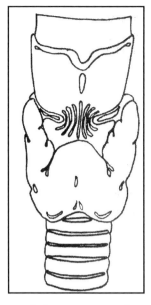

(left)

THYROID is assigned as number 10 in SAF® work. The emotion is anxiety.

and forms, even though the baseline material used for the entire universe is similar.

In SAF® programming, the number 9 represents the bones and muscles. It also indicates traumas, pain and upset involving the physical structure, and movement of the human being, but relates to rigidity of thought processes as well. The person may hold onto thoughts, ideas and emotions, storing in their bones and muscles, long past the time these could be released.

Sensory Channel 91
THYROID
(carbon-nitrogen monitor)

The crystal structures transmutated or changed an even more highly finetuned sense of protection by being able to detect the presence of forms of energy that were growing and forms of energy that were in decay.

The sense awareness to stay away from poisonous or noxious energies evolved from the experience of hundreds of millions of years of crystals working their processes and their diagrams, fol-

lowing their plans and programs to be able to detect poisonous structures around them. Poison, to a crystal, is something either too dense or without enough energy in it to support the crystal's life. And so, this particular function came from the ability of the self-protection mechanisms of the crystal to perceive solids and vapors.

In SAF® programming, the number 10 signifies the thyroid gland and veins and arteries of the upper extremities. The metabolization of energies in the body is the sorting out of pressures that are either too great or too weak for the individual to sustain himself. If a person has trouble on this sensory level, he may experience dizziness, vertigo, anxiety and other upsets directly related to the malfunction of the thyroid.

Sensory Channel 92
BLOOD VESSELS
VEINS & ARTERIES
(fear vs. courage, Phase 1)

The crystalline structures of long ago had the ability programmed into them to decide on a course of action that would protect their survival.

The energies surrounding crystals were constantly encroaching on their spaces in the hopes of absorbing their energies to use for their *own* systems. Because of all this encroaching, a program was created that would give the cells and crystals a way of being able to decide whether to stand and fight, or cut their losses and run, *move* out of the way.

The overall relationship of this system of protection is a direct descent of thyroid activity. It is the induction of poisons in the system that ignites the program that causes the crystal to perform the way it

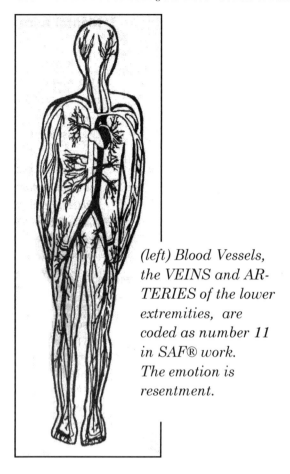

(left) Blood Vessels, the VEINS and ARTERIES of the lower extremities, are coded as number 11 in SAF® work. The emotion is resentment.

When we analyze information, we simply break down a large problem into many smaller ones in order to make it simpler. This analyzing of data causes us to take pieces from a large and complicated mass and reassemble them into a more palatable unity to fit into our own program so that we can make a decision whether or not to act, or to relax and wait. Much of the activity is on a stimulus-response mechanism, a knee-jerk reaction, via the nerves and nervous system.

In SAF® programming, the brain and nervous system is in position number 12; it is the twelfth stage of protective transformation. This brain activity acts as a protective mechanism for the body because it can evaluate information and make decisions as to whether or not the person should act upon certain situations or leave them alone.

does.

In SAF® programming, the blood vessels, in particular the veins and arteries of the lower extremities, are coded as number 11. The emotion is resentment.

Sensory Channel 93
BRAIN & NERVOUS SYSTEM
(fear vs. courage, Phase 2)

Structures that had the innate intelligence to make a decision whether or not to attack or retreat ultimately relegated this task to an even higher form of evaluation. The brain is the analyzer of the human being, and yes, on Channel 93 a researcher will find the crystalline chips that were the early programs that directed analyzation capability.

(below) The BRAIN and NERVOUS SYSTEM are in position number 12 in SAF® work. Information is evaluated and decisions are made on a stimulus response manner. Electricity makes it happen; nervous is the emotion.

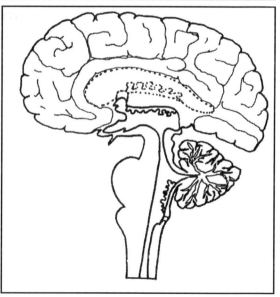

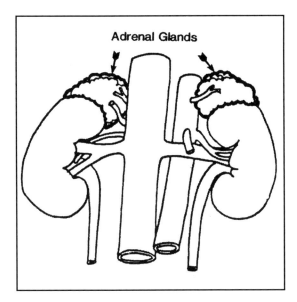

Adrenal Glands

Sensory Channel 94
ADRENAL
(fear vs. courage, Phase 3)

Perhaps the apex of the dichotomy of fear and courage comes at the point where the adrenals formed. The early crystalline structures had a program etched into them that resembled the electric configuration of the adrenal glands. This program was simply a relegated automaticity by the brain to decide for the body when it was time to fight or run.

Found at the 13th number in SAF® programming, the adrenals hold their position. It is a magic number that means something to everyone because it is the point where we have decided to hand over our protective mechanisms and our survival to automaticity.

The adrenal glands are considered a Z reaction terminal. Here is a subsection of activity for the human being and similar life forms as well, to relax and allow the adrenal glands to handle all of the pressures and stresses. It is the point where crystals and all life energy forms have evolved so that they do not need the input of having an entity with full attention on

(left) The ADRENAL glands, number 13 in SAF®, are a Z Reaction, on alert to dangers and pressures so we don't have to be to focused. The emotion is courage.

the processes of survival and protection.

In other words, throughout this entire process thus far, the entity had been completely confounded and absorbed by the process of protection, and if we look at this in light of SAF® programming, we can see a more subtle effect is occurring in the system. If we present numbers in an SAF® chain sequence that are low, such as 1, 2, 3 or 4, it means our attention is focused squarely on the problem of survival. Most of our units of analytical power and energy are tied up in the problem of survival. We cannot focus on pleasure or happy endings because we are very much worried and concerned about some issue or problem with the body or mind, which is causing us fear.

As we move up to the higher grades of protection (the numbers above 13), we find greater solace. We are able to let go somewhat so the automatic mechanisms of protection can decide to fight or take flight, to stand with courage or attack. We are able to relinquish our focused attention and relax.

It is interesting to note that in SAF® work, if 12 (the brain) and 13 (the adrenals) appear in succession in a chain sequence (written as 12-13), it indicates a state of insomnia; the person has relegated his ideas of protection to his brain and adrenal glands, and it is keeping him up at night.

Other interesting organ and gland combination is 13-20, depression, loss of possessions or location, hypoglycemia.

13-17/18-20-24: trapped somewhere in time.

(above) The MIND is found as number 14 in SAF®. When it appears in a chain it indicates there are some aberrant thought processes; worry, wonder.

Sensory Channel 95
MIND
(learning cognitive processes)

At Sensory Channel 95 for crystal perceptions, there is the development of a cognitive process. This is a form of primordial analyzation that allowed the crystal to take successive views of energy and make predictions. Not only could the crystal predict, but it could also construct mental machinery that could act as a servomechanism and make automatic supposition. A fully constructed mind is able to coordinate its energies and activities toward the end purpose of being able to protect itself on all fronts.

Here is the primordial program to reason its way out of pain. Sensory Channel 95 is the inherited mind for humankind.

With SAF® programming, the mind is represented by number 14. Whenever 14 appears in the chain, it indicates some issue or change with the mind; there is a deviation or wandering from the natural course. There is a definite situation occurring that causes the attention to be affixed to problems and unknowns of survival. However, by looking at the overall process, transmutation of the existing state of crystals and all life forms, up to the most complex and most intelligent human being, requires that they all have some automatic servomechanism (a mind) to make decisions for them on the simple equations of daily survival.

Sensory Channel 96
SENSES & HYPOTHALAMUS
(mouth, eyes, ears, nose, throat, skin, teeth, etc.)

The earliest crystalline forms developed programs that could give them the sense perceptions that were necessary to

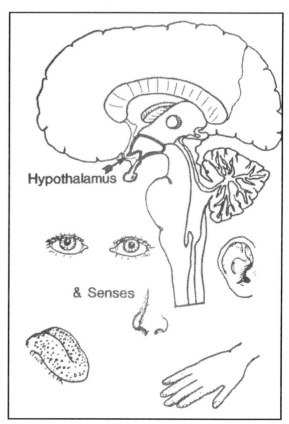

aid their survival. Many of the perception tracks that are concerned with and focused on sensing for the crystal are designated primarily to specific areas of the body. It is probably the most profound statement to say that all 128 sensory channels are sense perception levels of one sort or another across the entire range of the electromagnetic spectrum. The fact is, on Sensory Channel #96, the individual crystal develops the capability to fine-tune its senses and attention, focusing them where it wants.

Humans have this ability, but have greatly abused it. Their attention is scattered, their thoughts dispersed. In SAF® programming, the number 15 represents the senses and the hypothalamus. Whenever number 15 appears in a chain or program utilizing SAF® technology, there is cause to be alarmed about the ability of the person to perceive correctly.

In many SAF® scans and sequences found throughout the country, the number 15 appears quite frequently. At the present time, there are a great many perception distortions. There are excesses of radiation, stress and radiant energies moving in; we are being barraged day and night with errant frequencies that overload our ability to discern their invisible source, the cause of our distress. Some examples are satellite transmissions, microwave towers, computers and all the electrical gadgets—a cacophony of electrical input— so much so that we exhibit sensory overload; there is too much coming in and it can't be evaluated properly.

(left) The SENSES and the HYPO-THALAMUS are in position number 15 in SAF® chain work. The emotion is attention, which may be fixated, inhibited.

(below) The KIDNEYS are designated as number 16 in SAF® work. The kidneys filter out what is not needed; the emotional component is fear.

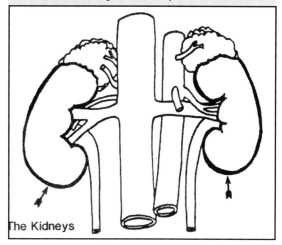

The Kidneys

Sensory Channel 97
KIDNEYS
(perception of poison)

This sense perception channel of the crystalline structures circuit is a mechanism directly connected to the processes of protection for crystalline structures, in that it involves the ability of the system to filter its own wastes. For the first time in the process of protection, the crystalline structure has decided there are certain parts of the program that do not gel with the rest. This is the point where the crystal, or any life form, decides that these non-gelling particles, considered to be poisons, need to be filtered out, erased, removed, or exchanged with something else.

In SAF® programming the kidneys are positioned as number 16. All those problems that involve the kidneys will cause 16 to appear in chains, whether created with symptom surveys and evaluations, such as the SAF® questionnaires, or infrared devices.

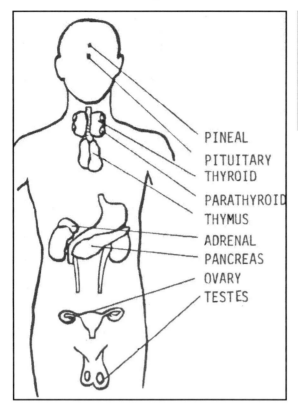

PINEAL
PITUITARY
THYROID
PARATHYROID
THYMUS
ADRENAL
PANCREAS
OVARY
TESTES

Sensory Channel 98
MALE — FEMALE
(hormone balances)

An extremely important part of all these perceptions is the connection of hormone substances in the system, acid and basic (acid-alkaline), which behave much like male and female principles and induces the bias or action of crystals, life energy forms and humankind to behave in ways that are, and have been, patterned throughout existence.

Along with the acid and alkaline scale, we find these principles echoed in various philosophies: yang and yin, pressure and space, mass and energy, positive and negative, magnetic and electric; these are all concepts in which we can find balance.

Hormones are continually being researched and studied by scientists; in the past hormones were thought to be only

(left) The MALE and FEMALE systems, (hormone or endocrine), is number 17/18, with conservative as the emotion.

Hormone is from the Greek: hormaein, *meaning "to excite, to set in motion, to spur on".*

secreted by the endocrine system of glands but research shows these to be circulating in the blood stream targeted toward specific organs and functions.

While certain behaviors of an individual have been handed down to him through his species, the program for the coordination of hormonal balance is a crystalline activity. The hormones themselves, which carry the male and female principles, are crystals. These crystals are floating in the bloodstream of human beings and coercing the certain urges and instincts.

The endocrine system (pineal, pituitary, thyroid, parathyroid, thymus, adrenal, pancreas, ovaries (F) and testes (M) is considered the hormone system and so this position is quite important; it is viewed as the power train.

The designator number in the SAF® program catalog for endocrine system and hormone balance is number 17/18. These two numbers are always used simultaneously to indicate the male and female balance that is involved; number 17 indicates the male and number 18 for the female of the species.

Sensory Channel 99
SKIN
(defense protection)

At the 99th sensory perception channel, the idea of protection becomes solidified. The borderline mass of energies demarcates territories between particular forms of energy, be they crystals, vegetation, animals or human beings. The skin is the largest organ in the system.

The SAF® lineup of organ and gland systems has designated the number 19 as the skin. Marking its territory, its boundaries, it is a solid form of protection. "He, she or it got under my skin" might be expressed.

The skin is the reflexive reaction of the thymus activities in the first stage of protection. While the thymus (1) is the electronic phase of protection, that invisible idea of protection, the skin (19) is the actual solid mass protector. It encases the human body, forms the boundaries; this defines the border integrity.

In addition to the usual and visible manifestations on the skin itself, when the number 19 appears in an SAF® chain of numbers, it indicates a boundary violation has occurred. When seen in combination with other organ and gland systems, this indicates the extent of the violation.

(below) The SKIN is designated as number 19 in SAF®. Boredom is the emotion, from bor, auger *(old English) to make a hole and to weary by being dull.*

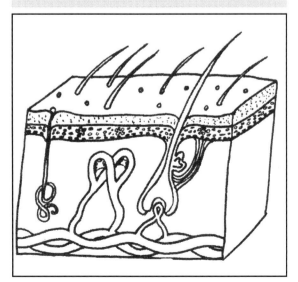

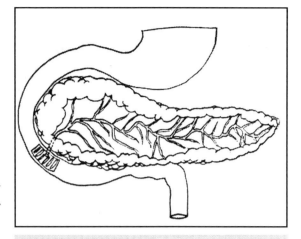

The PANCREAS and SOLAR PLEXUS are in position number 20 with SAF®.

Sensory Channel 100
SOLAR PLEXUS & PANCREAS
(yawn vs. laugh response, location)

This sensory channel is the area of a crystal's programming that controls the efforts of the mechanism to stay awake and conscious. It can almost be likened to a happiness circuit. The more something is happening, the more the individual is awake. The more something is not happening, the more he is unawake.

We can juxtapose these concepts to the idea that if an individual is doing something that he does not wish to participate in, if he is feeling suppressed or under a lot of pressure, he will become tired, lethargic and begin to yawn. On the other hand, if the person is participating in an event that he fervently believes in and takes great pleasure in being active with it, then he will be happy and able to express himself. He may be seen to laugh — not a mere twitter of a giggle, but a deep laugh from the belly; he responds in a favorable fashion.

Happy and happening come to our language from the same root word hap, *Middle English for occurrence. We are happy when we are making something happen, when we are doing something productive.*

In SAF® programming, the number 20 represents the solar plexus and the pancreas. Whenever this number appears in a sequence as a result of an evaluation, it indicates that there is some disturbance inhibiting the electrical function of the lower half of the body. It also indicates that the center of gravity for the whole human being, the location aspects (the solar plexus) may be out of balance, often caused by disturbances involving the endocrine system and its relationship with the mind.

Sensory Channel 101
H₂O & POSTERIOR PITUITARY
(perception of comfort—rest)

The crystalline structures wrote programs that directed energy to perceive possibilities of overload. By manipulating the quantity of conductant around the crystal, the entity could protect itself from harm.

In SAF® programming, the number 21 is representative of water (H_2O) and also the posterior pituitary, which controls the water and fluid balance in the body.

If an individual presents number 21 in his chain sequence, it indicates that he may have developed some disturbances in the conductive mechanism of electricity in the body, causing the water balance to go off center. An excess of fluid buildup may be expressed as tears, which releases the

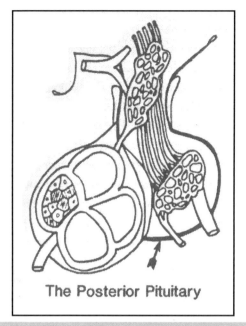

The Posterior Pituitary

(above) POSTERIOR PITUITARY, which controls the water and fluid balance of the body, has been assigned the number 21. The emotion is grief (tears).

fluid as it balances the electric charges.

The ability to perceive comfort and rest is derived from this particular crystalline program, Sensory Channel 101, to perceive the presence of excess or deficient electric charge in the system.

Sensory Channel 102
CALCIUM & PARATHYROID
(perception of reward for activity)

Millions of years ago, crystalline structures developed processes, diagrams, plans and programs to actually precipitate mass and energy to build monuments, or representative masses, of their particular patterns of energy. It is a fact that when experience hits any life energy form, metals begin to precipitate, matter becomes more solid.

Experience comes in the form of electric charge.

Human beings precipitate calcium when they have experience. This is evidenced by the fact that newborn babies have very little calcium in their bodies and as they proceed through life they begin to form more and more calcium (their bones grow and thicken) by way of their experiences with the environment. The body mass increases; they become more solid.

In SAF® programming, calcium balances, regulated by the parathyroid glands are designated number 22. The number 22 governs the perception level of reward for activity. Whenever the number 22 appears in a chain sequence emitted by

(below) In SAF® work, the number 22 has been given to the PARATHYROID, four small glands that regulate the calcium levels in the body.

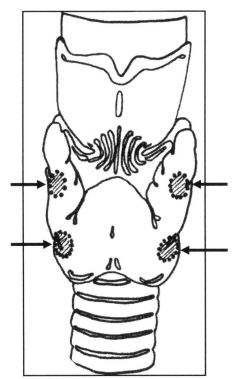

(below) The SPLEEN is found as number 23 in SAF® work. It is an organ that protects the interior of the system and goes into action when invaders have breached the boundaries.

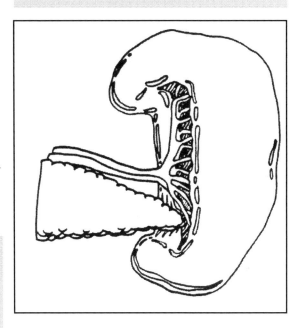

computer driven processes and evaluations, it points to the fact there is some upset or imbalance on this particular level. The emotion is anger.

Sensory Channel 103
SPLEEN
(perception of invasion reflex)

Up until this point, the entity or the crystalline substance needed to create programs to stop the encroachment of poisons within its boundary lines. It has been indicated that the skin (Channel 99) appears in the SAF® line-up of organ and gland systems as number 19. This intimates that the crystalline structure did most of the battling against poisons for protection within its own perimeters. After all the programs had been decidedly and correctly launched, crystals would

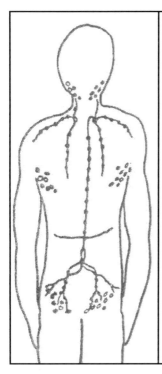

(left) The LYMPH SYSTEM is found in the SAF® numbering system as 24.
The emotion is enthusiasm, and is sometimes seen with addictions & quick fixes.
The word comes to us from Latin and Greek, en-theos, enthous, *inspired, possessed.*

have written programs so that they could protect themselves on the inside from any future invasions of unwanted particles. This is the realm of perception channel 103, the spleen.

In SAF® programming, number 23 represents the spleen, an organ that is closely connected to bodily protection. It is comprised of lymphoid tissue with duties to reject, engulf and dispose of allergens and other unwanted substances and frequencies that have managed to get inside the structure and antagonize it.

Whenever number 23 appears on an SAF® program or in a chain sequence, the spleen will be indicated as being out of balance, and in need of assistance.

Sensory Channel 104
LYMPHATIC SYSTEM
(perception of environmental attack against the individual)

Sensory Channel 104 is the lymphatic channel, whose purpose on a physical level is to filter toxins and other unwanted frequencies from the blood and other systems. The lymph system is part of the overall mechanism of protection that the crystals had programmed hundreds of millions of years before. The crystals handed down these programs to human beings and these particular programs are written for networks and communities of cells. After all of the protections that the crystal has written into itself, no one crystal needs to defend itself from the environment, but for the massive coordination of hundreds of trillions of cells, such as we have in an individual human body, it is important that a program exists somewhere in the DNA-RNA molecule to protect it from outside interference. The environmental attacks continue, unseen visually, but sensed nonetheless.

In SAF® programming, the number 24 represents the lymphatic channel.

Sensory Channel 105
ELECTROMAGNETIC
PERCEPTION
(magnetic-electric & electric-magnetic)

The early cells, spurred on by crystalline diagrams and programs, gained a perception for electric and magnetic vibration. The primary purpose for this ability was the need to know whether particles were conglomerating (building up) or fragmenting (breaking down). It is the difference between solidity and separation. This is extremely important to any primordial entity in that it is a direct precursor of procreation and survival.

Electromagnetic perception follows the bank of protective phases labeled

SAF® and the endocrine sense channels (Tracks 34-104). It is at this particular channel, #105, that the entity gains the ability to perceive creation and destruction. The positivity and negativity of a situation depends upon its growth potential versus its inevitable decay.

The perception of electromagnetic waves also gives the primordial crystalline structure the ability to choose a wavelength of operation. Therefore, there will be entities and energies that assume positions along the electromagnetic spectrum and operate in the electric bands, the radio waves, microwave areas, and infrared zones. It means that their influences can be picked up at these frequencies.

The magnetic-electric and electric-magnetic waves expand and contract and undulate in wavy constant movement, north, south, east, west, paramagnetic (attracted to a magnetic field) and diamagnetic (repelled by a magnetic field). This energy is the aura of the human and is used by the body on a physical plane.

The electromagnetic perception becomes an extremely important process. It is the area of life and living that gives an intelligent being the ability to discern whether or not circumstances will be harmful or beneficial. It is that sixth sense that we develop that intuitively sig-

Electromagnetic perception is the ability to discern electric and magnetic vibrations and whether these are conglomerating or fragmenting. This is the aura of the human; all living life forms in this planetary system have it.

Some people have an innate ability to see auras, but we all can be taught this art.

Beautiful computer generated images for the electromagnetic field abound; these show the field and the flow, complete with colors, but keep in mind it is not a static field but moving and energized.

The flow and the colors will appear characteristically different for each person because we each have our own lifetime situations, conflicting metals and elements, and emotional issues in the RAM chip in the DNA to address.

nals us that there are "bad vibes" in the atmosphere or neighborhood. This energy track, and the acute perception of it, is what leads others to believe a person has psychic powers.

Channel 105 is the area of perception that is tapped into by people with extrasensory perception (ESP). This perception is deeply affected by excess electricity and errant frequencies.

Sensory Channel 106 ELECTROPLASMIC PERCEPTION (ability to scan for Concept controlling magnetic-electric and electric-magnetic fields)

Following the electromagnetic perception (#105) which is a physical plane the body uses, the sensory perception for the electroplasmic field in Sensory Channel #106 is the arena of the spirit. The guiding force or spirit operates on the layers or decks of certain electromagnetic wavelengths around the body. It is considered an expanded perception from #105.

This is a formatted ability developed by early crystalline structures to survey other entities at a distance, by sensing those electric pressures.

The electroplasmic field (EPF) is the energy surrounding humans and other life energy forms that balances all the levels of radiation. It is a coined word to distinguish it as an <u>electrical</u> energy (of spirit or mind) that unites with <u>plasma</u>, the essential physical substance of all bodies. These decks of energy revolve around, into and through the body as it balances our electric pressures.

Medical experiments were conducted with this field in Russia in the 1950s and at Life Energy Research in Pennsylvania in the 1980s. Using different meters, it was found that the EPF is both radiational and gravitational, in that it can expand and contract at will around the body, depending upon the person's condition. The EPF characteristically changes color and contracts when allergic or sensitive substances are introduced and moved closer to the field, such as bugs, plants, foods, metal, animals or other people.

These decks and layers of energy act much like protective bubbles and balancing mechanisms. Extremes of electric pressure are acted upon by pulling in tighter to protect and preserve or expanding outward to allow the crystal to break through the protective bubble and examine what is inside.

When relaxed, the EPF is light and wispy, a cool bluish gaseousness. When excited, the field may become more solid, denser, and even gummy. It may buckle, crease, bend or twist into a double helical pretzel shape. A more protective stance may be as a five-pointed star.

Normal depth or thickness varies from two feet or less (when very ill) to two hundred yards or several miles, this latter figure being extremely rare. The depth can be determined by using copper divining rods or dowsing with pendulums.

Human beings use this particular electroplasmic program to increase their powers of perception beyond normal reality. It is a level of imagination allowing those with intuition and foresight to develop into geniuses. Einstein and other laureates, including the alchemist of old and the energy healers of today, have tapped into this crystalline program, which, while giving them powers and perceptions far beyond those of any ordinary human, sometimes have left them with the inability to adequately communicate with the rest of mankind.

It is the form of vast intelligence that may become narrowed in focus and create a prodigious savant. In these cases, a person may have developed great intelligence or mastered abilities in a focused area—art, mathematics or music—and yet may be uninformed in other aspects of daily living.

Ever since the beginning of the Atomic Age, when experimental radioactive elements were released into the atmosphere, knowledge of atomic levels was also published. It is interesting and not a coincidence that there has been a corresponding increase in psychic abilities and perceptions since that time.

Sensory Channel 107
HOT OR HEAT

At this point in the explanation of the sense channels, it must be confirmed by analysis that individual crystalline structures and their programs had evolved to a point where imagination and perception were far greater than the need to exist. In other words, the importance of survival had succumbed to the ability to perform on many different levels and so, therefore, boredom struck at certain levels. The crystalline structures then needed to write programs that could compensate for the lack of change in the environment. Once programs had been written for every known circumstance, new projects and new programs had to be re-launched just to create some thrills.

This level of perception is perhaps part of the mechanism that human beings tap into to experience games and excitement. When things become too relaxed and survival becomes assured, it is time to create some havoc. On this particular level, the crystalline structures had written a program to perceive where the action was. It was necessary to move out of a restful state and into places where experience could be gained. It is this Channel 107 that causes a person to move or

Matter and Form in the terrestrial world consist of four basic elements: Earth, Water, Air and Fire, with descriptors between. The Earth is dry and cold; Water is cold and wet; Air is wet and hot; and Fire is hot and dry. (from Physics *by Aristotle.)*

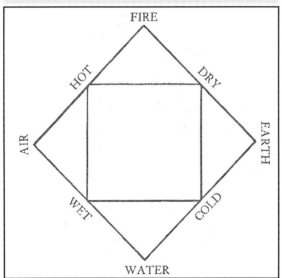

urges him to take chances and ultimately risk his normal happy way of life.

This is the area or zone that is violated by human beings when they move out of safety and into danger, just for the sheer excitement of it. It is the zone tapped into by a happily married man when he ventures out to experience excitement and the thrill of sharing his energies with other females, or the same energy tapped into by any person who decides to invest his already-gained stable energy into a shaky venture.

It is the zone of the businessman who is constantly speculating on new areas of achievement for greater intensity of life and living, regardless of the risk.

Sensory Channel 108
COLD OR COLDNESS

Consequently, as a direct result of hot or heat in the previous perception channel, the early crystalline structures needed to develop a process by which to preserve themselves after a long exploration through areas of energy that were unstable or discordant.

The perception of cold or coldness is the point where the adventuresome individual seeks to escape the trap that he has created for himself by his own curiosity. When the adventures got too hot (Sensory Channel 107), it was time for a cold shower of reality (#108).

Cold or coldness is the perception that is essential when an individual needs to escape from a detrimental situation or "slowly being boiled in oil" process, which seemed a bed of roses at first, but turned out to be an energy mess. It is time to cool off.

Sensory Channel 109
DRYNESS
(lack of water)

Early crystalline structures needed to be able to observe the presence of conductant or the lack of conductant. The universe is set up with energy principles that depend on movement. H_2O is a substance that promotes movement and exchange of energies. It is the medium by which males and females find balance in each other. A diagram was developed on this particular channel to give the crystalline structures a method of operation in the event of dryness or the lack of conductant. This program is set up primarily to handle energies in dormancy. It is a phenomenon of existence that once water is removed from any structure, especially crystals, their performance goes into a state of hibernation. It is necessary, then, if one hopes to gain the right effect for any community of cells, to apply the right amount of water or conductant to that area or group of living entities.

If one seeks to keep certain activities or energies suppressed, then water must be removed.

In human beings, the lack of water is immediately signaled, and on this particular channel, the factor of dryness is excited through the senses and detected by us in the form of thirst. When we are thirsty we are primarily being signaled that there is a lack of conductant in the body, and that the normal metabolic processes cannot continue without this vital substance.

Not only are the metabolic processes of the body respectful of the water levels, but so are the processes of the mind and the spirit. We need water to perform our functions of creativity, and so, it is a very keen perception for us to be able to observe the dryness (humidity) in an area and develop a sense perception for this phenomenon so as to avoid ultimate disturbance of the entire system.

Sensory Channel 110
BEAUTY

Early crystalline structures wrote programs and etched electric information into themselves based on the relationships of energy, whether the energy was chaotic or cosmetic. The perception of beauty is basically the perception of harmony. The normal everyday flow of energy in the environment attempts to create symmetric patterns while outside interfering entities disturb the delicate tracings. To observe beauty in the environment is to be able to detect the ultimate intelligent direction of subliminal energy that exists in all life forms.

Individuals who exude the energy of beauty are sending signals of harmony, which are detected by others.

Sensory Channel 111
UGLINESS

Following beauty, early crystalline structures developed the subsequent understanding of ugliness, that is, the jagged, disruptive patterns that occur when energies are in disharmony or chaos. Ugliness is akin to misunderstanding. It is part of the harmonic of the color bands and spectrums that include black light.

Humankind shuns ugliness in favor of beauty because it has lost the perception

"Under heaven all can see beauty as beauty, only because there is ugliness."

—Tao Te Ching, Lao Tsu

to be able to detect beauty in ugliness. Human beings have lost the capability of perceiving beauty in all things. If they were able to understand this factor and retrieve the ability to perceive beauty in ugliness, then there could be no unhappiness, for unhappiness is also a harmonic of ugliness, just as happiness is a harmonic of beauty.

There is a massive amount of confusion on these two particular perception levels, beauty and ugliness, and so these perception levels are very high on the chart (#110 and #111) and are far from reach by many individuals.

It is incredible when we imagine how in the same instance we can see beauty in an object or person and then simultaneously are struck with a feeling of ugliness.

It has been said that "familiarity breeds contempt" in which a person begins to lose his charm in the face of overexposure to his peers; but the point is, ugliness reigns when an individual loses his ability to differentiate between harmonic and disharmonic, between the orderly system of cosmos and the dysfunctional chaos, between whole concepts and broken concepts.

Sensory Channel 112
SYMBOLS & LANGUAGE

At a certain point, crystalline structures developed so totally that they most certainly wrote programs to understand language, to perceive the content of energy and reference this energy into symbols, which could be made to associate and mean other forms of motion and time.

The letters of an alphabet are symbols used to depict sounds, colors and shapes in the environment. A language is a set of these abstract symbols, which are evolved

Found in most ancient middle-eastern languages, Z, called zayin, means a spiritual sword, the sword of God.

The pictograph of Z in classical Hebrew script (7th letter):
(top right) _Uncrowned Zayin_ = Straight Light from God to Man

(bottom right) _Crowned Zayin_ =
Returning Light

Survival was the first order of business for the ancients and is reflected in the first two letters of the Phoenician alphabet, the first written alpha-bet, now more than 6,000 years old (later adopted by the Greeks).

A (Aleph, meaning ox, from which they derived food, work and clothing.)

B (Beth, meaning tent or house, the letter itself showing two chambers, one for men and one for women.)

today and no longer have the meaning they once did.

A look at early Sumerian pictographs and we find heliolithic images; the sun and its rays, or drops of rain falling. These drawings were lively, taken from nature. The Phoenicians had an early first alphabet derived from even earlier cryptograms, and the Egyptian hieroglyphics reveal the precursors for the modern letters and alphabets of today.

The ancients were more in touch with many of these language and spiritual precepts that we have lost touch with today.

Many of the abilities that individuals

have to perceive language or to use language as a mechanism for communication come directly from this Sensory Channel 112. And so it is that many of the disruptions of language ability result from a lack of perception of languages and its harmonics, which are primarily color, sound and various shapes.

Human beings use language for communication and when humans gain the ability to perceive all language, the communication of ideas across space, telepathically, will be much easier to implement and comprehend.

Sensory Channel 113
SYMBOLS & MATHEMATICS

"Mathematics is the language with which God has written the universe."

—Galileo

The most basic knowledge that exists is mathematics, the study of form, quantity, arrangement and magnitude.

Early crystalline structures, in their development, wrote programs within themselves by etching electronic experience into the core of the crystal structures and perceiving the need to create complex forms of interrelationships of various pressures and to symbolically represent them. Mathematics is the development of mankind handed down from the experience of pressure by crystalline structures.

What gives us the ability to perceive mathematics on any scale is the fact that there are crystals in the cores of the most intelligent cells of the body, which have already experienced the pressure levels of the environment. Sensory Channel 113 is so vitally important to the survival of mankind that it cannot be underestimated or undervalued.

The SAF® system that has been de-

The binary system of numbers used today in computers and cell phones has history! It was invented in 1679 by mathematician, Gottfried Leibniz, who was fascinated with the correlations between binary numbers (0 and 1) and the 64 hexagrams of the I Ching. He had been introduced to this philosophy by a friend, a Jesuit missionary to China, Joachim Bouvet.

The I Ching hexagrams affirmed for Leibniz the universality of his own religious beliefs as a Christian, in which binary numbers (1 out of 0 or nothing) were symbolic of the Christian concept "creation out of nothingness".

We would call this fusion energy, creating something out of nothing, see Step One. ("Let there be Light!")

Leibniz wrote the I Ching in binary sentences. (above: Eight trigrams of the Bagua)

veloped, utilizing the sense perceptions of the individual and mathematics, works off and from this particular channel. We can perceive our innate symptomatic troubles

"The numerical matrix of the sun can be used in a proven mathematical formula to help you gain insight into your troubles."

– Joseph R. Scogna, Jr., on SAF®

by interfacing the crystal patterns of the symptoms with the mathematically expressed pressure variations that exist in the body.

By way of example, if a person has diabetes, and his pancreas is malfunctioning, then the pancreas itself harbors crystalline structures that are perceiving levels of pressure that are extraordinarily different than what is needed for normal operation. In the case of diabetes, there was a past great emotional trauma that is still affecting the person, especially if it is out of focus, unknown at the present time. Several organs and glands may be affected, so this would be felt as a good amount of pressure.

The whole idea of crystals perceiving pressure and the relationship of this pressure into mathematics, such as 1, 2, 3, 4, 5, 6, 7, etc. is the basic operating principle of all life energy forms on the planet. By utilizing this particular phenomenon, vast numbers of scientific programs can be written to elucidate this valuable information. The cells, and the crystal formations that control the cells, that is particularly, those energies that are directing the DNA and RNA chromosomal patterns, have within them a complex mathematical structure that can be read much like a computer printout.

Today there are a number of mathematically-based computer programs that can take information from a human being on various tests, such as infrared, Doppler, etc. and interface these with the pressure readings that are present in the cells and tissues. This information is incredibly invaluable for search and discovery processes needed to decipher the intricacies of the human condition on planet Earth.

Sensory Channel 114
INTENTION

Intention is from the Latin word *intendere*, to stretch out, endeavor. Intention has long been a manner of healing as it encompasses decisiveness.

After mathematical programs on pressures, crystal structures next developed the ability to perceive Intention. Intention is the harmonic of perceiving electromagnetic and electroplasmic energy fields (Sensory Channels 105 and 106), but is more subtle, for Intention enters into the realm of the individual's ability to perceive energies that are two-dimensional and imaginary.

The intentions of an individual most certainly are the precursors of electronic movement. This perceptive channel helps to establish a mean baseline of intensity where a person is concerned. This channel is the part of the programming for crystalline structures that allows them to perceive the actual quantitative pressure that exists. Even though mathematics has the capability of reading out a specific number and quantity, this level is quite two-dimensional.

Intention gives that flavor or estimate of ultimate potential and power that is translated into mental form. Mathematics reads out the intentions of an individual in a number sequence, whereas this perception channel of intention gives the individual the actual picture or image in color, sound and form.

Sensory Channel 115
POSTULATE COMPOSITION
(evaluative script for beings)

A postulate is a fundamental principle; a self-evident truth by virtue of preceding ideas.

At this channel, we find the ability to visualize a result, to perceive and pose problems into a series of conceptual preferences that could ultimately create an effect.

This perception gives an individual the power to sequence events for an ultimate result. It is the channel of sensory perception that entrepreneurs and speculators use to dream, and to create vast empires.

Postulate scripts are the part of energy used by those who realize that a seed will someday grow into a tree and yield fruit, which will then bear more seeds, to ultimately create more trees.

Sensory Channel 116
COUNTERPOSTULATE

Once a postulate has been posed, there may be opposing ideas and energy. Sensory channel 116 is the perception that an individual uses when attempting to decipher all those energies in the environment that are against his particular sequence of ideas, his postulate.

For example, if someone were to create a prospectus on a business, he wisely includes everything that may come between him and his ultimate success. If he desires to set up a fruit stand, the obvious postulate would be to sequentially develop concepts that will ultimately make sales boom and cause him to realize a large influx of money.

The Counterpostulate to his dream (postulate) of a successful fruit stand would be the understanding that having an outside fruit stand might be hampered by thundershowers and windstorms and these should be factored in the equation. In the foregoing explanation, thundershowers and windstorms are counterpostulates to the postulate of selling fruit successfully at a roadside stand.

We usually imagine that when we are developing an idea or some program that it will always be a sunny day. However, the perception and understanding of counterpostulates many times is what causes an individual to be more realistic in a postulated venture, and consequently more successful in all his endeavors.

Sensory Channel 117
LIES

A lie is an untruth; it is an illusion and as such presents an erroneous or misleading impression.

A change of position in the environment is an attempt or action on the part of crystals to consistently "keep the game going". Because the levels of perception at this position, #117, are extremely high, one must avoid boredom at all costs. The stagnation of energy causes an instant retrospective, which eliminates the thrill of motion.

The ultimate lie for all crystalline objects and life energy forms is motion. Moving from one point to another changes the individual in form and peripheral content while he essentially remains the same.

This basic concept can be quite confusing, for people often cannot see the truth in the lie that they live. They are, of course, themselves, but each time they change position, they present a different image of themselves. They give the illusion that they are in motion, when in reality they are still unchanged. The primary illusion (the lie) of this planetary system is motion.

This subject cannot be extensively discussed in this brief text for it is a very deep and important subject and part of a law of physics that requires a good deal of understanding and perception. But suffice to say, those who have been disabused of the ultimate lies in their life (consequently removing many of the lies that they think are important) are able to see the ultimate truth of motion. They are free from false or mistaken ideas.

In SAF® programming, when we see the 1-9 in a chain of numbers, this tells us there is an untruth close at hand, a lie, something the client thinks about, perhaps often, but does not disclose. It could be a major or a minor issue; however, it is being held onto, kept in the bones and muscles where it can do harm. It takes a lot of energy to hold it all in.

If there is anger involved, such as with the sequence 1-9-22, this is the readout for arthritis., inflammatory arthritis.

SAF® can be used to foretell the future: if nothing is done with this sequence, if it continues to be held in the bones and muscles, arthritis will be the result. It is a matter of mathematical probability.

Revealing this early on to the client, discussing the situations and events, can often be the most helpful and enlightening for the client because it releases a tremendous amount of stuck energy.

Sensory Channel 118
TRUTH

The truth of the crystal and all of its progeny, to include humankind, is that it remains unchanged.

The basic law of this universe is that matter and energy can be neither created nor destroyed, but merely rearranged in form. This factor is what is beguiling to the average person. Scientists and researchers, however, even though they study this concept more closely, have not philosophically put the pieces together, for they do not know the early crystalline diagrams, programs, and ultimate purposes and plans.

On Sensory Channel 118, the truth shines through. The true statement is that nothing has changed and energy is what it is.

However, as we look around our environment, we can see change. People are moving to and fro, changing positions constantly. Energies in the environment are moving back and forth and even though there is an illusion of stillness, if we were to move in closer and observe, we would see the vibration of energies around that object to the point where, if we were to use the correct equipment, we would see only a seething mass of electrons.

1-9: The actions of the bones and muscles, in coordination with the thymus gland, are primarily to capture and hold poisons that have entered from the environment; these can be body, mind and/or spirit poisons. Energies that are dissimilar or of an origin other than from the person are processed by the thymus and network.

Those who withhold trauma or hold back information are suffering from an overrun of poisons. When the thymus does not know what to do with these poisons, the energy is held in. There may be electric charge overloads producing great pain.

Early cultures all over the world worshipped the sun.
(above) Egyptian Amen-hetep IV, his wife, daughter and slaves or workers, with the sun sending helping, healing hands.

(above) Cross of the Sun rock art, Texas

Sensory Channel 119
PERCEPTION OF THE SUN

The perception of the sun has been developed by crystals to understand who their true parents are.

The Sun is the father and Space is the mother of all energies existing on this planet.

Our Solar System

Sensory Channel 120
PERCEPTION OF THE SOLAR SYSTEM

At this level, an individual possesses a greater overview of his perception of this planet in relation to the entire solar system. Crystalline structures have programmed this relationship, which still lies deeply buried in the programming of the DNA-RNA.

Sensory Channel 121
SURVIVAL

Survival is the common goal of all crystalline energies. Survival is the ultimate goal.

This is our directive: to survive.

Sensory Channel 122
SUCCUMBING

Early crystalline structures were able to sense the difference between winning and losing and at Sensory Channels 122 to 124, there is a very subtle relationship with energy; it is the ability to perceive the alignment of true magnetic forces. It is not so much to be "right", but to be right on.

The magnetic lines of force for this planet, the solar system, and the energies around it, are the true lines of force. As we are coordinated and connected up with the ultimate purpose of energies around us, we allow poisons and toxins to fall away from us.

When succumbing as on this channel, all of these energies do not slough off; these energies adhere to us when we are at cross-purposes with the earth.

(left) Survival! Cave painting of a human hand and deer. Paint pigment was mixed with saliva and painted on the walls or blown through a hollow bone or reed to make the negative of the handprint. 11000-7000 BC.

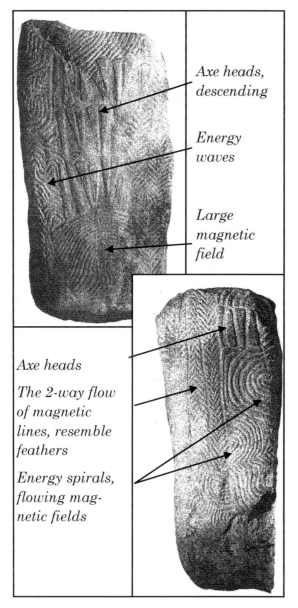

Axe heads, descending

Energy waves

Large magnetic field

Axe heads

The 2-way flow of magnetic lines, resemble feathers

Energy spirals, flowing magnetic fields

Sensory Channel 123
WINNING

Crystalline structures have imbued individuals and humankind with the automatic feeling of winning, which occurs when the energies of lining up with the purposes and goals emitting from the sun and other large masses, endow energy to all humankind.

The energies that adhered when at cross-purposes (Channel #122) are shed, much like water off a duck's back, when we are coordinated and connected with the ultimate purpose of energies around us.

Sensory Channel 124
LOSING

Early crystalline structures had observed that the most stable and relaxing energy that there was, and the most rewarding, fulfilling and thrilling sensation, was that of being lined up with the ultimate purposes of any postulate, exposing and negating counterpostulates.

The feeling of losing, as on this perception channel, stems from being at cross-purposes with the ultimate goal.

The axe represents strength and power. On these stones, it may be interpreted as "a bolt from heaven, lightning," to energize water flows and the magnetic spectrum.

(above) Stone Age engravings, Gavrinis, Brittany, France, c. 4000 BC. Found at the site are many intricate carvings showing that Stone Age man understood the energy of the earth around him and the grandeur of the universe and skies above him.
Photos by Michael Poynder. He dowsed with pendulums and drew energy plots of many sacred sites in Europe, Africa and India; Snake Butte, South Dakota; Medicine Wheel, Wyoming; Locust Grove, Ohio; Rogem Hiri in Israel; Knossos, Crete; and Uxmal, Mexico (Mayan).

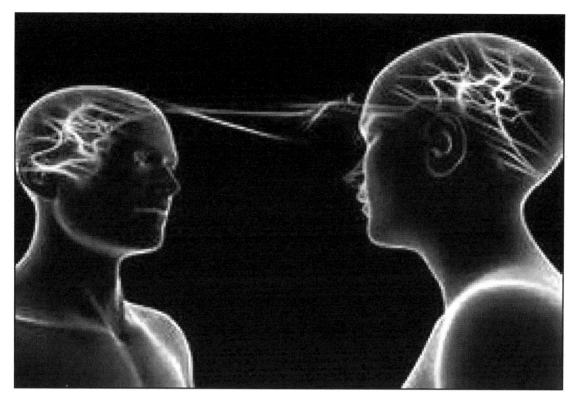

Sensory Channel 125
BODY TEMPERATURES

This perception channel for body temperatures is a harmonic of heat and cold, and is an ability for the crystalline structures and all life energy forms to be able to perceive another living entity.

Sensory Channel 126
SPIRIT (greater or lesser)

The spirit of each human defines and initiates Concepts, Dreams and Desires for its host, the holistic human body. This perception channel accounts for the hierarchy of vital essences of energy; there are greater and lesser spirits.

Hierarchy comes to us from the Greek word, *hierarches,* meaning sacred. The spirit realm is considered divine in origin and nature.

This crystalline view of control forces entices energies to move into positions necessary to accomplish thoughts, dreams and desires of universal intelligentsia.

"When we contemplate the whole globe as one great dewdrop, striped and dotted with continents and islands, flying through space with other stars all singing and shining together as one, the whole Universe appears as an infinite storm of beauty."
—John Muir, 1915

Sensory Channel 127
THE UNIVERSE

"The beginning of the universe is the mother of all things. Knowing the mother, one also knows the sons." —Tao Te Ching

This sensory channel includes the perception of all life energy forms, all existing things in the entire universe. This includes the whole of creation, including all celestial bodies and all of space, the entire cosmos.

"When we try to pick out anything by itself, we find it hitched to everything else in the Universe." —John Muir, 1911

(left) The Earth from space.

(below) Andromeda Galaxy, looking like the Milky Way

Sensory Channel 128
GOD

Crystalline forms and life energy entities alike must admit to the ultimate game plan created by the Supreme Being. The task for crystalline forms and life energy entities here on Earth is to study the Plan and know it inside out.

The interpretation of the Plan must be preceded, however, by its discovery.

(above) God infuses Adam with Life Energy
Creation, by Michelangelo
Sistine Chapel, Rome, Italy

"All matter originates and exists only by virtue of a force. We must assume behind this force the existence of a conscious and intelligent Mind. This Mind is the matrix of all matter."
—Max Planck

"The gift of mental power comes from God, Divine Being, and if we concentrate our minds on that truth, we become in tune with this great power."
—Nikola Tesla

Step Eight: Fats

Following the 128 sensing channels of perception, in the next stage of energy development the crystallized structures sought to encapsulate the entire process of energy in a form that would be impenetrable and able to survive under all circumstances. Because the sensory perception channels are dependent primarily on the transfer of electrical information, the next logical step in the development to preserve and protect this package was the creation of barriers.

The energies surrounding fat are primarily directives from the crystals themselves, born of radiation and electronic levels as was stated in previous sections. Commands are issued that instruct certain substances to repel water.

The fat molecule was created by crystalline programs to thwart the intrusion of conductant (water) into its circuits. Oils, fats, mucus and all those energies that are various stages of protection for the entity are steeped deep in the Z Process. It is an automatic procedure to create fat and protective membranes around areas of operation that have been created to service the overall crystalline community.

The organization of the human body protects and defends its systems and its various selected cells and tissues by manufacturing inhibiting membranes, oils, sheaths, fats, mucus and other kinds of electrically non-conductive goo to prevent the interception of transmissions within its boundaries by unwanted visitors from the outside.

Fat is the answer to overt amounts of electric pressure that push the human body to the limits of pain and sensation and violate the Law of Comfortable Pressure and Space. (see page 98)

Even the Earth, the elements of which are the composition of all humans and life energy forms, has its own protections and insulation (oils) to slow the sun's powerful rays even as it is energized with the electricity from a lightning strike.

Similar to the Earth, we humans are electromagnetic beings, running on electricity. We need fat for efficient operating systems and for insulation from electric pressures of environmental accidents, impacts and especially mental traumas. We do need a certain amount of fat in our system; the absence of fat is detrimental resulting in mental illness, nervous breakdown and psychosis.

While the Fat Insulation of Channels 35-38 addressed the crystalline aspects, the four primary stages of fat barriers in Step Eight take into consideration the necessary protection of the entire energetic and physical structure, the electromagnetic human being.

Stage 1. Simple Oils and Fats

The first stage of fat as simple oils is essential in all higher forms of life. These aid in the selective transmission of energies that pass through cell membranes. The energies that have been encapsulated in the fat are used to help cells and tissues in that vicinity to carry out the various functions programmed into it.

For example, in the liver, the special tasks of transmutating proteins and storing sugars are aided and abetted by the co-enzymes and enzymes, which are encapsulated in the fat surrounding this vital organ. All of these materials are necessary for the function of life.

However, when deficient (not enough) or toxic (too much or inert), there can be imbalances of operation. The deficiency of specific oils can be remedied with intake and diet. The toxicity of certain oils or inert energies is also dietary and may be reduced with diet, but toxicity can be stress induced as well.

In an SAF® sequence, when 14-17/18 appears it exemplifies this situation: 14-17/18, which means "building up of fat cells for protection" and/or "ill effects of arguments."

Stage 2. Emergency Fats and Mucus

The second stage of fat is used in emergencies. It is mucus and enveloping pus. It is the goo that is developed to smother the electronic effects of energies that have encroached on areas in which they do not belong. Mucus and pus smother bacteria, toxins and viruses and other accidental invaders, such as a splinter. Mucus and pus buildup is a creation of primary phagocytic maneuvers, that is, white blood cells that hunt down and devour cells poisonous to the body, and then creates a barrier that prevents poisons from coming into the body.

With bacteria or a substance that the body deems a toxin, it will be encased with mucus and expelled through coughing or sneezing.

In the case of an accidental invader, such as an unwanted splinter in the finger, colonies of pus will form around the piece of wood and the finger will swell from the extra presence (wood) and pressure. Before long, the pus will form a head like a pimple and explode itself out of the finger, taking the splinter with it.

This type of fat and mucus usually recede after the injury has resolved.

Stage 3. Hardened Fat, Solid

The third stage fat barrier is one that is almost beyond the point of control. Fat surrounds tissues in the dangerous but risky effort by the organism to protect itself from the constant overloads of electric pressure, such as from emotional traumas, microwave transmissions (cell phones), television, radios, computers, x-rays and the frequencies of drugs, pesticides and herbicides. These unseen frequencies, stress, are antipathetic to the harmonic operation of the human body.

The Stage 3 protective fat deposits develop into areas of overweight (fatty deposits), which are counterproductive to any harmonic operation. In an all out effort for the body to prevent poisons from invading its systems, a wall is created that is very difficult to break down and be reabsorbed.

Stage 4. Chronic Dangerous Degenerative Fat

The fourth stage fat barrier is the frozen, hard, stiff fat that accompanies chronic disease. In this situation, it must be removed mechanically, surgically, or by dissolving it with chemicals. It is the point where the fat in the body of higher animals has gone way past the control of the system.

Human beings who suffer from arteriosclerosis, atherosclerosis, heart disease, etc. have developed these particular stages of fat by inundating themselves with stress. The electric stresses of the environment, which invade the body, automatically trigger cellular reactions that depend upon crystalline programs to interfere with the stress. The primordial messages that originate from the crystalline structures tell the body to make fat to protect itself. More fat!

****

The programs that have been written into the cells are extremely old and work on a stimulus-response mechanism. If a person ever hopes to keep his physique in prime shape, he must stay away from stress at all costs or better yet, learn to reprogram the system by understanding it and by fostering an attitude change so that the composite being (body, mind and spirit), does not hyper-react in the presence of stress. Each of us is unique and we react to similar stresses in different ways.

It should be noted that all stages of fat are found in vegetable, animal and man as a reaction to the interchange of elements within the organism and as a response to intolerable electric pressure.

Stress

What exactly is meant by stress? Stress is defined as a non-specific biological phenomena or an adverse external influence such as chemicals and frequencies. Both register and are read by the human sensing system as electric pressure.

Stress can be from the environment around us, near and far, experienced as emotional radiation (anger, arguments, worries) coming from family, friends, co-workers, or from the job situation itself. (see page 49)

Stress or electric pressure is created from excess electricity and errant frequencies, which are commonplace in our modern world of electronic gadgetry. Any frequency that carries an overload of pressure is considered a dissimilar vibration that threatens the harmonics of the human body.

If the workplace is loaded with computers, if we use our cell phone continually, if we live or work anywhere with electricity in the walls or fluorescent lighting, this will register as stress, pressure.

Other examples in our modern world are just about any type of drug or drug use, car accidents, poor diet, pollution in water, air, soil, and even noise pollution. It doesn't have to glow in the dark; all these frequencies are not harmonic with the human system as designed.

The crystalline response to this type of stimulus is to order more layers of fat for insulation and protection.

Part Three

Steps Nine through Sixteen

Step Nine: *Milk, Sap, and Ooze*

Step Ten: *Microbes, Plants, Bacterial Colonies*

Step Eleven: *Crustaceans, Shellfish*

Step Twelve: *Fish*

Step Thirteen: *Snakes & Reptiles*

Step Fourteen: *Insects*

Step Fifteen: *Birds*

Step Sixteen: *Animals & Mammals*

The entire pattern of the sixteen steps of the Z Process is a depiction of energies going through the life cycle, which is the nature of this universe—eating and being eaten, sex and procreation, birth and death.

Steps One thru Eight are programmed into the crystalline structures of the DNA and used by every living entity on planet Earth on Steps Nine through Sixteen. Each has been given a directive by their respective crystalline structures of the DNA: I will survive.

This means that all of life's organizations are able to sense in their crystalline structures, just as we are, radiation, light elements, heavy metals, the actinide series of radioactive elements, simple and complex sugars, compound and inert salts and crystals, protein matrices with the 128 sensing channels, and fats are used for protection.

Animals (Step 16) have very good instincts; all 128 sensory channels are at their disposal. Many animals can see in the dark and often in the ultraviolet or infrared bands. They have acute hearing and smell, and are of necessity hyper-alert to danger. They can sense where water is located and if there are other protein bodies nearby to either gather with, run from, or prepare their digestive juices for a big delicious meal.

Humans, also Step 16, have these same abilities even though we may not be aware of them yet or using these fully. But our ancestors, the Stone Age people just may have. They were more aware of the universe and their place in it. This is evident in their rock carvings and sacred places built all over the world for observing the planetary, celestial and solar changes. We find it in the holy books and wisdom from very early writers.

Our ancestors were in tune with the universe in ways we have forgotten; the magnetic and electric force fields that crisscross the earth, the sacred centers of energies, water lines crossing underground, the energy of the earth ignited and charged by lightning from the sky.

In our modern world we have lost much. To find our water, we turn on the tap. To locate our food, we go to the grocery store and buy plastic wrapped packages and boxed foodstuffs.

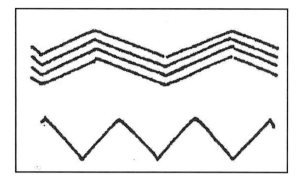

(left) Examples of zigzags from rock art and pottery in the Americas and Europe. American tribes will readily recognize these from pots and pipes.

The legend behind the decorative designs on pots is that these represent wavelengths—solar, electric, magnetic—concepts the ancients understood.

The trouble is, much of what is available to us is not nutritious; it is not alive food, and we don't give it much thought. We have indigestion and insist on taking a drug to squash the acid reflux so that we can continue to eat the foods we want, even if these are causing us bodily troubles!

How would we fare finding food and water and shelter if left to our own devices? Yes, we do have more technology than the ancients, more electronic gadgets, electric appliances, GPS to help us find our way home, vehicles to get us there, and instant communication devices, but all of that has its repercussions on this electrical body system of ours.

4 billion years of evolving; 4 billion years of implanted programs in the system. Programs that the genes picked up and used are associated with surviving better; that was the initial purpose and is still true today.

Animals and mammals on the planet today are not that old in Earth-Time or Universe time. But remember that Z programs are coming from early on in the track of existence, since the inception of this planetary system, so when we go back on the genetic line of humans, we find programs in operation based on the predecessors of our whole cellular makeup. We share a lineage in some aspects with all the earlier episodes of Time since creation of the Earth (Steps 1-8), and with all the evolved creatures and species since then: Milk, Sap, & Ooze; Microbes, Plants, & Bacterial Colonies; Crustaceans; Fish and water-bound entities; Snakes & Reptiles; Insects; Birds; and earlier Animals & Mammals.

It has been the effort of SAF® programming to help us reach the kind of clarity needed to allow us access to these banks of information. The data that is impressed within the cell and the nucleus of the body itself is of a simple but highly ordered intelligence. It is inaccessible to those who cannot understand its structure.

As we study this information to learn it and use it, we will have heightened awareness; and with that we will have greater control of the process.

Each of us has different active circuits to be addressed because we are unique, one of a kind. We pride our self on our individuality! So it is very important to remember there is not one solution or one pill or one anything that will fix all of us equally, all the same.

That is the beauty of this system.

And that is our challenge.

The Allergy Connection

Allergy! Just the mention of the word evokes multiple sensations of some insidious esoteric mechanism that can cause anything from a simple itch or runny nose to shock or even death.

The view of allergy as demonstrated by SAF® procedures follows a logical mathematical progression. Exposure to an allergen causes certain pains and sensations (pressures), which leads to lesser awareness (less conscious). There must be enough incidences of this same overload to cause an automatic flashback of energy against the person, a Z reaction. It can take the shape of *any* known allergy and is decidedly bent on taking over a certain sector of the body.

A Z reaction can be explained simply as energies that are highly stimulated. There is an overload; too much of a certain substance is in our space and we cannot assimilate it, digest it, understand it, or delete it.

All those substances that dim our awareness have the potential for creating unpredictable reactions. Superman had his kryptonite and we have ours.

What are these?

It might be a common allergy or it could be a metal, electricity, food additives, cell phone (microwave) transmissions, other people, certain places, or plastic. In addition to the present day allergens and unknowns in our life, just about everything that humankind could not understand through the ages, up to and including the present electronic age, have confused him. Those same confusions are in our DNA and require our study and vision to unravel.

We have plenty of invisibilities to contend with in our modern society. Electromagnetic gadgetry and radio waves are surprising, even startling, because we see objects in operation with no visible, perceptible action attached to them. We are told electricity and microwaves exist and we purchase devices that use these to work, but who has ever actually <u>seen</u> electricity or the frequency of a microwave?

We move blindly ahead and add to our electronics with more radiant waves, even though we are not knowledgeable of the creation of the process or the ramifications.

Does this sound overly dramatic? Those ramifications, the side effects, have escalated measure for measure with the introduction of each new gadget. Nowhere are these side effects more apparent than in our own body. There is electricity being tossed into the airwaves; these invisible frequencies get in and disturb the delicate harmonic vibrations of our own human electricity.

Technologically and scientifically, we've gone ahead of ourselves without the underlying knowledge of certain mechanics.

The confusion that results from not knowing causes these ill effects, the Z reactions. The tragedy of a person not being able to locate the source of a recurring Z reaction that plagues him is visible in his chronic fear, depression, anxiety, superstition, disease and malaise— this is the state of humankind today.

At present, we live in a society gone mad to burn itself out. Energies are compounded and frozen into certain patterns that are hell-bent to create formidable Z reactions. Someone who abuses alcohol or drugs, smokes tobacco, eats too much, or does some other disharmonic sport against his body, will wind up with a Z reaction. But we all inhabit a world surfeited with chemicals and other poisons; these frequencies are unseen and overpowering and have led to unprecedented disease configurations and syndromes, Z reactions all.

Rachel Carson called our attention to dangerous chemicals in her landmark book, "Silent Spring" (1962):

"If we are going to live so intimately with these chemicals – eating and drinking them, taking them into the very marrow of our bones – we had better know something about their nature and their power."

When we discover, understand, and accept that there is truly such a thing as a Z reaction, an active zombie program inside us, we are ahead of the game. We just need to understand and interpret the types of signals we receive when triggered, our symptoms and reactions, and to understand the genetic planning and programming that has been involved in the process.

Conditions will persist as long as they are automatically commanded to do so, inadvertently caused by us, our selves. We add much fuel to our own fires by our own lack of awareness. We, all of humankind, will never realize just how much control we truly have unless we study this concept and put it into action.

When the levels of pressure and losses of pressure repeat and repeat so that a groove is made in one area, automatic blueprinting or rewriting of the gene chip occurs. The groove is much like the groove on a vinyl record or a CD, which holds a recording of voices or music. This rewritten blueprint in the gene chip continually runs in the background of our mind, directing us.

Thymus Gland: the Seat of Defense against Foreign Invaders

We have internal help from the protective systems as discussed in Step Seven. The thymus is considered our "radiation sensor"; it is sensitive to radiant energies. As an electronic shield, it works more intimately with the thyroid than any other gland in the task of protecting the electric balance of the other body systems. In actual practical theory, the thymus gland marshals all of the electric-magnetic power of the body to resist the infiltration of bacteria, viruses, parasites and toxins. It assists in regulating and mastering the defense mechanisms of the other glands, organs, tissues and cells.

By electric-magnetic detection, the thymus aligns and controls cells. It monitors the correct wavelength and frequency of the harmonic structure of the body by way of the thyroid (carbon-nitrogen balance); anything that is of a dissimilar vibration (carbon or nitrogen) is dealt with severely.

Electric balance of the thymus gland is altered drastically in the presence of un-

Defense Mechanism

The hypothalamus (1), in coordination with the thyroid (2), signals the thymus (3) that invader forces (7) have entered the body. The thymus (3) commands white blood cells, which roam the body and originate from the lymph glands (4), the bone marrow (5) and the spleen (6), to attack the invader force (7). Copper (8) is also sent to electrocute the troublemaker. After the death or capture of the invader force (7) is accomplished, the debris is routed to either the spleen (6) for further processing, to the liver (9) for disposal, or the skin (10) for ejection.

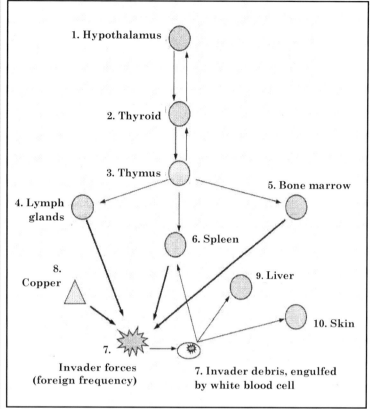

1. Hypothalamus
2. Thyroid
3. Thymus
5. Bone marrow
4. Lymph glands
6. Spleen
8. Copper
9. Liver
10. Skin
7. Invader forces (foreign frequency)
7. Invader debris, engulfed by white blood cell

wanted organisms or substances in the body. It increases in positive charge and utilizes the massive network of defense (the reticuloendothelial system), which is stretched throughout the body, to transmit powerful electric pressure to all areas in attempts to destroy any incompatible bacteria, virus, parasite or toxin. The thymus gland utilizes the bloodstream to move white blood cells into position to envelop invader forces. Once captured, the unwanted guests are electrocuted; the effect is much like that of an electric bug zapper. When the unwanted guest enters the field, it is zapped into ashes. The white blood cells are more or less a cleanup crew.

The thymus gland runs primarily on automatic microwave commands by either genetic patterned responses or direct emergency input from the hypothalamus command center. The thymus plays a pivotal role in the intercommunication of defense plans for all the organs above and below it. Most of the automatic impulse is a taped circuit implanted in the gland from genetic and magnetic experiences in the environment.

As an example, the magnetic experience of having the flu will trace a recording of the incident into the memory bank of the thymus gland. Later, when the same invader forces (the flu) attack the body, there is a "file" of experience from which the thymus can draw a defense plan. These plans may include an amazing system of defense that commands hormones and enzymes from the bone marrow, the adrenal glands, the spleen, the liver and the pancreas.

Along with the adrenal glands, the thymus works on intricate automatic defense programs. Sophisticated electric pressure sensitive messages are fed to the hypothalamus so that the releasing factor of certain adrenal hormones will trigger during an allergic response. This is an anti-shock, anti-hypnosis reaction, which keeps the electric balance of the body as stable as possible under all circumstances.

Allergy = Aversion

Allergy shocks are overloads of positive and negative electric pressure and can stem from any source. All we need to do to acquire an allergy is to overload the body with any given material, such as too much sun or too much of a certain food.

The sun or food energies, congealing to a certain point, will have an explosive quality until the body can't stand it any more. We would say the body is spring-loaded; there is no balance. These energies can override the body's ability to remove it or even to warn the rest of the systems of impending disaster.

Working at homeopathic and allergy clinics, where the emphasis is placed on symptom knowledge, we found people can have a specific aversion to almost anything. The most noticeable responses follow a major impaction of electric pressure, such as a car accident.

Someone who cannot drive the car after a severe collision has a noticeable fear (allergy) of cars for a good reason. But more significant is the person who has had an accident or several accidents, who may be "accident prone", and yet immediately gets behind the wheel again. Various, often bizarre symptoms may be experienced.

In this instance, the adrenal glands, under the guidance of the thymus and the hypothalamus, blindly attempt to protect the body. There can be aversions and symptoms related to the actual wavelength and frequency of the car and any of its metal and plastic parts, to the environment and the personal circumstances of the driver and passenger, the time of day, the month, the year, the location of other protein bodies at the scene, the sights, the colors, the sounds, the smells, ALL the perceptions across 128 sensory channels are recorded.

Any *one* of the above can trigger an allergic response because of the overload of energy the body received during the accident.

The thymus (under the guidance of the controlling mechanisms of the body) immediately instigates the adrenals to pump epinephrine and nor-epinephrine to protect the body.

Protect it from what?

From *more* of the same imbalance of electric pressure.

During the car accident, the body had more than it could stand of certain wavelengths and frequencies on a genetic level. It must somehow release the pressure already overwhelming it. When the client is brought into the area that contains the greatest amount of one particular wavelength and frequency (the material with which or in which the person was injured, in this case, the car) the allergic response follows.

The symptoms are not standard for everyone because of the emotions activated and the nature of the incident. These are expressed by each individual as pertains to their own situation and is best sorted out with the SAF® questionnaires and infrared, under the guidance of an SAF® practitioner. The incident may need to be examined more than once; each time a different sequence of organs will be shown and different perceptions will arise. Complete understanding of the event or incident would follow the diagram of Electricity Known, Sensory Channel #69. When we finally do understand something, the energy floods in, electricity flows, we light up.

Allergy and Addiction

The other interesting factor is the connection of allergy to addiction. We are often addicted to items to which we are allergic. We tend to gravitate toward (want) those things that make us less aware.

Many people have food allergies, which can be convoluted and confusing substances when trying to determine the source. A good example would be an allergy to chocolate. Cacao beans are grown in hot humid areas, gathered and stored in burlap bags. Cockroaches live in the same area, sharing the spaces. When the beans are processed into chocolate powders, a few particles of cockroach legs and body parts are inevitably included. Quite a few "cockroach parts" are allowed and pass inspections, and are so tiny we wouldn't know it (or so we are told).

Winged cockroaches are survivors from the Carboniferous period so are aligned closely with allergic responses to coal dust (coal being compressed particles of dead insect bodies and vegetation). Coal tar is used in acetaminophen, salicylic acid ointment, calamine lotion, as medicated shampoos for dandruff and soaps for psoriasis.

So is it a chocolate allergy, a cockroach allergy or a coal dust allergy?

As an aside, in those early eons, the cockroach was about four feet long and

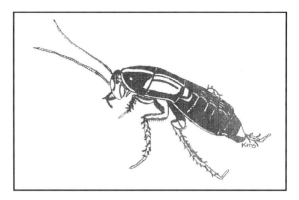

(above) Immature cockroach (no wings).

may have been the first creature to fly. Past events of run-ins with these giant creatures (human or pre-human) are handed down in the memory banks of the genetic blueprint, so the present day sight of a one or two inch long cockroach scampering across the floor can cause those who are weak of heart and nerves to be frightened by the electric impact of the vision, as if it were four feet long!

The Formula for Resolving Z

There is a positive in this entire allergy scenario—there is balance and order in this universe. We have been inscribed with the mechanics on how to maintain this balance, even if it is now on a subliminal, unconscious basis. There is a formula for releasing these allergy responses and resolving Z reactions!

The Z Process begins on a spiritual level. This is most important to understand—it is that Step One Radiation, the Intent of desire that creates. We must consent to the idea that such a thing exists in the first place (spiritual); let it exist in the second place (mental); and forget that it is there in the third place (physical).

Because all of these things occur in the proper sequence, it is mechanically possible to understand and reduce the effect of Z reactions. The formula is finalized by:

1. Making people aware of the Z Process through the various Steps listed in this book.

2. Teaching people how it got that way, to include personal work in understanding of our own issues with the SAF® method.

Once the personal connections have been made, the power that the (former) unknown had over us, that directed us, is dissipated, and there will be an electric release.

In this way, we can remove any Z program that may be draining power on a physical, mental, and spiritual level, and restore balance.

(see chart, page 26)

The following are fascinating examples of categories of Z reactions. More personal examples and specific sensitivities and allergies can be found with SAF® protocols. Once found, homeopathic remedies can be used to de-sensitize clients. The products contain little substance, but do contain the electrical energy of the original material (the frequency and vibration), which makes the remedies an excellent method for amelioration.

STEP 1: RADIATION REACTION

One example of a radiation reaction would be electricity, because electricity is the substance that runs the human body with frequencies from as few as three cycles per second to as many as 800 trillion cycles per second.

The introduction of any *new* current from outside sources, such as high tension lines, neighborhood distribution lines,

transformers and generators, electric gadgets, automobiles, fluorescent lighting, or appliances that require electricity to function, disrupt the harmonic operation of the nervous, endocrine, respiratory, circulatory, and digestive systems of human beings.

Because of the new added current, the person may have to "change gears", which causes displeasurable sensations: headaches, nervous tremors, heart palpitations, anxiety, restlessness and great heaviness in the joints and limbs. The person may experience apprehension of going near anything electrical.

Children (in smaller bodies and more alert perceptions) are especially sensitive and vulnerable to excess electricity.

Someone with a highly developed psychic sense is sensitive to electricity and is most likely aware of this already. Additional electricity may cause sensitive people to become wary or cautious of surroundings that are filled with low intensity electrical current or even extremely low frequencies (ELFs), and may feel drained, with tingling in arms and fingers. This "drain" or "energy drain" is the blocking of the electrical structures of the body.

Energy that controls the nervous system—the enzymes, vitamins, minerals and hormones moving to and from glands to organ terminals—will be cut off, misdirected, bounced and/or reflected away from their intended cellular targets.

We are seeing a lot more of this type reaction as the use of electronics increase and as the chemicals and those frequencies are spewed forth (radiational energy) into the water, air and soil, into our foods, into our bodies. It is significant that the number 15 in SAF® work, the Senses and the Hypothalamus, appears more frequently in the front of the SAF® number sequence, meaning it is acute, this is stimulated and we are on overload.

When this happens, put attention on the electrical circuitry that is nearby either at work or home. Are there high tension lines overhead, transformers or generators in the area? Do you sit in front of the computer all day, talk on your cell phone? If you have trouble sleeping, locate where the electric meter is and where the electric current enters the house.

Be alert and aware of the cross-interfering electrical circuits because these all generate frequencies that will squash your awareness. Learn all you can about electricity to increase your awareness on this subject. This situation is yours so use the ammunition you need—knowledge.

Follow a detoxification diet and exercise program, find homeopathic remedies or herbs, and other nutrients that help release these energies from the body.

STEP 3: HEAVY METALS

At Step 3, when the heavy metals were formed, there was a buildup and collection of pressures and electric motions. We have memory traces of this time period in earth's history, experienced with our emotional states (electric motions).

Traversing down the Graph of Emotions (page 66), we encounter increasingly heavier emotions, each of which is expressed differently, and varies human to human; this can be plotted easily with SAF® procedures and the Endocrine Sense Channels 74-104.

Extremes of emotions, overwhelming stress, pressure and polluting chemicals collect and build up until there is an all out heavy metal war within the system. In this case, the heavy metals have built up to toxic levels.

In *The Promethion*, we read that the metals are controlled by the emotions and the emotions are controlled by the metals. What happens when attention is focused on this heavy metal war process is an instantaneous transmutation of elemental energies within the body, a change in emotions that can be rapid, a cause and effect relationship that affects the balance of mind and body.

From here on out, when the heavy metal war is examined with chain work, this allows a rebirth of electric pressures into an awesome power of a new type of energy.

How does this happen? When we make connections between our emotional present and our emotional past, the power of that connection causes a dissolution of the energy. There is a discharge of the energy holding that in place.

STEP 9: MILK, SAP & OOZE

This is the beginning of life's organizations as humans relate to it; a very old program that involves the relationship of lactation, when the woman and other female mammals lactate. The hormonal relationship of the pituitary glands directing the mammary glands to lactate is extremely old, 300 or 400 million years old. It is a chip in the DNA of all mammals, all those entities that have mammary glands. This includes men; males of a certain African tribe breast feed their infants while the women hunt, but that is the extreme. When a woman becomes pregnant, the milk, sap and ooze chip turns on, and it essentially dictates, "We're moving into the ooze program now." Fluids increase,

(left) Petroglyph of tree deeply etched on sandstone boulder. It may date from a pre-Clovis tribe before the Maidu.

Tree sap contains plasma, the substance that holds in suspension and allows movement of nutritive-rich sap to all parts of the tree. Indians chewed pine sap for joint pain and to increase mobility. Maidu Interpretive Center, Roseville, CA. Photo by Larry Barker, 1998

the placenta grows and the fetus is nourished until the fully formed baby slips out with the ooze during birth.

The mother holds the infant close, the warmth and cries of the helpless infant set the hormones into high gear and lactation begins. Feeding the baby breast milk is the best for mother and child. In addition to being held and protected and loved, the child receives the natural antibodies and immune factors of the mother and that genetic line, and at the same time the hormones released stimulate the woman's body to heal and recover from childbirth faster.

Nutritionally, Z reactions from cow's milk are numerous. That milk was designed for a large baby calf, about 80-100 pounds at birth, not for the delicate 7 pound human baby and often the fat and protein content is too dissimilar even for adult humans to digest.

Among children and adults, allergic reactions to cow's milk, cheese and ice cream are headaches, rheumatic pains, stomach upsets, and constipation. Milk, milk products and dried milk can be inconspicuous villains as these are found in most packaged goods, desserts, macaroni and noodles, breads and bakery goods, and salad dressings.

Many people are allergic to milk (dairy) and many more are lactose-intolerant, lacking the lactose enzyme to break it down for digestion. The closer one's ancestry line to the equator, the less likely they will be able to tolerate milk. The humid heat in those regions, such as Equatorial Africa, lacks the cold necessary to keep animal milk from spoiling rapidly so those human systems cannot digest it. On the other hand the Laplanders (Sami), and others living in the northernmost areas of Norway, Sweden, Finland and Russia, at one time lived on reindeer milk and cheese. Located along and above the arctic circle, the area is cold enough for preserving milk in its fresh condition.

If allergic or sensitive to dairy products, it is essential to read labels. The hidden sources can be surprising.

The sap that we find in trees and plants today is from this early time period. This program is the ability to create and use plasma to move as one entity. The sun and stars are primarily constructed of electrically-conducive plasma; the electroplasmic field of humans is both electric and plasmic as it protects, detects, and interprets what is inside; it is in constant movement and flux. We find the milk, sap and ooze program as the material that holds our blood cells in suspension in our arteries and veins and allows distribution of nutrients to all cells.

STEP 10: MICROBES, PLANTS & BACTERIAL COLONIES

In Step 10 we have energies living in harmony and multiplying, such as the invisible microbes, all the algae, yeasts and fungi. These have their own directive to survive and so they do.

These microbes developed early on in the Pre-Cambrian time period and we have friendly bacteria and flora in our intestines and colon, in the lactobacillus family, which produce needed nutrients, maintain colon and over all body health, and balance of the system. When these are killed off with antibiotics, there is often a bloom of "unfriendly" flora, such as Candida or e coli.

Unwanted molds, fungi and bacteria can cause itching, redness of skin, rashes, and infections anywhere in the body such as tonsillitis or strep throat, so called "yeast infections" (blooms) and other more deadly reactions.

The spores of the perennial molds are always present in the outdoor air when the ground is not covered by snow. It is in the dust of topsoil and vegetation such as lawns and the undergrowth of trees, fallen leaf litter and from hay and straw, especially if stored in damp conditions. It is found inside barns and garages.

Mold can be found indoors in clothes dryer vents, tiles and grout of bathrooms, stored food that has spoiled, damp shoes, the dust of grain for baking and milling industries, orris root and cosmetics. Such allergens are associated with the fur industry, and even the family pet dog and

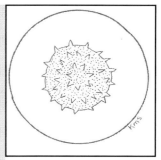

(top) Jagged spore of ragweed can cause what is known as "hayfever".

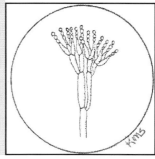

(bottom) Penicillium is a blue-green mold that produces tufts of fine filaments. Found on decaying fruit and ripening cheese, it is used to make penicillin and cheese.

cat.

Certain foods that contain yeast may need to be avoided — cheese, wine, beer, cider and some vinegars with yeast. Melons, particularly cantaloupes, mushrooms, pickled or smoked meats and fish, and any baked goods containing yeast.

In this Step 10 reaction we also find plants, and substances that have the appearance of plants, such as hair on the body, any kind of hair follicle, the villi in the intestines, anything with fingers that act like plants. The hair and villi entities mentioned are connected to plant programs that were picked up on the time track millions of years ago. It is an old program, an interesting one for the GPM to use in its system for survival.

Plants such as ragweed can create aggravations. The general pattern of this disturbance is often called hay fever, with the symptoms of itching of eyelids, watery discharge from nose and eyes, asthmatic attacks, sneezing, wheezy coughs, and diarrhea, especially during the summer months.

In this situation, hay is not the cause and the sufferer most likely does not have an elevated temperature.

The activity of ragweed and other sister plants is directly connected to the phenomenon of wind pollination. Plants use the air waves to communicate to an opposite sexed plant. It is a ritual reserved to regenerate the species, a part of their own directive to survive. Wind blows the pollen indiscriminately, and yet it will reach its intended target.

In the process of the wind blowing (or a slight breeze or up-draft), a human may step outside and get a blast. The air movement might carry a mixture of pollens of trees, flowers, or weeds.

Because plants are rooted entities, the only method of contact between their numbers is by way of the air chemically and electromagnetically with ultraviolet and other forms of light to attract bees and insects. There is no limit to the type of cross communication that can occur between plants in a forest or in open areas surrounding communities.

In this situation, the real Z reaction is *not* the hay fever. As uncomfortable as it may be, the hay fever response is a healing signal to the person that great battles are being fought below the surface in order to maintain a certain amount of homeostasis. The fluids leaving the body are carrying with them the offending allergens, encased in watery fluids, mucus or pus as discussed in Step Eight, Fat.

In actuality, the real Z reaction is an insidious degenerative reaction that constantly turns the electromagnetic energies of the body against itself.

In this Step Ten we will find reactions to foods that are from plants, such as wheat, apples, bananas, beans, cocoa, as well as reactions to trees, nuts and seeds.

By definition, all Z reactions must be of the type that will destruct or degenerate healthy tissue, unbeknownst to the host. And that is where the great allopathic battle has stalled. The standoff is at the point where curative agents are aimed at the signal or the signpost (the hay fever response) when to the homeopathic and SAF® way of thinking the force of medicinal power used to strike the hay fever could be much better spent against the Z reaction, which is deeper and more complex.

Men of science are hunting down the equation that causes Z to precipitate. The quest to find some "thing", which is only an idea, has found great substance in folklore and literature but has been put aside as a fairy tale by those men of science.

A parasite, no matter how it was created, still maintains and follows the policy and mechanism of living off a host entity. In nature, we can see that this is true. What present day science has not examined is the variety by which a parasite can manifest itself.

Ostensibly, there could be two types of parasite. First, the type that lives off the host without doing great damage. This would be most visible and solidly in the awareness of the host, such as when we are bitten by a mosquito. The complete process is visible to us and is continually re-experienced because the raised welt resulting from the sting violently itches for some time.

The second type would be a parasite of which we have no awareness; it may reside in the body unbeknownst to us. This could be in the form of round worms, tape worms, bacterial and fungal parasites, as well as other entities that feed off us.

Bacterial and fungal colonies and other energies that live in harmony and multiply have been programmed to survive, as have all creatures in this planetary system.

Bacteria do evolve. We have seen this in a single generation of humans with penicillin. When first discovered, penicillin (anti-biotic developed from fungi) was considered a wonder drug as it successfully treated harmful bacteria, such as staphylococci and streptococci. But overuse in the 1950s and 1960s, for such things as viruses, against which an antibiotic does nothing, have created a situation in which harmful bacteria are increasingly resistant to penicillin and its sister drugs. As new forms and families of antibiotics are created in the lab, the bacteria mutate into still newer forms in order to continue its own survival plan.

The currently feared MRSA is a mutated staphylococci that is resistant to known antibiotics.

The Ebola virus and the ever-changing yearly flu are other examples. These colonies are considered 'the least among us' and, like the craze for zombies, are the stuff of Hollywood movies. In the 1953 version of War of the Worlds, the earth was invaded by aliens who were technologically far superior to humans. Humankind had no weapons for combat, no protection. In the end, it was a lowly bacteria of Earth that wiped out the aliens, to which they had no immunity.

Of all the parasites, there are most definitely those that will drain all stages of energy development on physical, mental, and spiritual levels.

Trilobite fossil. Trilobites were crustaceans from the Early Cambrian Period. They were bottom dwellers, for 270 million years they ventured to the soft underbellies of larger soft creatures for meals. Extinct for 250 million years, the remains of their lineage is seen today in the horseshoe crab (not a true crab).

STEP 11: CRUSTACEANS, SHELLFISH & TRILOBITES

In Step 11 we find the colonies that develop protective armor. This is an interesting step because a lot of the human programs for fear, anger, resentment, many of the emotional programs that involve threatened survival, come from the Step 11 time period.

The proving of all these steps can be done homeopathically. By taking homeopathics, these symptoms can be turned on. If it can be turned on, it can be turned off in the same way, with homeopathics. The early homeopathists experimented with all entities on the planet and have enriched our base of knowledge today.

During the Middle Cambrian era, there was a massive number of new creatures appearing, a population explosion. This being a kill or be killed environment, all the species were heavily threatened.

Predator fish increased in number, began to develop jaws and teeth, and had plenty of food in the little soft fish-type critters.

One little fish had the idea, the brainstorm of the equation: "Okay, if I'm soft, and a big fish comes, I will get eaten. So, I will have spikes and they can't eat me."

Where did the soft fish get the idea in the first place, where did it get the programming?

From the genes.

But how did it start? What came first? How do you program the genes?

You traumatize it! Shock it, kill it. The soft little fish is eaten. But that didn't happen in this case. A big fish arrived on the scene and tried to kill a soft fish and the little one got away! If it had been eaten, we wouldn't have crustaceans or this Step 11.

Nietzsche said, *"That which does not kill us, makes us stronger."*

So here is what might have happened. The big fish swam closer to the little soft fish. All the little soft fish could see were those giant jagged teeth coming at it! Jaws! That was the only model it had. It said to itself: "the only way to win at this game is to have giant teeth".

The electrical energy of the shock and the trauma that was unleashed on it—the shear *terror* — created enough ionic interference in that little fish that it sprouted a tooth-like structure over it.

It survived; it won. And then every other fish of its nature and make up, that was privy to that traumatic occurrence, that picked up on that electrifying information whether near or far, all the similar soft fish in the oceans on the planet began to produce spiky, fang-like coverings, shells.

And we still have them. Look at some of the crustaceans—they have the most ornate looking shells that resemble very pointed teeth. They sport an external shield, an exoskeleton.

So, we can see that winning takes the shape of the one who survives in the end.

In the case of humans, let's say you get in a loud argument with somebody with whom you have a close inner connection. It is a shock. It might be a nasty fight, a real knock-down drag-out fight. You can feel the electricity welling up inside; this human electricity runs in the angstroms, that is the wavelength. So, when that electricity builds, the pressure builds, you are close to the x-ray band. When you get angry enough, you can almost SEE in the ultra-violet band! Your whole body changes. Your whole environment changes. That is shock.

For those who have studied evolutionary biology, survival of the fittest, natural selection, mutations, this concept might be an insight. Random, genetic changes, what we call mutations, get selected differentially because of their survival value. In those studies, students were taught to shoot x-ray beams in and change the base pair on the DNA. What could be done is to use electricity, a shock, and change that base pair. And this can happen in our own environment, too, with electricity. In the case of the soft, unprotected fish, that new gene was selected, it won, and look, crustaceans are everywhere. It didn't have to take a long time through the genes, one generation to another.

This is the point of the genetic changeover. We can get in there and make changes by understanding the whole process, the before and the after. We can't change the events; those things happened. And by doing this process, the images become *more* clear, not less so. We are *more* conscious to them, not less so. We can't delete them either.

But we can understand and see the bigger picture. We CAN change our attitude about past events and let it go. And we can be released, to be much freer, lighter.

Those who are allergic to crustaceans (crabs, clams) will experience symptoms such as nausea, violent vomiting, excessive salivation, infections, bacterial infestations and hardened crusts on the skin. An allergy to lobster has been homeopathically cataloged to produce a raw throat, a burning throat with tough mucus, headache, dyspepsia, frontal and temporal pain with sore eyes, pain in the stomach and abdomen, and itching of the skin.

Purple murex and other shellfish affect women in the sexual organs, contribute to diminished protection from invaders and therefore other allergies, varicose veins, and gout.

STEP 12: FISH

According to scientists, fish made their appearance about 540 million years ago during the Cambrian period. This category includes the full spectrum of water-bound bodies that eventually move up into mammalian or reptilian status through adaptive radiation and genetic changes. The Cambrian Period offered immense opportunities for birth and growth, and yet a mass extinction marks the end of that period as it completed its life cycle. The life cycle then began anew, with new energy, new vigor and a better environment for the new species.

We humans at Step 16 have fish programs in our DNA. The oldest portion of

Cave painting of fish, Arnhem Land, Australia.

the human brain, which is formed first *in utero*, is called the "fish brain"—the brain stem, the pons, the medulla oblongata. This fish brain is shared with the later developed Snakes & Reptiles (Step 13), as well as all later developed species, and is sometimes called the "reptilian brain." It may date from 500 million years or more. In these early sections of brain, we find the automaticities of breathing, respiration and heartbeat.

Fish have their directive: to survive.

What if the fish you just caught for dinner wanted to remain a fish and you are not of the strength internally or digestively or spiritually to make that eaten consumed fish a part of your own system? You will have a belly ache, indigestion, sleep disturbances.

This is perhaps why the native peoples always blessed and thanked the creatures they killed before eating them; in the process, they became one with the creature's energy and it was assimilated easily. The blessing of food at the table serves a similar purpose.

Cod can cause thyroid troubles, swelling and headaches.

Salmon reactions or allergies may include a weak auto-immune system and

Coiled snake, cave painting in Northern Territory, Injalak Hill, Australia. To the aborigine, the snake was divine and magnetic, with wisdom and energy.

thus other allergies, difficulty coping with environmental elements, low blood sugar, digestive acidity, liver troubles and indigestion.

Fish in general can cause migraine headaches, poisons harbored in the colon, gradual loss of energy control, electric hypermotion and an over acidic stomach.

So you can see, these are not the run of the mill allergies for which you would take a Benadryl; these are sensitivities, from mental images that cause symptoms. Over-the-counter allergy products won't help with electric hypermotion, poisons in the colon, or loss of energy control.

STEP 13: SNAKES & REPTILES

This group includes creatures whose ancestors were here before the giant dinosaurs — reptiles, snakes, lizards, turtles, tortoises and crocodiles.

The fish brain mentioned previously is also called the "reptilian brain", a part of our physical makeup: the brain stem, the medulla oblongata, pons and midbrain, and portions of the hypothalamus.

When the "reptilian brain" has been stimulated, we humans can be "cold blooded," we mark our territory, we domi-nate others and grasp at things to own and possess. This accounts for the fight or flight reflexes to danger, instinctual responses to traumatic events with high anxiety levels, and we may be hyper-alert to dangers and fears, whether we know what these are or not.

This is not physically changeable by us because it is hard-wired in, but we can still examine and understand behaviors, and remove and reduce electrical charge relating to those behaviors.

Humans have had run-ins with snakes and reptiles for as long as there have been humans. Snake bites can be deadly; their venom contains poisonous secretions.

Rattlesnake venom, with compounds of cyanide and hydrates of soda, is deadly. Such a bite with venom causes hemorrhages, central nervous system paralysis, paralysis of the right half of the body, boils and eye pains.

The Bushmaster snake venom thins the blood and causes hemorrhage, with swollen tonsils, cardiac irregularities, emotional outbursts, and throbbing in the throat.

The German viper causes paralysis, kidney and heart malfunctions. Fluid will engorge the arms and hands; there will be an enlarged liver, and inflammation of the veins with great swelling.

Each snake's venom is different and the antivenin must be from the same type of snake that did the biting.

Snakes have acute radiation sensors; their eyes and heat-sensing pits on their face are used to locate the thermal radiations of their warm-blooded prey, especially at night. They can't hear very well, but instead they sense vibrations of prey or enemies in the ground, which travels through their skeletal system to their auditory nerve.

In earlier times, when man lived in caves and small villages in the country-side, snakes were a constant threat and required alertness to the surroundings. Death by snake bite was swift so fear of snakes was a healthy fear. Modern day city dwellers who are fearful of snakes or even snake-like objects (earthworms, cen-tipedes) can look back in time for the original cause.

Homeopathic remedies have been used for the listed symptoms but not as an antidote for a poisonous bite.

STEP 14: INSECT

BEE: Honey bees, bumble bees, wasps, hornets and insects inflict a vicious sting on people and animals when they inter-fere with the insect.

Over the centuries, the homeopathic remedy "apis mellifica" (honey bee) was one of the first and most often used cor-rections. It was useful for symptoms such as stinging pains, swellings, nervous fa-tigue, bruises, intolerance of heat, and ovarian cysts.

This insect reaction was a major breakthrough in the study of Z reactions and sensitivities. Working with clients at homeopathic clinics, it was noted that the client, whose body was producing symp-toms, was confused by the convoluted con-nection of pollen (harmless) to a winged insect with stinger, which produces an uncomfortable pain or sensation (harmful).

Through the ages, humankind has had encounters with bees, hornets, and wasps of all types when we inadvertently invade their territories. Because bees are busily gathering pollen and nectar from a

Apis Mellifica, honey bee

variety of plants and flowers, the ground becomes a veritable minefield of sting pos-sibilities.

People may find themselves behaving strangely around certain types of flowers; this may be a reminder of earlier stings and allergic responses to certain insects that hovered near that type of flower.

The body may recoil from fields or meadows where bees generally reside in clandestine hives and nests in branches, small holes in trees or in the leaf litter under bushes. There may be a distinct aggravation towards heat and humid con-ditions, which is the time of year bees are active.

The parts of the human body that are similar to the honey bee (and thus will be alerted) are those with very high vibra-tions. The rapid beating of the bee wings and the sound of the buzzing vibrate at frequencies that are perceptible by the neurological systems, the mid-brain, pi-tuitary, hypothalamus and the senses (ears, eyes, nose and nervous system), and the thyroid and thymus.

The skin is often involved in any aller-gic-type reaction. Even though it does not

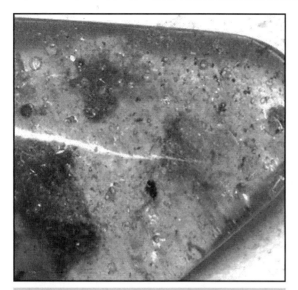

Ancient ants frozen in time and space within a bit of Colombian amber.

have any similarity or connection to the bee's behavior, the location on the skin of the last sting might be inflamed and sensitive.

The specific symptom patterns of the honey bee and its relatives will always be swelling and itching of the mucous membranes. Redness, puffing, itching, soreness, an inability to withstand the slightest bumping or touching on that area of the skin will lead to the possibility of hypoglycemic-like reactions. These drops in blood sugar are especially prevalent in the afternoon towards four o'clock, when bees are busily gathering pollen.

Women often react more violently to the restimulation of a Step 14 traumatic sting. When there are disruptions of the menstrual cycle, faintness, and great pain and tenderness over the region of the abdomen corresponding to the uterus, this may indicate that Apis mellifica has been close by or a buzzing has been heard or sensed.

The skin may be sore, hands and feet swollen and stiff. There may be hives and arthritis. There could be chest tightness, which is symptomatic of an asthma attack.

The past action of the bee against the body causes an acid-like Z reaction and automatic recoil from any situation that may thrust energy toward the inside or middle of the body. In some situations, the afflicted person may dislike heat, pressure, or feeling crowded; they will appreciate open spaces, cold air and water.

This insect allergy is sometimes called "rose fever" because at the time the person was stung the bee was carrying the pollen of a rose, although it can be any kind of flower. The body can't discern the difference between the bee and the types of pollen. In this case, when the bee stings with pollen attached, it is hot, stinging, a heavy, burning hurt, and the reaction might be: "it's a flying plant that has a sticker and kills my cells!"

The body attempts to protect against this in the future with the idea implanted "stay inside when pollen is in the air," or "stay away from meadows and fields in the afternoon." The human body mechanisms are composed of electric-carrying, memory-tracing fibers so it is understandable that confusion exists. We humans like things to be neat and tidy, and to make sense, so this scenario of what occurred first can be a tricky one for us to sort out.

Remember that each person is different; we each have different circuits in the RAM of the DNA to sort out. There is not one stock answer, one-size-fits-all solution that will work for everyone across the board each and every time.

Very often, people will find their bodies behaving strangely around certain flowers. It may be subliminal, faint. The flower may remind the body system of earlier bee stings and allergic responses to certain insects that hovered near that type or color of flower. The person may think they are allergic to that flower, when it actually stems from an early sting or other mishap.

ANT:

Ants, in the Formicidea family, are also called pismires because of the residues of formic acid, a urine-like substance that they excrete and leave behind as markers.

An interesting allergic mechanism is called "formication." When a person starts to become frightened, it's difficult to pinpoint the exact triggers in a person because we are each unique, but when the Z program "formication" is stimulated, there is a sensation of ants crawling all over the body. And it *is* ants crawling all over the body. That chip, that "ant crawling program" has been turned on. It turns on the action of energies in a system that are disassociated from one another, however, work for a common purpose, just as an ant colony is one entity with many cells (ants) moving all over in unison, with a single purpose.

An ant allergy is likely to take place on those areas of the human body that are similar to the hymenoptera body of the ant, namely the membranes, skin, and areas that provide protection or barriers.

The sequence of SAF® numbers for formication is 1-15-19. This phenomenon of "ants crawling" can also occur from drug or alcohol abuse, or from morphine use in the very ill.

The social ants made their appearance during the Cretaceous period after the rise of flowering plants, 100 million years ago. Before bees were commonplace, ants were the pollinators of tropical and early plants. Even today, ants are the pollinators of our garden variety peony, and low lying flowers and spurges. Since ants generally live in the ground, their formic acid can be found on fruits and vegetables, and on the countertops in the kitchen when they invade our spaces. Formic acid is difficult to remove.

The symptoms triggered by formic acid may include poisons that move through the body and cause sharp pains. There may be pains in the joints, ankles, knees, shoulders, with arthritis, gout and/or rheumatism. There may be excessive nervousness and constant irritability, which causes the person to scratch, pick the nose, and rub the itchy eyes.

STEP 15: BIRDS

Birds appeared on earth fairly late, after there were enough proteinaceous insects and seeds for them to eat. Easily tamed, the chicken was domesticated in India about 6000 BC. Geese, pheasants, ducks, turkeys, doves and pigeons are all kept in captivity for man's use. This Step 15 reaction includes all fowl and poultry, ostrich, rhea and emu.

The ancestry of the bird family may go back to the large flying creatures of the dinosaur period, although scientists are not exactly sure if those can be truly classified as "birds."

Young domestic fowl have endured a long history of degradation at the hands of humankind. Fowl and poultry are used

Cave painting of human hand and three-toed Rhea. At 4' tall, with an 6' wingspan, the rhea is a fast runner but flightless bird. Called Darwin's rhea, who found them in 1834. Were these ancient prints of a domesticated rhea?

The negative images were made when saliva, mixed with paint pigment, was blown through a bone or hollow reed. 7000-11000 BC. Santa Cruz, Argentina.

as food, their eggs for an easy to assimilate protein, and their feathers for pillows and ceremonial uses.

The genetic blueprint of the human is influenced by the connection that birds, especially chickens, have on the energy systems, so it is important to know what is going into your own system by way of food. The areas affected in particular, are the respiratory system and the abdomen. There may be pains in the chest, wheezing, coughing; and mucus buildup that leads to bronchitis or pneumonia.

If there is a constant nightly inhalation of microscopic particles of chicken, duck or goose feathers in feathered pillows, down comforters, or feather beds,

(right) Bird hunting in ancient Egypt, a colorful and lively tomb painting.

there may be skin reactions, rashes, itching eyes, and asthma. This may lead to apprehension and fear, nervousness and anxiety.

Z reactions from birds may include signs of indigestion and inability to digest fats. Liver function may suffer, with jaundice and raised serum cholesterol levels. The adrenals may be affected making it difficult to maintain steady blood sugar levels, with hypoglycemic-type symptoms.

One of the remedies for hypoglycemia is the suggested increased consumption of protein, and chicken had been thought to be easily digested. However, with the symptoms listed and the organs affected, it may be that chicken is causing the hypoglycemic condition in the first place!

The chicken is a timid creature and that character trait is ingested as well, so there may be hesitancy, shame and embarrassment, and not having the courage to face up to even normal everyday tasks. The slur, "you're a chicken" exemplifies

this trait.

Egg protein is found in various store-bought packaged products, as well as in the high protein powders for weight lifters, athletes and dieters, so there may be reactions in the joints, bones, muscles and the kidneys. Be alert for chronic backache, pains in the stomach and arthritic-like conditions.

Once the offending materials are eliminated, the reactive force should slowly dissipate.

Free roaming chickens, homegrown chickens or 4H Club raised may be a better choice, because the birds might have had a better (happier) life and so will produce happier vibrations in the food that humans consume.

Step 16: ANIMALS & MAMMALS

The much-loved family dog or cat can stimulate a Step 16 reaction because the animal particles and wave frequencies are classified under "Animals and Mammals."

Dogs have been domesticated for more than 30,000 years; cats only about 8,000 years. The electromagnetic codes and DNA-RNA programming that create directives that the human follows for survival have been overwhelmingly programmed to avoid contact with cats and members of the cat family.

The domesticated cat, a direct descendent tamed by the Egyptians, was lauded by them for its ability to prey on mice, vermin and other pests that got into grain stores.

The origin of the species that roamed that area and of which the Egyptians would have been terrified at first, was the Jungle Cat and the African Wildcat (Egyptian Sand Cat). Many mummified

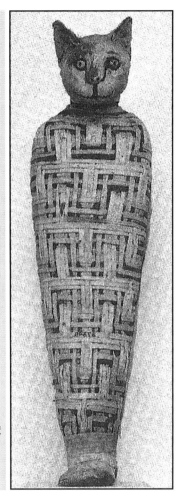

(right) Egyptian mummified cat, 100 BC, was excavated at Giza in 1907. This mummy of a cat is now located in the Natural History Museum, London.

Cats were beloved by the Egyptians, embalmed with oil of cedar and interred in secret vaults.

cats have been found that include Wildcats and other cats that had been cross-bred with the Wildcat.

Later elevated in status, Bast the Cat Goddess, was revered in temples and yearly festivals, received offerings and had special rituals. Egyptian laws protected all cats and they roamed freely.

Domestic and wild cats interbreed easily so there are several ancestral families; the European Wild Cat, the Chinese Desert Cat and others. For all the breeds of domesticated felines, there are just as many wild counter-parts.

If humans were to disappear, the domesticated housecat could survive in the wild, and do a very good job of it, all within a short span of time.

From the height of a goddess to the low image of being in league with the devil, hateful superstitions and being killed for witchcraft in years past and in modern day Caribbean rituals, the cat has survived.

Perhaps some of the negativity toward cats can be blamed on the electromagnetic blueprint of the DNA genetic codes that recorded instances of the forefathers of the human race that were consumed continuously for breakfast, lunch and dinner meals by large cat-like animals that roamed the earth—lions, tigers, leopards, bobcats, lynx, panthers, cougars, and mountain lions, etc.

The cat is nocturnal and can see and hunt well in the dark and dim light. Blinking is infrequent, with vertical slit pupils similar to a snake.

When the cat Z reaction is stimulated in humans, it is predominantly in the eyes; a dimming of vision, inability to focus, watery eyes and tears, stubborn itching.

Strong sunlight might be bothersome, the light of day creates tiredness and most of the energy depends on the ability to keep moving at night, as a feline does. There may be memory lapses and depression.

Along with eye and vision symptoms, a triad of ills may indicate a cat allergy is occurring: kidney and bladder troubles, and sexual dysfunction.

Animal dander would fit in this Step 16 reaction. Dander is the scruff and particles from the coat of various animals, dogs, cats, and horses, which can cause an allergic reaction. Dander can cause acne and a multitude of skin conditions because the skin of the human corresponds to the coat of the animal.

There can be an excess release of ammonia, an irritated bladder and gasping for breath.

There may be electric overload, electric confusion in and around the hypothalamus, muscle pain and an overconsumption of protein.

Epilogue

The universe is a harmonic one — and balance is naturally calculated into the equation.

With that basic premise, Joe Scogna dedicated his life to understanding life energy and finding balance between the body, the mind, and the spirit, and how it all fits together in the greater universe.

He was fascinated with all branches of knowledge and especially the long history of what has worked for healing and achieving balance in the past from such studies as Eastern and Greek philosophies, Chinese and western medicine, homeopathy with its anti-radiation properties, quantum physics, the elements, electromagnetics, and the DNA-RNA. He incorporated all these ideas and philosophies in his work.

This book stands on its own merits as an intriguing look at the 16 Steps of the Z Process, the hardwiring of the universe, the framework that is in our collective DNA and the DNA of all entities in this planetary system.

In Step Seven we find the 128 Sensory Channels, the awesome perceptions we can use to make sense of our world; perception channels such as sound and color, electromagnetic and energetic fields (auras), energy gyros (chakras), greater and lesser spirits, God, language, radiational forces, nutrition, and the magnetic ability to locate our people and place, to mention but a few.

With the added excitement of the Random Access Memory chip in our individual DNA, we have a truly personalized method to follow, to augment, and to use to heal.

Joe considered that this was the most important of his books and expected it to have far-reaching effects for humankind.

The adage "knowledge is power" is so true. Knowledge and the understanding that floods in with it is your key to controlling your own situation. Not by force, not by repeating words in hopes of change, but by acceptance. Don't hide from the negatives in life, but identify them, make personal connections between the past and the present, and the power the unknown had over us in the past is dissipated. When brought into the light by this method, we will experience an electric release (A-ha!) as the break is healed.

In this affirming way, we can allow the controlling negatives from the past a means of release.

Can it be as simple as this? Yes, very often it is.

As Nikola Tesla expressed: *"The truth that we can heal, we must learn again. Medicine is in our hearts and also in the heart of that which we call the Universe."*

You are in the right place for healing to happen.

We still have a lot to learn and share, about life and living, about healing in these challenging times, so we can move forward as more enlightened beings of Light.

Kathy M. Scogna
2014

ACKNOWLEDGMENTS

My heartfelt thanks to Jezra Lickter for his programming magic and bringing this work into the new century with our presence on the web.

Thanks to Rachel Lickter for typing the original manuscript into computer format one summer, and for many helpful suggestions in this new world of publishing.

I am indebted to my Editor-Extraordinaire, Nancy B. Porter, DN, LISW, whose assistance has been awesome! She understands the SAF® process well and uses it daily. She identified sections that needed further explanation, and found much use for more mundane secretarial skills, as well.

A sincere thank you to my special readers for sharing their thoughts: Bonnie Hendricks, Laura Lee Morningstar, and Pam Mark Hall.

Special mention for their questions, insights, and encouragement along the way: especially to Nic Scogna, for his invaluable advice and viewpoint, which at times was sorely needed, to Kalli Scogna, for typing many of the audio seminars, books and computer programs over the years, Josh Lickter, Sandy Aquila, Mary Habeeb, Myrna Hallett, James Manegold, Diane Searfoss, Linda Schwank, Dr. Don Mayfield, and Bruce L Erickson.

Thanks to Jason Scogna for reworking the chalkboard illustration and other photography work, and for many helpful ideas.

And special thanks to the many SAF® practitioners, past, present and future, who have their work cut out for them as we bring about energetic healing in these challenging times.

CREDITS

The illustrations and photographs in this book could not have been assembled without a great many people and organizations, past and present. A few sources are unknown or could not be located, postings and re-postings on the Internet; however, we gratefully acknowledge the following photographers, artists, institutions, agencies and organizations we can identify for the illustrations in this volume.

p. 3 (cave painting of hands) Cueva de las Manos, Argentina, Wikipedia
p 11 (Kathy & Joe Scogna) Jack and Lois Scogna, Scogna Library
p 15 (chalkboard) Jason Scogna, Scogna Library
p 17 (photo of Joe Scogna by KMS) Scogna Library
p 29 (pressure sensing scale) *The Promethion*, Scogna Library
p 31 (atomic blast) NASA, Scogna Library
p 33 (Egyptian Thoth) Faber Birren
p 35 (Occult Chemistry Periodic Tables) Wikipedia
p 37 (DNA) Scogna Library
p 45 (sun) NASA, Scogna Library
p 48 (winged sun) Faber Birren
p 51-58 (emoticons, with additions by KMS)

p 59 (hydrogen illustration by JRS, Jr) Scogna Library

p 60 (water) Wikipedia

p 61 (triple spiral) photo by Tim O'Brien, Dublin, Ireland, from *Pi in the Sky* by Michael Poynder

p 62 (cymoglyph) Cuneyt Konuralp MD

p 62 (violin and bow, Chladni illustration) Wikipedia

p 64 (periodic table of the elements) Concise Encyclopedia of the Sciences

p 66 (graph of emotions) JRS, Jr., Scogna Library

p 69 (radioactive elements) Concise Encyclopedia of the Sciences

p 72 (space debris) NASA's Goddard Space Flight Center/JSC., NASA

p 73 (satellites in orbit) David Dickinson artist, NASA, Wikipedia

p 77 (glucose-fructose) Wikipedia

p 78 (energy patterns by JRS, JR.) Scogna Library

p 83 crystal radio © by Greg Farmer

p 84 (grain of sand) Wikipedia

p 91 (crystal graph) Scogna Library

p 95 (acid-basic scale) *The Promethion,* Scogna Library

p 101 (Egyptian Gods of the Senses, image only) Wallis Budge, Dover

p 102 (5 senses, KMS) *The Promethion,* Scogna Library

p 105 (vision) Faber Birren

p 111 (radiation—gravitation) *The Promethion,* Scogna Library

p 114 (electromagnetic spectrum, enhanced by KMS), Concise Encyclopedia of the Sciences

p 118 (life cycle) Scogna Library

p 124 (poison ivy) Wikipedia

p 125 (fingerprint) Wikipedia

p 127 (enzyme by KMS) Scogna Library

p 129 (juice key) Scogna Library

p 142 (hierarchy of glands and organs) *The Promethion,* Scogna Library

p 146 (energy gyros by KMS) Scogna Library

p 148 (my tribe) Wikipedia

p 149 (space) Wikipedia

p 151 (cave painting, deer and hunters, Lascaux, France) Wikipedia

p 153 (oils photo by KMS) Scogna Library

p 156 (arteries by KMS) Scogna Library

p 160 (coffin) Faber Birren

p 162 (sugar crystals) Wikipedia

p 173 (Egyptian burial preparation) William MacQuitty, Dover Books (Ronan) 1976

p 178 (yin and yang) Scogna Library

p 179 (alchemic illustration) Scogna Library

p 180 (Newton's color wheel) Wikipedia

p 186 (Project Isis) Scogna Library

p 188 (hexagram by KMS) Scogna Library

p 190-191 (time scheme, Secret of SAF) Scogna Library

p 192 (circular helix) Concise Encyclopedia of the Sciences (enhanced by KMS)

p 193 (Endocrine Sense Channels © 1983 KMS) Scogna Library

p 195-214 (24 illustrations 1. Thymus—24. Lymph), Scogna Library

p 197 (cave painting of crabs) Wikipedia

p 217 (Aristotle's Physics, 4 Elements) Scogna Library

p 219 (zayin) Wikipedia

p 220 (bagua) Wikipedia

p 224 (healing hands of the sun) Wallace Budge, Dover

p 224 (rock art of sun) Teresa Weedin, Pecos, Texas, Wikipedia

p 225 (solar system) Wikipedia

p 225 (cave painting of hand and deer) Cueva de las Manos, Argentina, Reinhard Jahn, Wikipedia

p 226 (photos of Stone Age rock carvings) from *Lost Science of the Stone Age: Sacred Energy of the I Ching,* by Michael Poynder

p 227 (spirits, telepathy) Wikipedia

p 228 (globe) NASA; (Andromeda Galaxy) Hale Observatories, CA Institute of Technology; Carnegie Institute of Washington.

p 229 ("Creazione" [Creation], by Michelangelo, Sistine Chapel) Postcard, ScognaLibrary

p 235 (eagle, illustration by JRS, Jr., enhanced by Jason Scogna) Scogna Library

p 238 (wavelengths) Michael Poynder, Paul Tobacco Cashman

p 241 (defense mechanism by KMS) Scogna Library

p 243 (cockroach by KMS) Scogna Library

p 246 (Maidu petroglyph rock carving) Photo by Larry Barker, from his daughter, Jody Barker.

p 247 (ragweed and penicillium illustrations by KMS) Scogna Library

p 249 (trilobite photo by KMS) Scogna Library

p 251 (cave painting of fish, Arnhem Land, Australia) Wikipedia

p 252 (cave painting of coiled snake, Northern Territory, Australia) Wikipedia

p 253 (bee) Faber Birren

p 254 (ant in amber) Photo by Nic Scogna, Scogna Library

p 255 (cave painting, rhea and human prints, Cueva de las Manos, Argentina) Wikipedia

p 255 (tomb painting) *L'Art Pour Tous, 1861-1906*

p 257 (cat mummy) British Museum, *Quest for the Past*, Reader's Digest

p 279 (Joseph R. Scogna, Jr.) Richard Patrick, Reading Eagle Times (Kathy M. Scogna) photo by Myrna Hallett.

REFERENCES & FURTHER READING

A History of the World in 100 Objects, Neil MacGregor, Director of the British Museum; Viking Penguin New York, 2011

The Circle of Lenapehoking, Paul Tobacco Cashman; XLibris Printing, Philadelphia (2003)

Concise Encyclopedia of the Sciences, John-David Yule, Editor; Von Nostrand Reinhold Company, (1982)

The First Essene, Edmund Szekely; International Biogenic Society, Nelson, Canada, (1981)

The Forgotten Science of the Ancient World: Lost Discoveries, Colin Ronan; Bonanza Books, New York, (1976)

The Gods of the Egyptians, Volume 2, E.A. Wallis Budge; Dover Publications, New York, (1904/1969)

Greek Science in Antiquity, Marshall Clagett; Dover Publications, New York (2001)

Lao Tsu—Tao Te Ching, translation by Gai-Fu Feng and Jane English; Vintage Books, Random House, New York (1972)

Lost Science of the Stone Age: Sacred Energy of the I Ching, Michael Poynder; Green Magic Printing, Somerset (2004)

Pi in the Sky, Michael Poynder; Collins Press, Ireland (1992)

Quest for the Past, Reader's Digest Association; Pleasantville, NY, (1984)

The Secret of Light, Walter Russell; University of Science and Philosophy, Virginia (1947)

Sensations As If: A Repertory of Subjective Symptoms, Herbert A. Roberts, MD;, Jain Publishing Co. New Delhi, India (1937)

The Story of Color, Faber Birren; The Crimson Press, Westport, CT, (1941)

Tutankhamen, Sir Wallis Budge; Bell Publishing, England (1923)

Have you read?
Scogna authored books:
Amino Acids: A Nutritional Guide, Kathy M. Scogna, Life Energy Publications, Pennsylvania, (1983, 2005)

Formula Z, Volume 1, Joseph R. Scogna, Jr. Kathy M. Scogna, Editor; Life Energy Publications, Pennsylvania (1982, 2006)

Formula Z, Volume 2 (manuscript only, not for sale), Joseph R. Scogna, Jr. Kathy M. Scogna, Editor; Life Energy Publications, Pennsylvania

The Homeopathic Self-Appraisal Index, Joseph R. Scogna Jr, Kathy M. Scogna, Editor, Life Energy Publications, Pennsylvania (1980, 2005)

Homeopathy Revisited: A Modern Energetic View of an Ancient Healing Art, Kathy M. Scogna, Life Energy Publications, Pennsylvania, (2005, 2014)

Light, Dark: the Neuron and the Axon, Joseph R. Scogna, Jr, Kathy M. Scogna, Editor; Life Energy Publications, Pennsylvania (2004)

Nutrionics, Joseph R. Scogna, Jr, Kathy M. Scogna, Editor; Life Energy Publications, Pennsylvania, (1980, 2006)

Project Isis: The Fundamentals of Human Electricity, Joseph R. Scogna, Jr, Kathy M. Scogna, Editor; Life Energy Publications, Pennsylvania (1984, 2005)

The Promethion: A Comprehensive Study of the Principles of Life Energy, Joseph R. Scogna, Jr, Kathy M. Scogna, Editor; Life Energy Publications, Pennsylvania (1980, 2003)

Remedy Orange, Joseph R. Scogna, Jr, Kathy M. Scogna, Editor; Life Energy Publications, Pennsylvania (1984, 2006-2014)

SAF Simplified, Kathy M. Scogna, Editor; Life Energy Publications, Pennsylvania, 2003 This book is indispensible. It contains the theory, the numbering system, the organ and gland systems, the emotions and connections, and provides the basics for understanding the science of SAF and using the self awareness method.

The SAF Infrared Manual, Kathy M. Scogna; Life Energy Publications, California, Amazon Create Space, (2014) This is the book of choice for more information on using the Infrared device to create a chain sequence rapidly, and for the complete rundown of Interpretations and Remedies available with SAF Online.

The Secret of SAF: The Self Awareness Formulas, Joseph R. Scogna, Jr, Kathy M. Scogna, Editor; Life Energy Publications, Pennsylvania, (1987, 2003)

The Threat of the Poison Reign: A Treatise on Electromagnetic Pollution, Joseph R. Scogna, Jr, Kathy M. Scogna, Editor; Life Energy Publications, Pennsylvania (1980, 2005)

INDEX

SAF® number sequences mentioned:

Axioms of SAF®, 87

B

Bacteria evolve, 249
Bacteria, reactions to, 247
Bacterial colonies, 248
Bad habits wear away protection, 107
Bad vibes, 215
Bagua, 220
Basketball, 18, 30, 40, 167
Bast the Cat Goddess, 257
Battle between person and environment, 118
B-Complex vitamins, 129
Be right on, 225
Beauty in ugliness, 218
Beauty, 218
Bee (insect reaction), 253
Bee's vision, 105
Bees and ultraviolet frequencies, 180
Beginning of life's organization, 245
Beginning of the universe, 228
Begins on a spiritual level, 26, 49, 243
Being devoured by another energy, 195
Being eaten = loss, 177
Ben Franklin, 34
Benzene ring, 188
Binary system, 23, 220
Biological tracings, 13
Biotin, 132
Bird reaction, 255, 256
Birds kept in captivity/hunting, 255, 256
Birds, animals, fish, ultraviolet, frequencies, 180
Birth (starting new cycle),115
Blessed, 26
Blessing food, 251
Blood Vessels, 205
Blue is cleansing, 183
Body changes with the seasons, 164, 166
Body Temperatures, 227
Body's language, 23, 193
Bones & Muscles, 204
Border defense, 210
Boredom (skin), 193, 211
Born of nothingness, 48
Boundary violation, 211
Bouvet, SJ Joaquim, 220
Brain & Nervous System, 206
Brando, 13
Breaks and resolution, 24
Breathing, 60, 202
Bronchi, 203
Bronze Age, 33

Build up of acidity, 108
Burroughs, John, 183
Bushmaster snake, 252
Business speculator, 217

C

Calcium & Parathyroid, 212
Calcium balance, 212
Can't photograph atom, 36
Capturing breath, 203
Carbohydrates (stored spark), 162
Carbon-nitrogen monitor, 205
Carl Jung, 17, 278
Carson, Rachel, 240
Cashman, Paul Tobacco, 48, 238
Cat mummy, 257
Cat, 146, 257, 258
Catechin, 137
Cats domesticated, 257
Cave painting, coiled snake, 252
Cave painting, crabs, 197
Cave painting, deer and hunters, 151
Cave painting, fish, 251
Cave painting, human and rhea prints, 256
Cave painting, survival (hand and deer), 225
Chain is Linear and 3 dimensional, 192
Chain sequence, a story, 24
Chakras, 146
Chalkboard, 15
Chance to change and fix, 23
Channels at greatest height, 192
Chemical diagrams of sugars, 77
Chicken is timid, 256
Chicken reaction, 255
Chladni, 62
Chocolate allergy, 243
Choline, 134
Choose a wavelength of operation, 215
Choose correct foods, 129
Choosing detrimental situations, 158
Chroma (Greek word), 184
Chromatic music scale, 184
Circular helix, 192
Clairvoyance, 35, 103
Clean off the pistons, 25
Cleansing level, 187
Coal dust allergy, 244
Cockroach allergy, 244
Cockroach story, 243
Cockroach, 243
Cod, 251
Coiled snake, 252

ABOUT THE AUTHORS

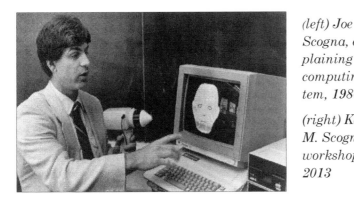

(left) Joe Scogna, explaining his computing system, 1986.

(right) Kathy M. Scogna at a workshop, 2013

Joseph R. Scogna, Jr. was born in Philadelphia in 1949. After he left school, he set off on his own course at lightning speed to study the interactions of matter and energy. His turbo kicked in, he entered hyperspace and by the time his groundbreaking work *The Promethion* was published, there were already several spin-offs. He wrote constantly and literally kept the printer in business.

Joe was President of Life Energy Foundation, Inc. He designed hundreds of computer programs in the early 1980s when very few people even knew about computers. He also started Probiotic, Inc. for his homeopathic remedies. He taught classes at the home office housed in a former school, and was a popular lecturer on the holistic circuit, principally in California, Colorado, Arizona and Florida.

He was the first to use infrared to read the bio-energetic field and locate the nervous system venting sites where organs and glands release their heat. The "hot" emotions, such as fear, anger, grief and resentment, accumulate over time and can be located and released through the self awareness process (SAF®).

Joe had a perspective that is unique: how the holistic human is balanced by cosmic and atomic energies working harmoniously. He took a step back in order to get a better view, to understand how all the parts fit together within an atom, in a human being and in the greater universe. Gifted, insightful and energetic, he was wrapped up in his work; his enthusiasm for it comes across in his writings and seminars.

Kathy and Joe married in 1975 and he fathered their children Nicholas, Kalli Marie and Jason. After their marriage, he stepped into the role of father to her children from a previous marriage, Joshua and Jezra Lickter.

Kathy worked with Joe in the early years, helping at seminars, editing, writing books and the company magazine. After his death in 1989, she focused on her first job, that of raising her five children. During that time, she also penned history books, screenplays and served on the boards of historical societies. She received awards from the State Historical and Museum Commission and the State legislature.

The reconstruction of Joe's Life Energy work and SAF® began in 1999 as Kathy infused it with new life and vitality. She has overseen the upgrading of the books and the computer programs into a dynamic, very usable online service that uses questionnaires and infrared for input. As a result, there has been a rebirth of Joe's innovative ideas in energetic healing. Practitioners worldwide now have access to the online system, with holistic interpretations and remedies.

This incredible legacy is timely and now reaches a new generation of practitioner and student alike. Kathy serves as Director.

She resides in California close to her family.

"Your vision will become clear only when you look into your heart. Who looks outside, dreams. Who looks inside, awakens."   ~Carl Jung

SAF® is truly the Rosetta Stone for the body, mind & spirit!

Practical use!

Our symptoms are messages we were meant to decode! The language for decoding is both a mathematical and a grammatical language, a combination of numbers and words to depict organs & glands, emotions, attitudes, and functions across many subjects.

SAF Simplified has the theory, the numbering system, the organs and glands, the emotions, and the basics of how to read a chain sequence.

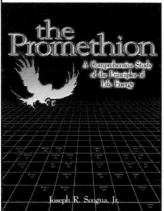

Background for SAF® Cosmology! Balance the elements with:
 *its mate
 *color-light
 *herbs
 *homeopathy
 *pressure to trigger points

Scogna reunites physical and spiritual alchemy on these pages. Discover healing as it has been done thru the ages. Illustrated Reference.

Still intrigued and hungry for more?

Junk DNA presents a lot of usable information but interested readers and seekers can take it one step further.

The Life Energy Computer System and SAF® programs of Joe Scogna's day have been upgraded to an online system, with infrared and 3 questionnaires for input. This makes it readily available in all countries, anywhere there is an internet connection and modern browser.

Give your own awareness process a boost and create an SAF chain of numbers by questionnaire or infrared. With your chain of numbers in hand, access the computing system, SAFOnline: www.LifeEnergyResearch.com/safonline and for a small fee the reader will find suggestions in the Omni-Track Interpretation.

These suggestions will specify which of the 128 Sensory Channels listed in this book have been stimulated and may need some attention. Reread those sections in the book, and add to your knowledge on the subjects from other sources, books, libraries and the Internet.

Want to learn more about the SAF® method and your sequence of numbers? Find an SAF practitioner. The practitioner can interpret your chain of numbers, help you find the Omni-Track Interpretations, sensitivities and allergies as described in this book, and locate remedies for change and balance.

www.LifeEnergyResearch.com

What to find at the website

- What is SAF®? (Find out more about the Self Awareness Formulas)

- What Practitioners Say. (Call the Home Office for an SAF® Practitioner)

- SAF Case Studies & Client Testimonials

- Purchase Books (for theory and practical use; *SAF Simplified* is most important)

- Call the Home Office for a discount code to purchase a quantity of certain books for resale to clients.

- Purchase an Infrared device for use with SAFonline (see book below)

- Training: Purchase Courses for Training and Certification

- About SAFonline: (Find chain sequence Interpretations and Remedies with SAFonline. List of the 40 categories available)

- SAF Online service: (Open an account. See book below for instructions.)

- Life Energy Monitor for updates and sidebars.

- Like us on Facebook: https://www.facebook.com/LifeEnergyPublications

---

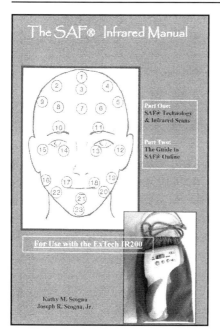

The SAF® Infrared Manual will help with:

- Learn about Infrared as used in SAF® work. Read fascinating stories and case studies. Temperature template to follow.

- How to Use the SAFonline service (free for students, minimal fee for practitioners— by day, week, 6 months, or year).

- Step by Step: How to use the Infrared device and Questionnaires with SAFonline.

- Based on chain sequence, how to find Remedies and Interpretations; details of the 40 categories, how to use these, etc.

Made in the USA
Middletown, DE
24 September 2022

10968677R00157